MURDER HOUSE

JAMES PATTERSON is one of the best-known and biggest-selling writers of all time. His books have sold in excess of 300 million copies worldwide and he has been the most borrowed author in UK libraries for the past nine years in a row. He is the author of some of the most popular series of the past two decades – the Alex Cross, Women's Murder Club, Detective Michael Bennett and Private novels – and he has written many other number one bestsellers including romance novels and stand-alone thrillers.

James is passionate about encouraging children to read. Inspired by his own son who was a reluctant reader, he also writes a range of books for young readers including the Middle School, I Funny, Treasure Hunters, House of Robots, Confessions and Maximum Ride series. James is the proud sponsor of the World Book Day Award and has donated millions in grants to independent bookshops. He lives in Florida with his wife and son.

Also by James Patterson

STAND-ALONE THRILLERS

Sail (*with Howard Roughan*)
Swimsuit (*with Maxine Paetro*)
Don't Blink (*with Howard Roughan*)
Postcard Killers (*with Liza Marklund*)
Toys (*with Neil McMahon*)
Now You See Her (*with Michael Ledwidge*)
Kill Me If You Can (*with Marshall Karp*)
Guilty Wives (*with David Ellis*)
Second Honeymoon (*with Howard Roughan*)
Mistress (*with David Ellis*)
Invisible (*with David Ellis*)
The Thomas Berryman Number
Truth or Die (*with Howard Roughan*)

A list of more titles by James Patterson is printed at the back of this book

JAMES
PATTERSON
& DAVID ELLIS

MURDER HOUSE

arrow books

3 5 7 9 10 8 6 4 2

Arrow Books
20 Vauxhall Bridge Road
London SW1V 2SA

Arrow Books is part of the Penguin Random House group of companies whose addresses can be found at global.penguinrandomhouse.com.

First published by Century in 2015
First published in paperback by Arrow Books in 2016

www.penguin.co.uk

A CIP catalogue record for this book is available from the British Library.

Typeset in 10.5/13pt Berkeley Old Style
by SX Composing DTP, Rayleigh, Essex, SS6 7XF

Penguin Random House is committed to a sustainable future for our business, our readers and our planet. This book is made from Forest Stewardship Council® certified paper.

Printed and bound in Great Britain by Clays Ltd, St Ives plc

To Matt, Libby, and Zach Stennes

Prologue

BRIDGEHAMPTON, 1995

WHEN HIS EYES pop open, it is still dark outside, the air cool and crisp through his window. Normally, he wouldn't be up for another hour yet, but he could hardly sleep last night waiting for today. He's not sure, in fact, that he slept at all.

He sees the long, narrow trombone case in the corner of his bedroom and his heartbeat ratchets up. All those rehearsals, all those hours of practice until his hands and shoulders ached, until his head throbbed, all of that preparation comes down to today. It's finally here!

He quickly brushes his teeth and puts on his Halloween costume. He picks up the trombone case and his school backpack and heads downstairs quietly, not wanting to wake his mother.

He rips open the cellophane and drops two Pop-Tarts into the toaster and pours himself a glass of milk. He drinks the milk but doesn't touch the pastries. His stomach is churning too wildly. He will eat later, after his performance.

It is still dark, a nip in the fresh air, as he leaves his house, backpack over his shoulder, trombone case in his left hand. At the end of his street, he looks to his right, where a half mile away he can see the fog of the Atlantic, dark and endless. His eyes invariably move to the house by the ocean, perched up on the hill, the haunted mansion that, even from a distance, scowls at him.

No one ever leaves alive
The house at 7 Ocean Drive

A shiver runs through him. He shakes it off and turns left, moving north on Ocean Drive. He alternates the trombone case between his left hand and his right, because it's heavy, and he doesn't want it to affect his performance today.

He perks up as he approaches the school from the south end. The morning air begins to warm, a refreshing break in the chill. The sun peeks through the treetops. Leaves of assorted colors dance in the wind. He stifles the instinct to skip along like an eager little boy.

But he's no little boy. It's not like he's eight or ten anymore.

He's the first one here, just as he planned, alone with an acre of grass, nothing but an expanse of open field, leading up to the baseball diamond and playground to the south of the brick building. No trees, no shrubbery, no brick walls, nothing for the length of half a football field at least.

He turns toward the woods on the east side and finds

his perch. He opens the trombone case and removes the rifle, already fully loaded.

He holds the rifle in his hands and takes a deep breath to calm his nerves. His heartbeat is at full throttle, catching in his throat, bringing a tremble to his limbs.

He looks at his *Star Wars* watch, which he is wearing over his Halloween costume. The first bell, the warning bell, will come soon. Some of the students will arrive early, congregating near the back door, dispersing into their little cliques or tossing a football or Frisbee around. The playground equipment, for the younger kids.

But it's not the younger kids he wants.

He looks back at his watch, where Darth Vader tells him the time is drawing near. He wanted to dress up today as Darth, fitting for the occasion but too clunky with the oversize helmet—visibility through the rifle's scope was nearly impossible when he tried it out.

He loses himself in his thoughts, in his fantasies, in the dancing leaves, and suddenly time has crept up on him. They are arriving. Small kids holding their parents' hands, bouncing with animation. Older ones walking together. Superman and Batman and Aquaman, vampires and clowns, kittens and bunnies, Cinderella and Snow White and Tinker Bell, Pocahontas and Woody from *Toy Story*, Ronald Reagan and Simba from *The Lion King* and Mr. Spock—

—and the oldest ones at the school, the juniors and seniors, a few of them with some obligatory face paint or semblance of costume but generally too cool to dress up like their younger classmates—

"Showtime," he says. He heard that word in a cable

movie he wasn't supposed to watch and thought it sounded cool. His body temperature jacks up beneath his costume.

"Showtime," he says again as he raises his rifle, but this time he finds his voice, strong and confident, and then everything changes, like the flip of a switch inside him. A sense of calm sweeps through him, itself exhilarating: Look at him! Look at him patiently walking out from the tree cover, rifle raised, aiming and firing and clicking in the next round, aiming and firing and clicking, *aim-fire-click* while he walks toward the unsuspecting masses. The pop of the rifle, with each pull of the trigger, is the most invigorating sensation he's ever felt.

Jimmy Trager howls in a combination of pain and surprise as his back arches and he staggers to the ground. Roger Ackerman, that asshole, clutches his arm and tries to run but stumbles into the leaves.

Visible in the clearing now, he drops to one knee to steady himself as screams and cries fill the air, as fifty, sixty kids scatter in all directions like cockroaches, bumping into one another, tripping over one another, dropping their school bags and covering their heads, unsure initially which way to run, heads whipping in all directions, only knowing they should run, run, run—

"By the trees!" one parent yells.

"The parking lot!" cries another.

He fires and clicks in the next round, *aim-fire-click,* while panic propels the population of students like a strong gust of wind. Their squeals are like music. Their terror is his oxygen. He wishes this moment would never end.

Six hit, seven, eight in the clearing near him. Another half dozen farther away.

And then he raises his rifle with a dramatic flair and takes a moment, just a moment, to savor the delicious scene, the power he holds, the havoc he has created. It's like nothing he's ever felt. It's beyond words, this rush, this thrill coursing through him. And then his vision blurs, and it's a moment before he realizes it's not the wind causing it but his own tears.

There are probably a dozen pellets left in his BB rifle, but he's out of time. Faculty will pour out of the building any second. The STPD will be called. And he accomplished what he wanted, anyway. Just some superficial pellet wounds.

But wow, was that fun!

And I'm only twelve years old, he thinks. *You ain't seen nothin' yet.*

Book I

BRIDGEHAMPTON, 2011

Chapter 1

NOAH WALKER STANDS carefully on the roof of his house, takes a moment to ensure his balance, and removes the Yankees cap from his head to wipe the sweat off his brow under the scorching early-June sun. He never minded roofing work, but it's different when it's your own roof, the place you're renting, and the only reason you're doing it is the landlord will take six months to get to it, and you're sick of water spots on the ceiling.

He runs his hands through his thick, wavy hair. *The Matthew McConaughey look,* Paige calls it, noting that he has the physique to match. He's heard that comparison for years and never thought much of it. He never thought much of what anyone thought or said about him. If he did, he sure as hell wouldn't still be living in the Hamptons.

He hears the crunch of car tires down the road, the hum of a powerful, well-maintained engine. The unpaved roads just off Sag Harbor Turnpike are uneven at best, sometimes bumpy and other times outright treacherous. Not like the roads by the ocean, by the forty-thousand-square-foot mansions where the elite like to "summer." Not that he should bitch too much about the blue bloods; he makes twice as much from May to August, doing their bidding, as he does the rest of the year combined. He fixes what they need fixed. He digs what they need dug. He stomachs their condescension.

"Paige," he says to himself, even before her black-on-black Aston Martin convertible pulls into his driveway and parks next to his nineteen-year-old reconstructed Harley. She's not being discreet. She should probably be more careful. But back here in the woods where he lives, people don't mingle with the wealth, so there's no real danger of this getting back to Paige's husband, John Sulzman. It's not like his neighbors are going to run into Paige's husband at some high-society event. The closest people like him have ever come to a tuxedo is watching penguins on the Discovery Channel. Same zip code, different world.

Paige floats out of her convertible with the same grace with which she always carries herself. Noah feels the primal yearning that always accompanies the first sight of her. Paige Sulzman is one of those people for whom beauty is effortless, a privilege, not a chore. In her white hat and polka-dot dress, one hand holding the hat in place in the wind, she looks every bit the Manhattan socialite she is, but she hails from upstate originally and has maintained a sense of proportion and humility.

Paige. There's something refreshing about her. She is

a natural beauty, with her shiny blond hair and killer figure, her softly upturned nose and stunning hazel eyes. But it's not just her looks. She has a sharp wit, the ability to laugh at herself, the manners of a well-raised girl. She's one of the most sincere and decent people he's ever known.

She's pretty good in bed, too.

Noah climbs down the back and meets her inside the house. She rushes to him and plants her lips against his, her hands on his bare chest.

"I thought you were in Manhattan," he says.

She gives him a mock pout with those juicy lips. "That's not much of a greeting, mister. How about, 'Paige, I'm *so* very thrilled to see you!'"

"I *am* thrilled." And he is. He first saw Paige three years ago when he was cleaning the gutters on the Sulzman estate. Her image lingered with him long after. It was only six weeks ago that the stars aligned.

The prospect of Paige has always been both exhilarating and terrifying. Exhilarating, because he's never met someone who could light that flame inside him quite like she can. And terrifying, because she's married to John Sulzman.

But all that can wait. The electricity between them is palpable. His big rough hands trace the outline of her dress, cup her impressive breasts, run through her silky hair, as she lets out gentle moans and works the zipper on his blue jeans.

"I'm going to leave him," she says to him between halting breaths. "I'm going to do it."

"You can't," says Noah. "He'll . . . kill you."

She lets out a small gasp as Noah's hand reaches inside her panties. "I'm tired of being afraid of him. I don't care what he—what he—oh—oh, Noah—"

He lifts her off her feet and they bump against the front door, pushing it closed with a thud, a sound that seems to coincide with a similar sound, another door closing outside.

Noah carries Paige into the family room. He lays her down on the rug and rips her dress open, buttons flying, and brings his mouth to her breasts, then slides down to her panties. A moment later, her underwear has been removed and her legs are wrapped around his neck, her moans growing more urgent until she is calling out his name.

He moves upward and works his jeans down, freeing himself. He braces himself over Paige and gently slides inside her, her back arching in response. They find a rhythm, first slow and then urgent, and the sensation courses through Noah, the intensity building, a dam about to burst—

Then he hears another door closing. Then another.

He stops, suddenly, and raises his head.

"Someone's here," he says.

Chapter 2

NOAH PULLS ON his underwear and scrambles to his haunches, staying low. "Are you sure your husband—"

"I don't see how."

She doesn't see how? John Sulzman has endless resources, more money than some small countries. He easily could have tailed someone like Paige, who is far too innocent to notice something like that.

Noah takes one deep breath; his heartbeat slows and his veins turn icy. He finds his jeans on the floor and fishes the knife out of his back pocket.

"Go upstairs and hide," he tells Paige.

"I'm not going anywhere."

He doesn't bother to argue the point. Paige wouldn't listen, anyway.

And besides, they're not here for Paige. They're here for him.

Noah hears movement outside, not voices and nothing deliberate, which makes it worse—they aren't announcing themselves. He stays low and slips out of the living room, but not before catching a glimpse through the window of bodies in motion, some rushing around the side of the house, others toward the front door.

A small army is descending on his house. And he has nothing but a roofing knife.

In the hallway now, he faces the front door. There is little point in hiding. If he hid, they'd find him, and they'd be braced for action when they did, their guns poised, fanned out in some defensive formation. No, his only option is to get them when they come in, when they think they're sneaking in on a lovers' tryst, when they think Noah won't be ready for them. Surprise them, hurt them, and escape.

He hears the back door slam open at the same time that the front doorknob turns slowly. They're coming from both directions at once. He has almost no chance.

But he has nothing to lose, he figures, as he tightens his grip on the knife.

He moves one leg back, like a sprinter locking into his blocks before a race, ready to spring toward the front door with his knife, as the doorknob completes its rotation, as his pulse drums in his throat, as the front door pops open.

He lunges forward, ready to sweep the knife upward—

—a woman, a redhead dressed in blue jeans and a flak jacket, a gun held at her side, a badge dangling from a lanyard around her neck—

—A badge?—

—he tries to halt his momentum, falling to his knees,

sliding forward. The woman spins and kicks up her leg, and Noah sees the treads of her shoe just before impact. His head snaps back from the kick. His body arches and his head smacks the floor, stars and jagged lines dancing on the ceiling.

"Drop the knife or I drop you!" she says evenly. "STPD."

Noah blinks hard, his heartbeat still hammering. *STPD.*

The police?

"Toss the knife, Noah!" says the redheaded cop as several other officers flood in behind her.

"Jesus, okay." Noah drops the knife to the floor. Blood drips into the back of his mouth. A searing pain shoots through his nose and eyes.

"Don't move!" the other officers yell at Paige. "Hands in the air!"

"Don't hurt her!" Noah says. "She didn't do any—"

"Noah, you resist me again and I'll put you in the hospital." The redhead puts her foot on his chest. Despite his predicament, and the pain drumming through his head, and the fear gripping his heart, he registers this cop for the first time, her striking ice-blue eyes, her shiny red hair pulled back, her confidence.

"What—what is this?" he manages. His initial reaction of relief—nobody's going to kill him—is short-lived, especially with the crew of cops flooding in from the back now. Ten officers, he guesses, all wearing bulletproof vests and heavily armed.

Why?

"You don't have the right to do this!" Paige shouts

from the other room. It comes out as half protest, half lecture, the kind of thing a person with money would say, someone who doesn't shrink in the face of the cops like others might.

About the only thing Noah can see, through his blurred vision, is the female cop staring down at him. He's in his underwear, flat on his back with her foot on his chest and a pretty good shiner developing from the kick to his face. But hearing Paige's cry sets off something within him.

"This is my *home,*" he hisses, his hands forming into fists. "You have a problem with me, knock on my door and tell me."

"We have a problem with you, Noah," she says. "Feel better?"

Noah's eyes catch Detective Isaac Marks, whom Noah has known for years, going back to school days. Marks doesn't give much of a reaction, save for a small shrug of one shoulder.

The redhead orders Noah to roll over. She cuffs him and yanks him to his feet. The sudden movement, coupled with the concussive effects from the kick to his face, leaves Noah's legs unsteady.

"This is ridiculous," he says. "Does Dr. Redmond say I took his Rolex again? Tell him to look in the couch cushions." It wouldn't be the first time one of the gazillionaires misplaced something and accused the help of pilfering it. A movie producer once had Noah arrested for stealing his golf clubs, only to realize later he'd left them in the trunk of his car. "And do you think you brought enough cops?"

"Is that why you rushed me with a knife?" asks the redhead. "Because you thought I wanted to question you about a watch?"

"He knows this isn't about a Rolex." Noah recognizes the voice before he sees Langdon James swagger into the house. He's been the chief of the Southampton Town Police Department for over fifteen years. His jowls now hang over his collar, his belly over his belt, and his hair has gone completely gray, but he still has the baritone voice and thick sideburns.

What the hell is the chief doing here?

"Detective Murphy," the chief says to the redhead, "take him to the station. I'll handle the search of his house."

"Will someone tell me what's going on?" Noah demands, unable to conceal the fear choking his voice.

"Be happy to," says the chief. "Noah Walker, you're under arrest for the murders of Melanie Phillips and Zachary Stern."

Chapter 3

THE FUNERAL FOR Melanie Phillips is heavily attended, filling the pews of the Presbyterian church and overflowing onto Main Street. She was all of twenty years old when she was murdered, every day of which she lived in Bridgehampton. Poor girl, never got to see the world, though for some people, the place you grew up *is* your world. Maybe that was Melanie. Maybe all she ever wanted was to be a waitress at Tasty's Diner, serving steamers and lobster to tourists and townies and the occasional rich couple looking to drink in the "local environment."

But with her looks, at least from what I've seen in photos, she probably had bigger plans. A young woman like that, with luminous brown hair and sculpted features, could have been in magazines. That, no doubt, is why she caught the attention of Zach Stern, the head of a talent agency that included A-list celebrities, a man who owned his own jet and who liked to hang out in the Hamptons now and then.

And that, no doubt, is also why she caught the attention of Noah Walker, who apparently had quite an affinity for young Melanie himself and must not have taken too kindly to her affair with Zach.

It was only four nights ago that Zachary Stern and Melanie Phillips were found dead, victims of a brutal murder in a rental house near the beach that Zach had leased for the week. The carnage was brutal enough that Melanie's service was closed-casket.

So the crowd is due in part to Melanie's local popularity, and in part to the media interest, given Zach Stern's notoriety in Hollywood.

It is also due, I am told, to the fact that the murders occurred at 7 Ocean Drive, which among the locals has become known as the Murder House.

Now we've moved to the burial, which is just next door to the church. It allows the throng that couldn't get inside the church to mill around the south end of the cemetery, where Melanie Phillips will be laid to rest. There must be three hundred people here, if you count the media, which for the most part are keeping a respectful distance even while they snap their photographs.

The overhead sun at midday is strong enough for squinting and sunglasses, both of which make it harder for me to do what I came here to do, which is to check out the people attending the funeral to see if anyone pings my radar. Some of these creeps like to come and watch the sorrow they caused, so it's standard operating procedure to scan the crowd at crime scenes and funerals.

"Remind me why we're here, Detective Murphy," says my partner, Isaac Marks.

"I'm paying my respects."

"You didn't know Melanie," he says.

True enough. I don't know anyone around here. Once upon a time, my family came here every summer, a good three-week stretch straddling June and July, to stay with Uncle Langdon and Aunt Chloe. My memories of those summers—beaches and boat rides and fishing off the docks—end at age eight.

For some reason I never knew, my family stopped coming after that. Until nine months ago when I joined the force, I hadn't set foot in the Hamptons for eighteen years.

"I'm working on my suntan," I say.

"Not to mention," says Isaac, ignoring my remark, "that we already have our bad guy in custody."

Also true. We arrested Noah Walker yesterday. He'll get a bond hearing tomorrow, but there's no way the judge is going to bond him out on a double murder.

"And might I further add," says Isaac, "that this isn't even your case."

Right again. I volunteered to lead the team arresting Noah, but I wasn't given the case. In fact, the chief—my aforementioned uncle Langdon—is handling the matter personally. The town, especially the hoity-toity millionaires along the beach, just about busted a collective gut when the celebrity agent Zach Stern was brutally murdered in their scenic little hamlet. It's the kind of case that could cost the chief his job, if he isn't careful. I'm told the town supervisor has been calling him on the hour for updates.

So why am I here, at a funeral for someone I don't know, on a case that isn't mine? Because I'm bored. Because since I left the NYPD, I haven't seen any action. And because I've handled more homicides in eight years on the force than all of these cops in Bridgehampton put together. Translation: I wanted the case, and I was a little displeased when I didn't get it.

"Who's that?" I ask, gesturing across the way to an odd-looking man in a green cap, with long stringy hair and ratty clothes. Deep-set, creepy eyes that seem to wander. He shifts his weight from foot to foot, unable to stay still.

Isaac pushes down his sunglasses to get a better look. "Oh, that's Aiden Willis," he says. "He works for the church. Probably dug Melanie's grave."

"Looks like he slept in it first."

Isaac likes that. "Seriously, Murphy. You're looking for suspects? With all you know about this case, which is diddly-squat, you don't like Noah Walker for the murders?"

"I'm not saying that," I answer.

"You're not denying it, either."

I consider that. He's right, of course. What the hell do I know about Noah Walker or the evidence against him? He may not have jumped out at me as someone who'd just committed a brutal double murder, but when do public faces ever match private misdeeds? I once busted a second-grade schoolteacher who was selling heroin to the high school kids. And a teenage volunteer who was boning the corpses in the basement of the hospital. You never know people. And I'd known Noah Walker for all of thirty minutes.

"Go home," says Isaac. "Go work out—"

Already did this morning.

"—or see the ocean—"

I've seen it already. It's a really big body of water.

"—or have a drink."

Yeah, a glass of wine might be in my future. But first, I'm going to take a quick detour. A detour that could probably get me in a lot of trouble.

Chapter 4

LANGDON JAMES CLOSES his eyes for just a moment and raises his face to the sun shining down on the backyard cocktail party. In these moments, with a slight buzz from the gin and the elite of Southampton surrounding him, he likes to pretend he is one of them, one of the socialites, the mega-wealthy, the trust fund babies and personal injury lawyers, the songwriters and tennis pros, the TV producers and stock speculators. He is not, of course. He wasn't born with a silver spoon, and he was always more street-savvy than book-smart. But he has found another route to power, through a badge, and most of the time, that is enough.

There are at least a hundred people in the sprawling backyard, most of them blue bloods, all of them here to support the reelection of Town Supervisor Dawn McKittredge and her slate, but really here to be seen, to eat elaborate hors d'oeuvres served by waiters in white coats and talk about their latest acquisition or conquest. They don't live here year-round, and the only relevance the governing authorities of the town hold for them is the rare zoning issue that may arise—water rights, land use, and the like—or in Chief James's case, the occasional drug bust or DUI or dalliance with prostitutes from Sag Harbor.

"Nice day, Chief."

Langdon turns to see John Sulzman. He's had a place on the ocean in Bridgehampton, a tiny hamlet incorporated within Southampton, for over a decade now. Sulzman made his money in hedge funds and now spends half his time in DC and Albany, lobbying legislatures and cutting deals. His net worth, according to a *New York Post* article Langdon read last year, is upwards of half a billion. Sulzman's on his third marriage—to the lovely Paige—and what appears to be his third or fourth Scotch, judging from the slurring of his words. He's wearing a button-down shirt with the collar open and white slacks. He is overweight, with a round weathered face and a full head of hair if you count the toupee, one of the better ones Langdon has seen, but still—don't these guys realize everybody knows?

"John," says the chief.

"I understand Noah Walker is in custody," says Sulzman, as if he's commenting on the weather. "I understand you were there, personally."

"I was." The chief takes a sip of his gin. No lime, no tonic, no stirrer. To all appearances, he could be drinking ice water, which is the point.

"I saw the police report," says Sulzman. "What was in it, and what was not."

His wife, he means. The chief didn't mention Paige

in the police report, thus concealing her presence from the media. John Sulzman probably thinks he did it to curry favor, but he didn't. There was no need to include her. She had nothing to do with the arrest, other than being a bystander.

But if Sulzman sees it as a favor—well, there are worse things.

"It's not a well-kept secret that you have your eyes on the sheriff's job, Chief."

Langdon doesn't answer. But Sulzman is right. The Suffolk County sheriff is retiring, and it would be a nice cap-off to Langdon's law enforcement career.

Sulzman raises his glass in acknowledgment. "Ambition is what makes the world go round. It's what drives men to excel at their jobs."

"I always try to do my best," says the chief.

"And I try to reward those who do." Sulzman takes a long drink and breathes out with satisfaction. "If Noah Walker is convicted, I'll consider you to have excelled at your job. And I'll be eager to support your next endeavor. Are you familiar with my fund-raising efforts, Chief?"

It so happens that the chief is. But he doesn't acknowledge it.

"I can raise millions for you. Or I could raise millions for your opponent."

"And who would my opponent be?" The chief looks at Sulzman.

Sulzman shrugs and cocks his head. "Whoever I want it to be." He taps the chief's arm. "And do you know who else is familiar with my fund-raising efforts? Our town supervisor. Your boss."

Chief James takes another sip of his gin. "Would that be a threat?"

"A threat? No, Chief. A promise. If Noah Walker goes free, there will be people in this community—maybe I'll be one of them—who will call for your head."

John Sulzman is not known for his subtlety. When you're worth five hundred million dollars, you probably don't have to be. So if Noah is convicted, the chief is a lock to be the next sheriff. If Noah walks, the chief can kiss his current job, and any future in law enforcement, good-bye.

"Noah Walker is going to be convicted," says the chief, "because he's guilty."

"Of course he is." Sulzman nods. "Of course."

This conversation should be over. It never should have started, but it should definitely end now. A guy like Sulzman is smart enough to know that.

And yet Sulzman hasn't left. He has something else to say.

"There's a . . . new officer on the case?" he asks. "A woman?"

The chief whips his head over to Sulzman.

"Your niece," says Sulzman, clearly pleased with himself for the knowledge he's obtained, and happy to throw it in the chief's face. "Jenna Murphy."

"Jenna's not on the case," says the chief. "She handled the arrest, that's all."

"I only mention it because I understand she had some issues with the NYPD," says Sulzman.

"The only 'issue' she had is she's an honest cop," Langdon snaps. "Truth is, the day she arrived, she was the best cop on our force. She's as smart as they come, and she's tough and honest, and she wouldn't put up with corruption she found in Manhattan. She wouldn't go along with dirty cops, and she wouldn't look the other way."

Sulzman nods and purses his lips.

"It's not her case, John," says the chief.

Sulzman appraises the chief, looking him up and down, then square in the eye. "I just care about the result," he says. "Make it happen. Make sure Noah Walker goes into a very deep hole. Or there will be . . . consequences."

"Noah Walker is going into a hole because—"

"Because he's guilty," says Sulzman. "Yes, I know. I know, Lang. Just . . . don't forget this conversation. You want me as a friend, not an enemy."

With that, John Sulzman makes his exit, joining some acquaintances under the shade of the tent. Chief Langdon James watches him leave, then decides he's had enough of this party.

Chapter 5

AS THE FUNERAL for Melanie Phillips ends, I say good-bye to my partner, Detective Isaac Marks, without telling him where I'm going. He doesn't need to know, and I don't know if he'd keep the information to himself. I'm not yet sure where his loyalties lie, and I'm not going to make the same mistake I made with the NYPD.

I decide to walk, heading south from the cemetery toward the Atlantic. I always underestimate the distance to the ocean, but it's a nice day for a walk, even if a little steamy. And I enjoy the houses just south of Main Street along this road, the white-trimmed Cape Cods with cedar shingles whose colors have grown richer with age from all the precipitation that comes with proximity to the ocean. Some are bigger, some are newer, but these houses generally look the same, which I find comforting and a little creepy at the same time.

As I get closer to the ocean, the plots of land get wider, the houses get bigger, and the privacy shrubs flanking them get taller. I stop when I reach shrubbery that's a good ten feet high. I know I've found the place because the majestic wrought-iron gates at the end of the driveway, which are slightly parted, are adorned with black-and-yellow tape that says CRIME SCENE DO NOT CROSS.

I slide between the gates without breaking the seal. I start up the driveway, but it curves off to some kind of carriage house up a hill. So I take the stone path that will eventually lead me to the front door.

In the center of the wide expanse of grass, just before it slopes dramatically upward, there is a small stone fountain, with a monument jutting up that bears a crest and an inscription. I lean over the fountain to take a closer look. The small tablet of stone features a bird in the center, with a hooked beak and a long tail feather, encircled by little symbols, each of which appears to be the letter *X*, but which upon closer inspection is a series of crisscrossing daggers.

And then, *ka-boom*.

It hits me, the rush, the pressure in my chest, the stranglehold to my throat, I can't breathe, I can't see, I'm weightless. *Help me, somebody please help me—*

I stagger backward, almost losing my balance, and suck in a deep, delicious breath of air.

"Wow," I say into the warm breeze. *Easy, girl. Take it easy.* I wipe greasy sweat from my forehead and inhale and exhale a few more times to slow my pulse.

Beneath the monument's crest, carved into the stone in a thick Gothic font, are these words:

Cecilia, O Cecilia
Life was death disguised

Okay, that's pretty creepy. I take a photo of the monument with my smartphone. Now front and center before the house, I take my first good look.

The mansion peering down at me from atop the hill is a Gothic structure of faded multicolored limestone. It has a Victorian look to it, with multiple rooflines, all of them steeply pitched, fancy turrets, chimneys grouped at each end. There are elaborate medieval-style accents on the facade. Every peak is topped with an ornament that ends in a sharp point, like spears aimed at the gods. The windows are long and narrow, clover-shaped, with stained glass. The house is like one gigantic, imperious frown.

I've heard some things about this house, read some things, even passed by it many times, but seeing it up close like this sends a chill through me.

It is part cathedral and part castle. It is a scowling, menacing, imposing structure, both regal and haunting, almost romantic in its gloom.

All it's missing is a drawbridge and a moat filled with crocodiles.

This is 7 Ocean Drive. This is what they call the Murder House.

This isn't your case, I remind myself. *This isn't your problem.*

This could cost you your badge, girl.

I start up the hill toward the front door.

Chapter 6

I'M TRANSPORTED BACK hundreds of years, to a time when you rode by horseback or carriage, when you lived by candlelight and torches, when you treated infections with leeches.

When I close the front door of the house at 7 Ocean Drive, the sound echoes up to the impossibly high, rounded ceiling, decorated with an ornate fresco of winged angels and naked women and bearded men in flowing robes, all of them appearing to reach toward something, or maybe toward one another.

The second anteroom is as chilling and dated as the first, with patterned tile floors and more of the arched, Old Testament ceilings, antique furniture, gold-framed portraits on the walls of men dressed in ruffled shirts and long coats, wigs of wavy white hair and sharply angled hats—formal-wear, circa 1700.

The guy who built this place, the patriarch of the family, a guy named Winston Dahlquist, apparently didn't have a sense of humor.

My heels echo on the hardwood floor as I enter the airy foyer rising up three stories to the roof. Every step I take elicits a reaction from this house, fleeting coughs and groans.

"Hello," I say, like a child might, the sound returning to me faintly.

The stairs up to the second floor are winding and predictably creaky. The house continues to call out from parts unseen, aches and hiccups and wheezes, a centuries-old creature drawing long, labored breaths.

When I reach the landing, it seizes me again, stealing the air from my lungs, pressing against my chest, blinding me, *No, please! Please, please, stop—*

—high-pitched childlike squeals, uncontrollable laughter—

Please don't, please don't do this to me.

I grasp the banister so I don't fall back down the stairs. I open my eyes and raise my face, panting for air, until my heartbeat finally decelerates.

"Get a grip, Murphy." I pass through ornate double doors to the second-floor hallway, where the smell greets me immediately, the coppery odor of spilled blood, the overpowering, putrid scent of decay. I walk along a thick red carpet, the walls papered with red and gold, as I approach the bedroom where Zach Stern and Melanie Phillips took their last breaths.

I step onto the dark hardwood floor and look around the room. Gold wallpaper is everywhere. Against one wall is a king-sized canopy bed with thick purple curtains and sturdy bedposts. The bed is dressed in a purple comforter and ruffle with velvet pillows, some of which are still on the bed, some of which lie on the floor. The dark wood dresser holds two pewter statuettes that were probably bookends for the thick volumes of short stories that also now lie on the floor. The statuettes, as well as an antique brass alarm clock, are knocked to the side on the dresser.

Opposite the bed, made of wood that matches the dresser, is a giant armoire. And in the far corner of the room, south of the armoire and west of the dresser, is the bathroom.

I remove copies of the crime-scene photos I xeroxed from the file. Zachary Stern was found lying facedown on the floor, his head turned to the right toward the door, his feet pointed toward the bed. Beneath him was a pool of blood and other bodily excrement from the horrific stab wound to his midsection. Several of his fingers were crushed as well. Melanie Phillips was found by the armoire opposite the bed, the back of her right hand touching the armoire's leg; she was lying on her stomach like Zach, her head to the left, her eyes open and her mouth frozen in a tiny o. She was stabbed more than a dozen times, in the breasts and torso and then in the face, neck, back, arms, and legs.

Now back to the scene. The comforter on the bed has been pulled back on the left side, showing a large blood pool where Zach was first stabbed while lying in bed. There is blood spatter on the wall behind the bed, and a thick sea of blood embedded in the floor where he died. There is blood spatter on the armoire and all over the nearby floor where Melanie lay as she died.

Two more facts: Judging from the fresh semen found

inside Melanie and on Zach's genitalia, it seems clear that the two of them had had sexual intercourse not long before they were killed. And as of now, barring DNA testing that is still pending, there is no physical evidence putting Noah Walker in this house—no fingerprints, no carpet fibers, no shoe or boot prints.

And now the theory the STPD and the district attorney are running with: Noah was obsessed with Melanie. He somehow learned of her affair with Zach and followed her here. We don't know how he got in. The front door should have been locked, and no damage was done to it. In any event, he lay in wait until they had completed their sexual intercourse, when they were relaxed, when their guard was down, to spring into the room.

Noah surprised Zach in bed, plunging his knife into Zach's chest and dragging the blade downward, causing a vertical cut of roughly five inches, tearing open the esophagus and stomach. At this point, Melanie, who was in the bathroom cleaning up, came out. Noah subdued her by the dresser, knocking over the books and alarm clock and stabbing her multiple times in the breasts and torso before throwing her to the floor by the armoire, where he continued to stab her from behind, slicing her cheek and ear and neck and then her back, arms, and legs. He then returned to Zach and threw him out of the bed and onto the floor, stomping on and crushing some of Zach's fingers in a blind rage.

I move to the corner beyond where Zach's body was found and squat down, trying to get the angle right and using the photos to make sure I'm accurate. Where Zach would have been lying on the floor, with his head to the right, his sight line travels beyond the edge of the bed to the armoire. I repeat the same exercise from Melanie's vantage point and get the same line of vision, from the opposite end.

I remove my compact from my purse and squat down by the leg of the armoire that Melanie's right hand touched. I curl the compact under the armoire and around the leg so I can see the back of it. As I thought, the wood is abraded—scraped and cut.

Ten minutes later, I'm walking on Ocean Drive toward Main Street, on my cell phone with Uncle Lang. "Melanie Phillips was handcuffed to the armoire's leg," I say. "He made her watch the whole thing. This wasn't an act of blind rage, Chief. This was a calculated, well-executed act of sadism."

Chapter 7

I GET BACK to my car and drive to see the chief, who is away from the office this afternoon (don't ever tell him he has the day off, because he'll spend a half hour explaining that the chief of police never has a day off). My uncle lives on North Sea Road in a three-bedroom cottage set back from the road and flanked with well-manicured shrubbery that always reminds me of a defensive military formation.

The front door is unlocked and open. It smells like it always smells in here, musty guy scent: dirty socks and body odor combined with the latest fast-food takeout he ate. A bachelor pad, ever since Aunt Chloe left him two years ago.

On my way to the back porch, I detour to the kitchen, open his fridge, and peer inside. Cartons of Chinese takeout, half a Subway sandwich in its wrapping, a twelve-pack of Budweiser with three cans remaining, a long stick of summer sausage, a pizza box shoved in the back. Oh, yes, and then a tall plastic container of sliced fruit that's packed to the rim, and a batch of veggie lasagna, still in the shrink-wrapped casserole dish, with only one square cut out of the corner.

I find Uncle Lang out back, sitting in a chair overlooking his lawn, a water sprinkler doing its thing, the air steamy as a sauna. Lang is wearing a button-down shirt and slacks and decent loafers. I'd forgotten he had that fund-raiser earlier today.

"Heya, missy," he says to me. His eyes are small and red. The glass of gin in his hand isn't his first of the day. He probably drank gin at the fund-raiser and pretended it was ice water.

I kiss his forehead and sit in the chair on the other side of the small glass table, the one holding the bottle of Beefeater.

"You haven't touched the fruit I cut up for you," I say. "And the veggie lasagna? What's the deal there? You preserving it for posterity?"

He sips his gin. "I don't like spinach. I told you that."

"Yeah?" I turn to him. "And what's your excuse for the fruit?"

He waves me off. "I don't know, it's . . . mushy."

"It's pineapple and melon and cantaloupe. You like them."

"Well, it's mushy."

"That's because you let it sit there for a week. I cut it up a week ago and you didn't touch it. Not one piece." I whack the back of my hand against his shoulder.

"Ow. Don't hit me."

"I'll hit you if I want to hit you. You're like a child.

You're like a little kid. That spinach lasagna is delicious."

"Then you eat it."

"Hopeless," I say. "You're hopeless. You know your doctor's appointment is next week. You think Dr. Childress is going to say, 'Congratulations, Chief, a month of eating meatball sandwiches and fried chicken and French fries did the trick—your cholesterol has plummeted!'"

Lang pushes the empty second glass over toward me and gives me a crosswise look. "Don't think I don't know what you're doing, missy."

"I'm looking out for the well-being of my only living family."

"No, you're *deflecting*. You call me up and tell me you've been to the crime scene, which you know you're not supposed to do, since this isn't your case, so you try to put me on the defensive about my eating habits."

I pour myself a glass of gin. One won't kill me. "Ten gets you twenty that the abrasions on the armoire leg came from a handcuff. He made each of them watch the other die," I say. "He immobilized Zach and he handcuffed Melanie to the armoire. He made them watch each other bleed out."

"Jenna—"

"This guy knew what he was doing," I say. "He stabbed Zach in a place where he wouldn't die instantly. I mean, he could have sunk that knife into his heart, or slit his throat. Instead, he stabbed him in a place that would cause incredible pain and a slow death. And when Zach made any feeble attempt to raise himself up, he stomped on his hands. And he did the same thing to

Melanie. Every time she tried to move, he stabbed her. She kicked her legs, and he stabbed her in the calf. She raised her free arm, and he stabbed her in the triceps—"

"Jenna—"

"These were sadistic, brutal torture-murders," I say, "not crimes of passion committed by a jealous lover."

"Crimes of passion can be sadistic, Jen—"

"Do you really think if Noah was in love with Melanie, he'd watch Zach have sex with her first? Why wouldn't he rush in while they were in the heat of it?"

"Hey!" the chief shouts. "Do I get a word in here? I've heard enough. There is protocol, and there is a chain of command, and nobody breaches that in Southampton. If you think just because you're my niece—"

"Of course I don't think that. And I'm just trying to help—"

"You're not helping. You're not helping at all!" The chief coughs into his fist, his face turning red. He needs to take better care of himself. I can make all the heart-healthy meals the culinary world has to offer, but I can't make him eat them. I can tell him to walk a couple of miles a few times a week, but I can't walk them for him. He ignores every bit of advice I give him. He openly defies me on a daily basis. So why do I love this grouchy old man so much?

"Why am I not helping?" I ask.

Lang polishes off his glass of gin and composes himself. "Because Noah Walker confessed," he says.

I draw back. "He . . . confessed?"

"Ah, the hotshot from NYPD doesn't have all the answers, does she?" Lang pours himself another inch of gin. "He confessed this morning. So don't you go writing up a report that I'll have to show a defense lawyer. Not when this thing is tied up in a bow."

"Noah confessed," I mumble, raising the glass to my lips. "I'll be damned."

"Noah Walker is guilty, and Noah Walker confessed," he says. "So do me a favor and move along."

Chapter 8

THE DIVE BAR is aptly named, dark in every way, from the dim lighting to the oak furnishings, with the Yankees on the big screen, mirrors behind the bar sponsored by various breweries, and nothing but some fried appetizers on the menu for those who dare eat. But the people are friendly and laid-back. It's a place to disappear, and disappearing sounds good to me at the moment. It started as a glass of wine, and then it became three, and I'm thinking it's five now. Once I started, I couldn't think of a good reason to stop.

This place is locals only—tradesmen and laborers and the occasional cop—which I prefer, because it's high season in the Hamptons and all the money's in town. Not that I don't enjoy seeing men with cardigans tied around their necks and women with so much work done on their faces that they've begun to resemble the Joker. Just not on my day off. And not after the day I've had, making a jerk out of myself in front of my uncle, the guy who gave me a second chance.

I should stop drinking. My thoughts are swimming and my mood is darkening. I'm still not sure I made the right move, coming to the Hamptons. I could have found something else to do in Manhattan, or I could have tried to find another big city and start over, even if I had to start at the bottom rung again on patrol. But my uncle the chief made me an offer, and nobody else was knocking down my door.

"Shit," I say, the word slow and heavy on my tongue. I check my watch, and it's nearing six o'clock in the evening. I haven't eaten anything since breakfast, and my stomach is hollowed out and churning. (Some might argue that's an apt summary of my life, too.)

"Whatever, man. Whatever! You know I'm good for it! How long I been comin' here?"

The small outburst comes from the guy at the end of the bar, whom I've managed not to notice since I've been here. Or maybe he just arrived. My brain isn't hitting on all cylinders right now.

He's dressed the same way he was today at Melanie Phillips's funeral, a dark T-shirt that I might otherwise use to wipe my kitchen counter, a green ball cap turned backward, his long, strawlike hair popping out on both sides and covering his ears.

"Jerry," I say to the bartender. That's a good bartender name, *Jerry*. "Put his beer on my tab."

Jerry, a portly guy with a big round head and a green apron, gives me a crosswise look. I nod and he shrugs, pulling on the lever to fill Aiden Willis's mug with a Budweiser he couldn't afford.

Aiden's deep-set eyes move in my direction. He

doesn't say anything. There may be a glint of recognition, if he noticed me at the cemetery. My biggest flaw as a cop is my bright-red hair. When I was undercover for a year and a half and didn't want to be memorable, I dyed it black.

I go back to my Pinot, trying to remind myself that I'm off duty but wondering if Aiden the cemetery caretaker will come over. When I glance back up a few minutes later, Aiden is still looking at me, his beer untouched. He doesn't acknowledge me in any way, just stares with those raccoon eyes. But even his stare isn't really a stare. His eyes move about, wandering aimlessly, always returning to me but never staying on me.

My cell phone buzzes, a text message. Ten mins away. R U at home?, the message reads. My hesitation to respond surprises me, but there it is. *Always trust your gut,* my father used to say. *Sometimes it's all you have.*

Well, Pop, I had a gut feeling about Noah Walker, and look where that got me.

I type in the address of the bar and hit Send. I look back to the corner of the bar, where Aiden's mug remains full of beer, but Aiden himself is gone.

I'm into my next glass, which now puts me at about five too many, if anyone's counting, when the door of the place pops open and a lot of people's chins rise. I don't even need to turn around to know it's Matty, who would stick out in this place like an oil stain on cotton. A moment later, an arm comes over my shoulder and playfully around my neck. His cologne greets me next, before his face is against mine. This is where I'm supposed to swoon with unbridled delight.

"Hey, gorgeous. What's with the depressing-bar thing?"

Matty Queenan is a Wall Street investor with a job I can't really describe because I've never really understood all the financial hocus-pocus these guys pull. All I really understand is that it's a game without rules: You pick a winner for your clients, then bet on them to lose behind their backs, and if everything goes to shit, the little guy will get screwed but the government will bail you out.

"Want a drink?" I ask Matty.

"Here? No. Let's go someplace decent."

I look at Jerry, who pretends he didn't hear what Matty just said.

"Seriously, Murphy. This place is a dump. I'm going to need a tetanus shot—"

"Keep your voice down." I'm standing now, whispering harshly in his ear. "People can hear you. You're being rude."

He takes me by the arm, but I pull away. "Jerry," I say, "I apologize for my rude friend, and please buy everyone a round on me." I slap a fifty on the bar, having already paid for my other drinks, and get some applause for the gesture along with some hard stares in my boyfriend's direction.

I hear my cell phone ring in my purse, but I'm too hacked off to do anything but storm out of the place, Matty not far behind.

Chapter 9

"WHAT'S WITH THE asshole routine?" I say to Matty as soon as I'm back in the sweltering heat outside.

"What's with being half in the bag before I show up? What's with hanging out in a seedy dive like that?"

I turn to look at my boyfriend of eleven months, the first two of which we spent together when I lived in the city, the last nine of which have been long-distance. I probably am a little tipsier than I should be, but he didn't even call and let me know he was coming until a few hours ago, when he was already on his way. That's Matty for you, always on his own schedule, just assuming I'll drop everything and jump into his arms when he shows up.

Okay, to be fair, it's not like I was working on my doctoral thesis or trying to end world hunger when he called.

I turn back to him. Matty looks like a Wall Street guy even when he dresses down, in an Armani sport coat, silk shirt, and expensive trousers, with Ferragamo shoes that would consume an entire paycheck of mine, his long hair slicked back. He's got the looks, no doubt. His confidence, more than anything, drew me to him when we met—guess where—at a bar in Midtown.

"Don't get me wrong," he says, moving to me. "I like you when you're tipsy."

I push his hands away. "Those people in there are nice folks. You insulted them."

He thinks for a moment, then puts a hand on his chest. "Then I will march back in there and give a bar-wide apology. Will that make Jenna happy?" He doesn't wait for an answer, instead raising his arm and checking his watch. "I just decided something," he says.

I guess I'm supposed to ask what. A few one-liners leap to mind.

"I just decided that this place is bad for you. You don't belong here. Just seeing you in the bar seals it. You need the city, kiddo. This place is depressing you."

"Manhattan would depress me," I say, even though in some ways, there's no place I'd rather be. There's no place like it in the world. But I got to know it through a cop's eyes, and seeing it otherwise now would be like a cruel joke every day.

"Well, we need to figure *something* out," he says as we reach his Beemer, fire-engine red with a beige interior. "This commute is a bitch."

"It'll be better after Labor Day, when the Rockefellers and Vanderbilts take off."

"Talk about depressing," he says as he uses his remote to pop the locks. "Summer's the only time this place is interesting. Hey," he says as I open the passenger door.

"Hey what?"

He nods at me. "Are you going to change? We're going to Quist."

For the first time, I take an inventory of myself. I'm wearing a sleeveless white blouse, blue jeans, and low heels. But even the nicest places—and Quist is the nicest, a hotel restaurant opened by some celebrity chef—have a pretty relaxed dress code in the summer.

"Let's swing by your place," he says. "Wear that lavender dress I bought you. Then you'll be turning heads."

"But I won't turn heads in this?"

He chuckles at his faux pas. "C'mon, you know what I mean. We're going to a five-star restaurant. You really want to look like that?"

I hike my purse back over my shoulder and remember my cell phone, the call I missed a moment ago. I pull out my iPhone and see that the call came from "Uncle Langdon," which I really should change to "Chief James" now.

Taking another look at my phone, I see that the chief actually called me twice, once a minute ago and once twenty-four minutes ago.

Still standing outside the car, I dial him back.

"Jenna Rose," he answers, the only person who's ever incorporated my middle name when addressing me. The only one who's lived to tell about it, anyway. "I was about to give up on you."

"How can I help you, Chief? Were you looking for my recipe for grilled asparagus? It's not that hard. Just grill the asparagus."

"No, missy, not just now. You wanted to work a homicide, right?"

I spring to attention. "Yes, sir. Absolutely."

"Then get your butt in gear, Detective," he says. "You just got a homicide. One you may never forget."

Chapter 10

"IT'S MY JOB. It's not like I have a choice," I say to Matty, his knuckles white on the leather steering wheel of his Beemer as we drive along the back roads. "A woman was murdered."

"It can't wait until after dinner? She'll still be dead."

I close my eyes. "You didn't really just say that, did you?"

The back roads are narrow and winding and unforgiving, two lanes at best, with no shoulders. Driving them in the dark is even worse. But without the back roads, the locals in Bridgehampton would collectively commit suicide during the tourist season, when the principal artery—Main Street or, if you prefer, Montauk Highway—is clogged like a golf ball in a lower intestine.

"I passed up Yankees tickets on the third-base line," he says. "Sabathia against Beckett in game one."

I know. I watched it in the bar. Sabathia got tagged for six earned runs in five innings. "It's my job," I say again. "What am I sup—"

"No, it's not."

"What do you mean, it's not—"

"Not *tonight* it's not!"

We find our destination, lit up by the STPD like a nighttime construction job, spotlights shining on the scene deep within the woods. The road has been reduced to one lane by traffic cones and flares.

Matty pulls up, puts it in park, and shifts in his seat to face me. "Don't act like you have no choice. There are detectives on duty right now. You're not one of them. You didn't have to take this assignment. You *wanted* it."

I pinch the bridge of my nose. "Sorry about your Yankees tickets."

"Jenna, c'mon."

I step out of the Beemer and flash my badge to the uniform minding the perimeter. I dip under the crime-scene tape and watch my step as I walk through the woods, with their uneven footing and stray branches.

It's a large lot, undeveloped land full of tall trees, with a FOR SALE sign near the road. Whoever did this picked a remote location.

Isaac Marks approaches me. "Bru-tal," he says. "C'mon." I follow him through the brush, my feet crunching leaves and twigs. "The guy who owns this lot found her," he says. "Nice old guy, late seventies. He was stopping by for some routine maintenance and heard a swarm of insects buzzing around."

I slow my approach when I see her. It's hard to miss her, under the garish lighting. She looks artificial, like a museum exhibit—*Woman in Repose,* except in this case, it would be more like *Woman with a tree stump through her midsection.*

"Jesus," I mumble.

The woman is naked, arms and legs splayed out, her head fallen back, as she lies suspended several feet off the ground, impaled on the trunk of a tree that has been shaved down to the point of a thick spear.

Technicians are working her over right now, photographing and gently probing her. The insects buzzing around her are fierce. She's suffered some animal bites, too. That, plus the look of her skin, gives me an approximate window on time of death.

"She died . . . maybe one, two days ago," I say.

Isaac looks at me. "Very good, Detective. At least that's what the ME is saying at first glance. One to two days."

"That's a significant difference, one versus two days."

"Yeah? Why?"

"Two days ago," I say, "Noah Walker was a free man. But one day ago, we took him into custody, and he couldn't have done this."

"You're connecting this with *Noah Walker?*" Isaac gives me a crosswise glance. "This is nothing like those murders."

I move in for a closer look at the victim. This nameless woman, hardened and discolored now, with the ravages of nature having taken their toll, is hard to categorize. I'm thinking she's pretty young, from the bone structure and lithe build. Early twenties, maybe, what appear to be nice features, and beautiful brown hair hanging down inches from the grass.

She was pretty. Before some monster impaled her on a wooden spear like a sacrificial offering to the gods, this woman was pretty. "No ID yet," says Isaac. "But we have a missing-persons from Sag Harbor that we think will check out. If it does, then this is . . ." He flips open a notepad and holds it in the artificial light. "Bonnie Stamos. Age twenty-four. Couple of arrests for take-a-wild-guess."

"She was a working girl." Not terribly surprising. The clients a prostitute serves come in all shapes and sizes, but it's like I felt when I was on patrol, approaching a car I'd just pulled over—you're never really sure what's waiting for you.

"This is totally different than what we found on Ocean Drive," Isaac says. "Those were a bloodbath. This thing is . . . what . . . posed, I guess. Dramatic. Like some ritual thing, some ancient Mayan ceremony. How do you connect these two crimes?"

I squat down next to the tree stump and gesture at it. "See the side of the tree and the surrounding grass and dirt?"

"I see blood everywhere, if that's what you mean."

"Exactly," I say. "Blood everywhere. Her heart was still pumping. *That's* how I connect these crimes."

"Not following."

"She was still alive when he did this, when he impaled her on the tree trunk." I stand back up and feel a wave of nausea. "The symbolism was incidental, a means to an end," I say. "He wanted her to die a slow death, Isaac. He wanted her to suffer."

Chapter 11

THE CHIEF HAS the porch light on for me when I walk up the steps to his house. The squad car that drove me here idles in the driveway. The door is open, and Uncle Lang has a bottle of gin and two glasses on the kitchen table. Dirty dishes are piled high in the sink just as they were earlier today, with evidence of meal choices—remnants of dried catsup or smears of brown gravy, a bit of hamburger. The floor could use a good wash, too. The clock on the wall says it's almost two in the morning.

My uncle doesn't look well. He's gained a lot of weight since Aunt Chloe left him two years ago. His face is splotchy, broken capillaries on his prominent nose, his eyes rimmed with heavy bags. He's wearing a wife-beater T-shirt that accentuates his added poundage, tufts of curly white chest hair peeking over the top.

"You don't look good," he says to me.

I kiss him on the forehead before I turn to the refrigerator. "I was just thinking the same about you. Still drinking, I see." I take another glance into his refrigerator. The fruit container still hasn't been touched, but a second square is missing from the pan of spinach lasagna.

I look back at him with an eyebrow raised.

"See?" he says. "I listen to you."

"Yeah?" I take a seat across from him. "And if I look through your trash, will I find an entire square piece of lasagna, without a bite taken?"

"Now you've insulted me. I'm insulted."

That's not a denial. But I can't spend every waking moment hectoring him.

"I'm serious, though," Uncle Lang says. "You look worn out. Are you still having nightmares?"

I shrug. It's been a thing, since I returned to Bridgehampton. Usually they come at night, the sensation of choking, the terror, the desperate cries. What happened to me today, at 7 Ocean Drive, was the first time it ever happened during daylight.

Lang pours me an inch of gin and slides the glass across the table. "Maybe you never should have come back here."

The thought has crossed my mind. It leads to another thought. "Why did my family stop coming here when I was a kid?" I ask.

The chief shrugs. "A story for another time."

"So there's a *story*. Something happened?"

Lang casts a fleeting glance at me, then deflects. "Did you move the body tonight?"

I nod. "We had to cut the tree from underneath her. Didn't want to separate her from the trunk yet. Never know what forensics might pick up."

"Good. Good that you moved her. I don't need to see photos in the *Patch* tomorrow. This is a dead hooker, Detective. Not a dead hooker who was split in half on a tree stump like some human *shish kebab*. Understand me? A dead hooker, to the media. That's it. Just another hooker *adiosed* in the Hamptons. That's a one-day story."

A one-day story. Appearances. Politics. There's an election coming up, and the town supervisor is already feeling heat from the Zach Stern / Melanie Phillips murders. Another sensational murder would just add pressure. It's good police procedure, too, not mentioning gory details to the press. In Manhattan, that plan never worked; the NYPD leaked like a colander. But here, it might.

"Your case has nothing to do with Noah Walker," Lang says.

Oh, Isaac, you little shit. Talk about leaks. No wonder the chief wanted to meet me tonight. Isaac must have sneaked away from me in a free moment and called him. So now I know where his loyalties lie. That little twerp.

"Too early to tell," I say.

The chief casts his eyes in my direction. He takes a sip of Beefeater and lets out a breath. "A few hours ago, you thought Noah was an innocent man, wrongly accused. Now you like him for the carnage in the woods, too."

"I don't like him or dislike him. Not yet. But it's possible the prostitute was killed while Noah was still a free man, not yet in custody. I'm just playing all the angles. That's what I'm paid to do."

He makes a noise as he finishes another sip. "No, you're paid to do what I *tell* you to do."

"I'm a detective," I say. "Once in a while, I try to detect."

The gin is sharp on my tongue, hot down my throat, leaving a delicious citrus aftertaste. Tastes better than it should. I take the bottle and pour myself another. "Let me ask you a question, Chief."

He shows me a wary look but doesn't speak.

"Why did we go in so hard on the arrest?"

"What do you mean?" He pours himself another drink.

"When we arrested Walker. The SWAT team. The automatic weapons. We were braced for a firefight. Noah didn't have any weapons."

The chief's jaw tightens, but he doesn't make eye contact with me. "Missy, you're lucky you're my favorite niece."

"I'm your only niece."

"Don't fuck with my case, Jenna." He slams down his glass. "I've got Noah Walker dead to rights. I need that solved. I've got orders from on high. You start tying this dead-hooker murder in with it, then we have to turn your report over to Walker's lawyer, and he'll play with that window of time—maybe two days, maybe three, maybe Noah was already in custody when the hooker got hers—and suddenly Clarence Darrow is saying that one person did both murders, and that one person couldn't have been Noah Walker."

"And what if that's true?"

My uncle gives me a look that I remember seeing as

a child, that look an adult gives when a kid is being adorably precocious, a combination of pride and annoyance. But in this case, the annoyance is outweighing the pride.

"Stay away from Noah Walker. Don't make your case something it's not."

"Just 'another hooker *adiosed* in the Hamptons,' right?" I push myself out of the chair. "I'm not going to do it. I'm following the leads wherever they go. You don't like it, relieve me."

The chief looks exhausted. He gestures toward me, the sign of the cross, absolution from a priest. "You are hereby relieved of any responsibility for the dead hooker in the woods."

"That's *bullshit*, Lang!" With the back of my hand, I whack my glass off the table, smashing it against the sink.

"Yeah? You wanna go for a suspension, too?"

"Sure!"

"Great! You're suspended without pay for a week."

"Only a week?" I yell, lost in my rage now, spinning out of control.

"Fine, then, a *month!* How about dismissal? You want me to can you?" The chief rises from his chair, directing a finger at me. "And before you answer that, missy, remember that being a cop is all you know. And I gave you a second chance. You'd think that would buy me just a little bit of loyalty from you, but oh, no!"

I shake my head, fuming. "I can't believe you just said that."

He waves me away with a hand. “One-month suspension, Detective, effective immediately. Now get out of my house.”

Chapter 12

FOR THE FIRST time in over a week, he breathes fresh air, he walks in grass, he wears his own clothes, he sees the sun, not over a concrete wall for one hour a day but out in the open. Noah Walker takes a moment to savor it before he steps into the minibus that will transport him to the train station for passage from Riverhead to Bridgehampton.

When he's home, he first takes a shower—no fancy shower-head or immaculate tub, but at least a healthy flow of water, without mold on the fixtures, without raw sewage bubbling from the drain, without having to look over his shoulder to wonder whether he was going to have an unexpected visitor. The biggest problem with Suffolk County Jail in Riverhead was the temporary nature of it all. Nobody in Riverhead had been convicted of a crime—if they had, they'd be in prison. Riverhead was just a pretrial holding facility for people with unaffordable bail or no bail at all, and thus there was nothing in the way of remedial programs or education, no recreational facilities, no pretense of nutritious meals. It was just walls, a handful of books, a chaplain on Sunday, shit for food, and an overpopulation of pissed-off detainees. He met someone inside, a guy named Rufus, who'd been in county lockup for over four years waiting for his trial.

None of that for Noah. He's demanded a speedy trial, his constitutional right. He can't stomach the thought of waiting months, even years, wondering.

Out of the shower, hair dripping wet, feeling warm and refreshed, he picks up his cell phone and hits the speed dial.

"Are you out?" Paige says breathlessly when she answers.

"I'm out," he says, thanks to her, and the checking account that bears only her name, that her husband doesn't control. "I'm home now."

"I can . . . I'll be there as soon as I can."

He feels a rush, a longing for her, tempered with fear. "Are you sure? What about—"

"I don't care. I'll figure something out. I'll tell him something. I don't think he knows about us. He's never said a word—"

"He knows about us," Noah says. Of course her husband knows. That has to be what's going on here. John Sulzman is a man of boundless influence. Influential enough to snap his fingers and have someone thrown in prison? Noah's no expert on backroom deals, but he doesn't doubt it.

"Well, I'm coming. I can't wait to see you!"

"Me too." Noah closes his eyes. "Just . . . be careful," he says.

Chapter 13

NOAH'S TOES CURL into the moist sand. He looks out over the Atlantic, black and restless in the dark, the post-rain breeze brushing his face. *This is what freedom feels like,* he thinks. *This is what I missed the most.*

He hears the familiar hum of the superior engine approaching. He stands and sees her Aston Martin pulling up in the lot. She pops out of the car and forgets to close the door. Noah is already running toward her.

No, he thinks, *she is what I missed the most.*

"I can't believe it," she manages as he scoops her up in his arms; she wraps her legs around him and grips his hair. Their mouths press against each other, more of a smash than a kiss. His body is charged with electricity.

"I didn't . . . kill those people," he whispers.

"You don't need to say that to me. Of course I know that." Paige strokes his face. "What can I do to help? Do you need money for a lawyer? A private detective?"

"You can't do that," Noah says. "John will—"

"I don't care about John. You need someone on your

side. I'll do whatever I have to do. I won't let you go through this alone. Tell me what you need."

"I just need you. That's all I need right now." Noah draws her close, breathes in her fresh-strawberry scent, takes in the warmth of her body. As long as he holds her, which could be five seconds, could be an hour, there is no criminal indictment, there is no prospect of life in prison, there is only Paige, the woman he loves, the woman who loves him.

And then he hears another vehicle approaching.

Noah raises his head. The beach had been empty, thanks in part to the lateness of the hour but more so to the rainfall an hour ago. The approaching SUV is not familiar to him. It stops in the middle of the small parking lot that serves as the end of Ocean Drive, positioned so that its headlights are trained on Noah and Paige.

Noah walks around the Aston Martin to stand between the headlights and Paige, a protective gesture.

"Well, shit, timing sure is everything, isn't it?" says Detective Isaac Marks, getting out of his vehicle. "Another case of coitus interruptus."

"What do you want *now*?" Noah's hands curl into fists. He moves toward Isaac.

"Easy, son, easy."

Son. Noah's always hated how cops talk to him, the condescension. But especially from Isaac Marks, who was the same year as him at Bridgehampton, and their history—and now he's calling Noah *son*. What a difference a badge can make.

"Just stop right there, Noah. I wouldn't want to

interpret your movements as a *threat*. Then I'd have to violate you, wouldn't I? Send you right back where you came from." Isaac nods in Paige's direction. "Of course, I could violate you right now for public indecency."

Noah, fuming, stands his ground. How much he'd love to wipe that smirk off Isaac's face. But that would be giving the cop exactly what he wants, to haul Noah back to Riverhead.

"Who's your friend?" asks Isaac, moving around Noah, shining his Maglite in Paige's direction. "Is that the same little honey from when we busted you?"

What an asshole. He knows very well it's Paige. This whole thing is because of Paige. It has to be. This has to be John Sulzman's doing.

"What do you want, Isaac?"

"That's Detective Marks to you."

"This is harassment!" Paige shouts. "We're not hurting anybody, we're not doing anything indecent at all! The only indecency here is the police harassing an innocent man. Don't you have anything better to do with your time, *Detective?*"

"Lady, let me give you a piece of advice," says Isaac. "I know it's fun to slum it once in a while and fuck the hired help, but your stallion here, turns out he's a vicious killer. Now, I don't know how in glorious hell he came up with the cash to bond himself out, but you better believe we're going to watch every move he makes, and we're not going to let him be alone with another woman after what he did to that waitress—"

"I don't know what's going on here," Paige says, frustration overtaking her composure. "But Noah is innocent, and it would be nice if the police department spent its time searching for a killer instead of following around someone who's out on bail."

"You're a real feisty one, lady, you know that?" Isaac shows her his teeth. "All the same, if we see you two together again, Noah gets violated and heads back to jail." He turns to Noah. "That simple enough for you to understand, Mr. Walker? See, lady, Noah here, he didn't do so well in school—"

"Oh, you want to talk about *school?*" Noah approaches Isaac. For a moment, it's like they're back on the playground, two kids, not a cop and an accused felon. "You want to talk about old times, Isaac? Because I've got a lot of stories. You wanna tell her how you got your nick—"

"That's enough, boy." Isaac raises a finger. "One more word, and it's back to Riverhead. Your choice."

Noah sucks in a breath. There's nothing he can say.

"There, that's better," says Isaac. "Mrs. Sulzman, you should be getting along now. Say good-bye to the Hamptons until next summer. Noah, he'll be at Sing Sing by then, but I'm sure you can find another boy toy, some gutter cleaner to pass the time."

With that, Paige breaks down, into tears and gasping breaths. Isaac swings his SUV in a three-point turn and drives away.

"Don't worry, I'll think of something," Noah says, holding Paige, touching her wet face. "I'll think of something."

And then, just like that, like the snap of a finger, he does.

Chapter 14

NO, PLEASE DON'T make me, I don't wanna—

Childish giggles, pressure on my throat, darkness, then light—

A bird, an angry bird with a hooked nose, standing upright—

Please don't make me—

I wake with a gasp, my head coming off the pillow, sucking in air, the sounds of giggling and desperate cries slowly fading, the pressure removed from my chest, hands no longer gripping my throat.

"Shit." My breathing finally slows. The clock says it's two minutes to seven. Who needs an alarm clock when you have nightmares every day?

I grab my iPhone and scroll through photos, spotting the picture I took of that little monument on the lawn at 7 Ocean Drive, that gray-and-black bird with the hooked beak and long tail feather. Yep, that was it, the same one from the nightmare. Great.

I shower, eat some toast and fruit, and chug two

glasses of water to work off my hangover, courtesy of the two bottles of wine Matty and I had last night as a send-off, my last night of forced vacation before I resume my job. Matty is long gone, having left my apartment around five this morning to head back to Manhattan; I have a brief memory of his aftershave and a kiss good-bye.

I go to work for the first time in thirty days. I feel like a tourist stepping onto foreign soil, the uncertainty of it all, especially of the reception I'll get from the natives when I show my face.

The Southampton Town Police substation in Bridgehampton is not exactly an intimidating place, nestled in the corner of an outdoor shopping mall called Bridgehampton Commons off Main Street, filled with chain shops like the Gap, Staples, Panera, a King Kullen grocery store, Victoria's Secret, and yes, a Dunkin' Donuts (I know, the jokes write themselves). The black patrol vehicles park in the south corner next to a row of tall recycling bins for clothes and shoes.

I park my beater in the back and walk into the substation, my bag over my shoulder and a general wariness in my gut. I get some mock applause from a couple of detectives who welcome me back after my one-month vacation. Isaac Marks isn't there, the weasel. He probably has his nose up the chief's ass right now.

Somebody tidied up my desk during my absence. Not that there's much to it, other than a photograph of my parents, and one of my brother, Ryan. There was a particularly nice shot of the entire family with Uncle Langdon and Aunt Chloe at Coney Island that I used to have on my desk at the NYPD, but I didn't want to emphasize the familial relationship here, with my uncle being the top dog. There's some resentment already, some whispers of nepotism about my hiring, though nobody could accuse the chief of favoritism after my suspension.

"Chief wants to see you, Murph." One of the administrative assistants, Margaret, drops a bunch of papers on my desk, mail and assorted paperwork.

"The chief's here?" Lang doesn't usually spend time at the substation, generally working out of headquarters on Old Riverhead Road.

When I enter his office, he seems to be expecting me, wiggling his fingers for me to come in and pointing to the seat opposite the desk while he finishes up a phone call. He finishes barking out directions to one of his deputies before hanging up and looking me over, a hand straying over his mouth.

"Sit," he says.

"I'm fine standing."

He folds his hands together. "When an uncle tells his niece to sit, she can say she's fine standing. But when the chief tells one of his detectives to sit, she sits. And right now, Detective, I'm your chief."

I look away, biting my tongue. He's right. Whatever else, he's right about this.

I take a seat.

"At least you didn't quit," he says. "I thought you might."

I toss my shoulders, like the statement is irrelevant. I'm not going to quit. That's the one thing I learned from the month I spent in Matty's condo in Greenwich Village, dining out and going for long runs, sleeping in and watching old movies, catching some theater and Yankees games. I love living in Manhattan, but I love being a cop more. And if I lose this job with the STPD, nobody will ever give me another chance.

Lang riffles through some paper on his desk. "There's a joint task force tracking heroin coming out of Montauk. You're joining it today."

My mouth comes open, but I don't speak. Look, it's not like I'm too good to work narcotics. My last assignment with the NYPD was working undercover on a major heroin ring. But I volunteered for that, because undercover work was a new challenge, and I'd come from Robbery-Homicide. Your basic narcotics task force—that's below my experience level. It's a clear step backward. And the chief, my dearest uncle, would know that better than anybody.

"Yes, sir," I say. "Anything else?"

"That's it."

I nod and push myself from the chair. When I reach the doorway, he calls out to me. I turn back and look at him.

"I'm having a salad for lunch today," he says. "And I've been walking a mile and a half every day for the last two weeks."

I don't smile. I'm not going to give him the satisfaction. "Why would a detective care what her chief has for lunch? Or what his exercise regimen is?"

He winks at me without smiling. "You're still my favorite niece."

I'm his only niece. But I won't take the bait.

"Don't worry, your favorite niece still loves you," I say. "But your favorite *detective* still thinks you're a horse's ass."

Chapter 15

"THE SUPREME COURT of Suffolk County is back in session," calls the bailiff. "*People versus Noah Lee Walker.*"

Noah shakes his head quietly. He hates it when they announce the case name. It's hard to feel like you have a fighting chance when it's the entire State of New York against you. And his full name—nobody's ever called him Noah Lee. It makes him sound like a presidential assassin or a mass murderer.

He's probably starting to look like one, too. In the three months since his arrest, Noah has not cut his hair, which was on the longer side to begin with. Now it falls in waves around his unshaven face. *USA Today* was the first to use the nickname Surfer Jesus, but now even the *Times* and Nancy Grace have adopted it.

"Mr. Akers?" The judge, an intimidating, steely-faced, silver-haired man named Robert Barnett, looks over his glasses at the prosecutor, Assistant District Attorney Sebastian Akers. Akers is a tall man with thick dark hair and the clean-cut good looks of a varsity quarterback or presidential candidate. But it's not just his looks; his presence, too, the confidence, the performance adrenaline; he's a man who seems to grow a few inches, whose voice lowers an octave, as he stands before a courtroom bursting at the seams with spectators and reporters.

"May it please the court," Akers says, buttoning his suit coat and positioning himself before the jury box. Fifteen sets of eyes—twelve jurors and three alternates—are fixed on the prosecutor. "Melanie Phillips was one of ours, born and raised in Bridgehampton. She didn't graduate at the top of her class and she hadn't yet attended college. But she had dreams. At age twenty, she worked day shifts at a seafood hut and took drama classes at night to realize that dream, the dream of becoming an actress. It may have been unrealistic. Sometimes dreams are. But this is America, and we all have the right to pursue our dreams, don't we? But Melanie—Melanie never got that chance. Her life, her dreams were cut short when she was brutally murdered, stabbed and slashed over and over again in a rental house by the beach three months ago."

Akers sits on that thought a moment, shaking his head with sadness. "Zachary Stern," he says, and the jurors pop to attention again. "Long time ago, Zach had the same dream. He was an actor. Never made it big, but did it for years, a few commercials here, a couple of television appearances there. And when he finally realized that being a movie star wasn't in the cards for him, he decided to help other people fulfill their dreams. He became an agent, one of the most successful in

Hollywood. And one day, while vacationing in the Hamptons, he met Melanie Phillips. He was going to sign her. Would he have made Melanie famous? Maybe. But we'll never know. Because Zach was murdered along with Melanie."

Akers turns sideways, so that the jurors can clearly see Noah at the defense table. Akers turns his head toward Noah and raises his arm. "That man, Noah Lee Walker," says Akers, jabbing his finger at him, "savagely killed Melanie Phillips and Zach Stern in a fit of rage, in the most brutal of ways. He sliced them open and left them for dead."

Noah shakes his head and locks eyes with the jurors. His defense lawyer said not to respond, to look composed and dignified, but he can't listen to that accusation without responding.

"It was a crime of passion, a crime of rage," says Akers. "A crime of jealousy. You see, Noah Walker was in love with Melanie. He didn't want to lose her to Zach Stern or to Hollywood. No, if you try to leave Noah Walker, this is the price you pay."

Akers nods to his assistant, who pushes a button. Noah's lawyer had argued desperately to keep this out of the trial, but the judge ruled against him.

The slide show that pops on the screen shows crime-scene photographs of Melanie, close-ups and full-body shots, her vacant eyes staring into space, her mouth barely open, a dozen cuts from a knife, some of them deeper, some superficial. The photos of Zach Stern aren't much better, perhaps less graphic but still horrific. The jury recoils at them, audibly gasping and murmuring.

Then the screen goes blank. Akers walks over to the witness stand. "You will hear from people who knew Melanie and Noah. They will sit in this chair and they will tell you about that relationship. They will tell you about Noah's obsession. They will tell you that Noah couldn't bear the thought of losing Melanie, that he was insane with jealousy." Akers walks over to the evidence table and lifts a bag. "You will hear expert testimony that this knife was stained with the blood of Zach and Melanie. And you will hear from Chief of Police Langdon James that he found this knife under a heating duct in Noah Walker's kitchen floor, along with a charm necklace that Melanie had worn around her neck every day of her life since she was six years old."

Akers takes a moment, waiting for his conclusion.

"And you will hear something else from Chief James. You will hear testimony that Noah Walker *confessed* to these murders, that when his guard was down, he admitted killing Melanie and Zach and explained exactly how he did it."

Akers turns again and points at Noah. "We will prove all of this to you, ladies and gentlemen, that much I promise you. And when this trial is over, we will ask you to give Melanie and Zach the only thing that you can give them now: justice. We will ask you to return two verdicts of guilty of murder in the first degree against Noah Lee Walker."

In ten minutes, Akers has summarized the whole thing in a way that makes Noah look obviously guilty. Akers has horrified them with the gruesome photos and appealed to their sympathy with the talk of Hollywood dreams dashed. Hell, he's even made that bloodsucker Zach Stern sound like a swell guy.

Noah sees it in the jurors' eyes, the way they follow the prosecutor as he returns to the defense table, the way they stare in Noah's direction with contempt.

He's going to need a miracle.

Chapter 16

"REMY HANDLEMAN," THE bailiff calls out into the hallway, summoning the prosecution's first witness.

Remy Handleman enters the courtroom and takes the witness stand. He is wearing a suit, but not one that he's worn before. The jacket hangs limp over his shoulders and the collar is too wide. Remy's probably never worn a suit in his life.

After he takes his oath, he runs a hand over his oily hair and fidgets in his chair, his hands likewise unable to find a comfortable place to rest. The behavior of a liar, a bad one, at least.

"Mr. Handleman," says the prosecutor, buttoning his coat at the podium, "is your appearance here today pursuant to a subpoena?"

"My appear—" Remy looks down at himself. "Somebody said I should wear a suit. Is that what you mean?"

Despite his predicament, Noah can't help but feel for Remy, who's too dim to understand why everyone's chuckling in the courtroom. Remy first came to Bridgehampton when Noah was a seventh grader. He was one of those needy kids who wanted everyone to like him and could never understand when they didn't, and never stopped trying. Noah tried to befriend him, even defended him a couple of times from playground beatings, but Remy never quite fit in. He smoked a lot of weed and sold some, too. He was known to the STPD long before they first busted him selling Oxy behind a diner off the turnpike about four years ago.

"Mr. Handleman, were you acquainted with the deceased, Melanie Phillips?"

"Yeah, I knew Melanie. I go into Tasty's for steamers, maybe a couple times a week."

"Tasty's was the restaurant where Melanie waitressed?"

"Uh-huh, yes."

"Take us back to the first weekend of June this year, Mr. Handleman," says the prosecutor, Akers. "Thursday, June second. Did you go into Tasty's that day?"

"Yeah, I did. I had lunch there."

"Who waited on you that day?"

"Melanie did."

"Did you see the defendant there on that day, at that time?"

"Yeah." Remy nods at Noah. "Noah was there. He was, like, like following her around."

"Melanie was doing her waitressing duties, and Noah was following her around?"

"Yeah."

"Did you hear them speak?"

"Yeah. Melanie was like, 'Leave me alone.' And Noah was like, 'Give me another chance, I love you,' stuff like that."

"Mmm-hmm." Akers nods with grave importance, as if the witness has just said something brilliant. Remy is anything but. But he's not so stupid that he couldn't recognize a deal when it was offered to him. Three months ago, the STPD busted him for the second time for selling Oxy, and the second bust was likely to mean serious prison time. It was awfully convenient, then, that he just happened to have information that would help the STPD solve one of the biggest murders the region had ever seen. Suddenly an eight-year sentence is pleaded down to twenty months, all because of his testimony today, his assistance in a high-profile double-murder trial.

"The defendant told Melanie he loved her?"

"Yeah."

"And he asked Melanie to give him another chance?"

"Yeah, he said, 'Give me another chance.' And she said it was over."

"She said it was over?" The prosecutor leans in, like the testimony is just getting interesting. "Did the defendant say anything else that you heard?"

"Yeah, he said, 'You don't just walk away from me.' He, like, grabbed her when he said it."

"He . . . grabbed her where?"

"Like, by the arm. She dropped a dish when he done it, too."

"He grabbed her arm and said, 'You don't just walk away from me'?"

"Right."

"And this took place just two days before Melanie was found dead?"

"Yeah, it sure did."

Sebastian Akers shakes his head, as if he's hearing this testimony for the first time and can't believe how damning it is. "No further questions," he says.

Chapter 17

WEEK TWO OF the Noah Walker murder trial. My first day attending, but it's packed wall-to-wall, as it's apparently been every day since it began. The Suffolk County Sheriff's Office has started a lottery for the general public's admission and a separate one for the media, though if you're a reporter, not drawing a lucky ticket just means you go to a spillover room down the hall to watch the trial on a closed-circuit television. Even coppers like me have a hard time getting in, but I know Rusty the bailiff—that's a good name for a bailiff, *Rusty*—so I got a spot in the fourth row, jammed between an older guy and a young woman wearing too much perfume.

I have a couple of days off after we completed our nine-week sting operation on the heroin trafficking, taking down over twenty people throughout Long Island, most notably a school principal at a private school in Montauk. I didn't have anything else to do, so after my five-mile run this morning, I decided to clean up and come see "Surfer Jesus" for myself.

There he is at the defense table, scratching his beard and whispering to his defense lawyer. The press was initially intrigued with the story because Zach Stern was a victim and it happened in the Hamptons, but Noah himself has now become as interesting as anything else to the talking heads on the evening cable channels—his swarthy good looks, for one, and also his rebellious attitude, refusing to wear a suit to court, opting instead for the desert-islander look with a white shirt and blue jeans.

Taking the stand is a man named Dio Cornwall, an African American in his midtwenties with a long skinny neck and braids pulled tight against his head. He's awaiting trial for armed robbery and had the pleasure of sharing a cell with Noah Walker during the week following Noah's arrest, before Noah bonded out.

"It woulda been the second, maybe third night," says Cornwall. "Guy just starts talkin', is all. Didn't need to ask him or nothin'. Just started talkin'."

"And what exactly did he say about it?" asks the prosecutor, Sebastian Akers, who could double as a Ken doll.

"Says she got hers." Cornwall shrugs. "Says the woman got hers."

"Did you ask him what he meant?"

"Yeah. He says, 'No bitch gonna leave me.' He says, 'I cut her up good. Can't be no movie star now.' "

Oof. That's not good for Noah. But then, nothing's gone that well for Noah, from what I've read and heard on TV.

I look at him, huddling with his lawyer, and again feel something swim in my stomach. When I met him, I made him for a guy who'd grown up rough, and who didn't hold the police department in high esteem, and yeah, someone I might like for a B-and-E or maybe an assault-and-battery. But a brutal killer? He just didn't ping my radar that way.

But it doesn't matter what I think anymore. It matters what twelve jurors think. The opening witness had Noah hounding Melanie at the restaurant where she worked, begging her to take him back and threatening her when she wouldn't. The forensics came next. The knife found in Noah's kitchen had traces of both Zach's and Melanie's DNA. A forensic pathologist testified that the knife had a slight jag in the tip that matched some of the cuts found on the victims.

There was no doubt, in other words, that the knife they found in Noah's house was the murder weapon.

And now this guy, Cornwall, the second person to attribute incriminating statements to Noah.

"When he said 'No bitch gonna leave me,' and that she 'can't be no movie star now,' did the defendant identify this woman by name?"

"Melanie," says Cornwall. "He said her name was Melanie."

Sebastian Akers nods and looks over at the jury box. Strong testimony for the prosecution, no doubt, but still—this guy Cornwall is no different than the first witness, a jailhouse snitch who'd probably sell out his grandmother to shave some time off his sentence.

Which makes the final witness all the more crucial

for the case. The witness being my uncle, Chief Langdon James, the one who found the knife in Noah's kitchen, and the one to whom Noah Walker confessed his guilt. Without the chief, there's the knife and two cons who'd say just about anything.

After the chief's done testifying, Noah Walker will be toast.

Chapter 18

LANGDON JAMES TAKES a hit off his joint and squints through the smoke at the cable news show, where four well-dressed lawyers are talking over one another, arguing about the merits of Dio Cornwall's testimony and the overall strength of the prosecution's case against "Surfer Jesus."

"If I'm Noah Walker's lawyer, my argument is that the prosecution's case is bought and paid for," says one. *"Remy Handleman and Dio Cornwall are criminals who would say or do anything to save their own necks."*

"But the case isn't over, Roger. The chief of police will testify tomorrow—"

With that, the chief sees his image on TV, a stock photograph taken of him over ten years—and forty pounds—ago, walking outside headquarters, his sunglasses on, hands on his hip, head profiled to the right.

God, where did the years go? That was a different time, in so many ways. That was before Chloe left. That was back when the job was still new to Lang, when he still considered it an honor, even a thrill, to wear the badge.

That was back when his niece, Jenna, still looked up to him, following his career path into law enforcement. He remembers all those nights when Jenna was still a young girl, after her father and brother died, when she would sit with Lang, how her eyes would widen as she listened to his tales of cops and robbers, good guys and bad, fighting for truth and justice. He remembers the swell of pride he felt on Jenna's first day at the academy, when he looked at her, eager to one day don a uniform and make the world a safer place.

The chief clicks off the TV and rubs his eyes. She's a good kid, Jenna. He wishes they hadn't clashed over Noah Walker. After all, she did what any good cop should do—pick up a scent and follow it—and he shot her down when she started to question Walker's guilt.

He hated doing it, dousing her flame that way. But as good a cop as she is—she has more instinct in her pinkie finger than most cops will ever have in their whole bodies—she doesn't always see the bigger picture. Noah Walker is guilty. He's sure of it. Rules and procedure and evidence aside, at the end of the day, that's all that matters.

Is the dead hooker's murder in the woods linked to the murders at 7 Ocean Drive? He doubts it. Hell, Jenna didn't even know for sure—it was just a hunch, an itch she was scratching. But he makes himself this promise: He will follow that lead—soon. Just not now. Not when Noah's defense attorney could play with it. After Noah is convicted, he'll personally check it out.

"Oh, Jenna," he mumbles to himself. Maybe she never should have come back here. The nightmares, the drinking—yes, he's noticed how much she drinks—it all kicked in since she came back here. Is that just a coincidence?

No, it can't be a coincidence.

Seven hours. He remembers it well. If there were seven hours in all the world he could remove, erase completely, it would be those seven hours from Jenna's life.

Seven hours of hell.

And her mother never let Jenna set foot in the Hamptons again.

Until she came back as an adult, to be a cop.

And he let her do it. He thought he was helping her, after she got run out of Manhattan. He thought he was doing a good thing.

He pushes away his notes on tomorrow's testimony. He's testified a hundred times in court. He knows the drill, the flow of the questioning, the way to frame his answers, the phrases to avoid, the importance of maintaining the appropriate demeanor. He stamps out the remainder of the joint, feeling a little stoned but not wanting to take it too far tonight, with the big day tomorrow. Seems like these days, he's always seeking some kind of lubricant to get through the evenings.

He kicks his feet off the bed and heads for the kitchen, for a glass of Beefeater. Just one glass tonight, no more, especially after smoking so much—

Something . . . something is wrong.

A shudder runs through him. He reaches the

threshold of the kitchen before he realizes that the *something*—a change in the pressure, a creak in the floor, a foreign heat source—is behind him, not in front.

He turns back just as the figure steps into the hallway from the bathroom. A man wearing a full mask, though Halloween is still weeks away.

"Wait," the chief says as he sees the weapon rising, training on him. "Wait, just hold on, let's—"

He feels the sharp pinch, the pure heat in his left upper thigh, an instant before he hears the *thwip* from the gun's suppressor. He doubles over but keeps his balance, yells, "Wait!" before another bullet tears through his left biceps. The momentum spins him around, and this time he loses his balance, falling to his hands and knees, crawling like a wounded dog away from his predator, who takes slow, deliberate steps behind him, tracking him.

The chief makes it into the kitchen, pushing off with his good arm and good leg. Another bullet blows through the bottom of his foot, ricocheting off the tile, and this time the cry he lets out is gargled, and he collapses to the floor. He tells himself to keep breathing, to avoid shock, and when he finally manages a pushup, his right elbow explodes from another bullet and he's down for good.

The floor is spinning, everything is upside down. The intruder now casts a shadow over the chief, seeming to be in no particular hurry for this ordeal to come to an end. The chief can do nothing but hope—hope that this man just wants to hurt him and not kill him.

The next bullet drills through his right calf. Langdon can no longer bring himself to scream.

Silence follows, a pause. For just that moment, the chief feels a surge of hope. He's been shot in the limbs, not the head or torso, no vital organs. Maybe the man will let him live. Maybe—

The chief feels a foot in his ribs, a gentle nudging. And then he hears the man's voice, slow and deliberate, icy-calm.

"I . . . need a few minutes," the man with the mask says. "Your fireplace . . . is really old."

Chapter 19

I CUP THE badge in one hand and slam through the double doors with the other. There are other officers already in the emergency room, who register who I am and point down the hall with looks of apology, sympathy on their faces. The hallway feels narrow and too bright, full of people in police uniforms or surgical scrubs. Someone tries to stop me and I say, "I'm next of kin."

There are rooms to the left, all covered with gray-blue curtains. A gurney pops through one of them, several doctors and nurses jogging alongside it, holding bags of fluids and calling out stats to one another.

An arm grabs me. Isaac Marks says, "They're taking him to surgery, Murphy. He—"

"Call Aunt Chloe," I tell him.

"I did already."

I pry my arm free and follow the doctors. "I'm his niece," I say when they object, and I position myself between them and the elevator so they can't stop me.

Uncle Langdon looks foreign, ancient, a mask over

his face for oxygen, a bulge in the covers by his lower torso. I take his right hand in mine. "I'm here, Lang," I manage, yelling over the commotion.

His hand squeezes back. The elevator opens and we all go inside. I angle between two medics who don't resist, allowing us as private a moment as they can possibly give us.

"You're going to be fine," I whisper, my face close to his.

Lang slowly raises his arm, like he's doing a difficult biceps curl, his hand finally reaching the oxygen mask. He pulls it down to his chin. "Jenna Rose," he says, the words thin and whispery.

"I'm here," I choke out.

"You're . . . a good cop."

"I learned from the best." I place my hand delicately on the top of his head, tears streaming down my face, my throat hot and full. "I'm so sorry I questioned you and said all—"

"No." His eyelids flutter, and his head turns ever so slightly back and forth. "Don't ever stop . . . questioning . . . look up . . . Chloe . . . look . . ."

"I will—Chloe's on her way—"

"Okay, we have to go!"

The elevator doors part. I press my lips against his forehead. "You're my favorite uncle." I squeeze out the words through a sob.

One side of his mouth curves just for a moment; a tear slides down his temple into his ear. "I'm your . . . only uncle," he whispers.

And then we are separated, a tug on my arm holding

me back, my uncle wheeled off to surgery, my view of him narrowing as the elevator doors move toward each other and then shut.

Not Lang, I think. *Not Lang, too. No. Please, no.*

When the elevator doors open again, I hear Isaac Marks's voice, talking to another cop. "Five gunshot wounds to his extremities," he says. "And then he heated up a fireplace poker and drove it through his kidney."

I turn in Isaac's direction, not looking at him, the words echoing between my ears. *Shot in the extremities and speared with a poker.*

Tortured. Just like Zach Stern. Just like Melanie Phillips. Just like the prostitute impaled on the tree stump in the woods.

"Oh, Murphy." Isaac's hand rests on my shoulder. "You okay?"

I don't answer. I can't speak.

"It's going to be hours before he's out of surgery, Murph. Maybe—maybe get some fresh air. Get away from this place for a while. But take the back exit. The press is gathered out front. The chief was supposed to testify tomorrow against Noah Walker."

Noah Walker.

I stagger toward the rear exit, into the humid night air, where I finish the long hard cry that I started in the elevator. I don't cry much, but when I do, it's a heaving, gasping avalanche. I fall to my hands and knees and let it all out, the images from my childhood rushing back, Langdon holding me in his arms after Dad and Ryan died, showing up on weekends at our house in the Bronx, always with a little toy or gadget for me, always ready with stories about the bad guys he put away.

Not Lang. Please, God, I know I've doubted you, but I'll do anything now, anything at all, just please, please don't take him away.

And then, after some amount of time I can't quantify, it stops. I get up and brush myself off. The soft tide of sorrow running through my chest turns hard. My senses readjust, back to alert, cop-alert. My vision clears. My nose stops running. My muscles tense.

Noah Walker.

I check my magazine for bullets, then reholster the weapon.

Hours, Isaac said. That will be more than enough time. Noah Walker's house is only a half hour away.

I shove my star deep in my pocket. I won't need a badge tonight.

Chapter 20

NOAH WALKER'S HOUSE is dark. If he's home, he's pretending to be asleep. But he won't have to pretend much longer, and this time he'll never wake up.

The night is sticky but peaceful, nothing but some stray insect sounds. I trot gingerly over the gravel driveway on the balls of my feet and cross around to the back of his house. There is a small yard that borders on heavy woods, an afterthought of a concrete slab with a barbecue grill covered by a hood. The back door is less secure than the front, especially after we busted through it during the arrest.

The door comes open with minimal noise. I shine my Maglite into the back room—a couple of motorcycle helmets, an old Corona typewriter, an easel with a canvas of a seascape, boxes stuffed with clothes and knickknacks, an antique desk in the corner, some framed artwork resting against a wall.

I move into the hallway, my flashlight and gun at eye level, moving them in tandem while I shuffle forward along the tile, surveying room after room—the kitchen, the foyer, the living room.

I stop. Listen. The house groans. The wind outside plays with the trees.

Now the attic bedroom. The only room left.

I try my weight on the first stair and it complains to me. I take every other step, crouched low, slowly transferring my weight onto each new stair like a spider approaching prey, keeping the light beam down.

My eyes are now level with the second floor, my body still below it. I listen for any sounds. There is no such thing as silence in a house. But this house, suddenly, is silent.

I take a step up into the attic, a large open space. I throw the beam of light onto a bed right in front of me, with the covers pulled back and a pillow indented in the middle. I swing to my left when something strikes me, sharp and violent, cracking me in the cheek, knocking me sideways to the right, sending fluorescent stars through my eyelids. The Maglite skitters across the floor, sending a crazy pattern of rolling circles of light against the wall. I remain standing but unbalanced, staggering, disoriented, and all I can think is—

Duck.

I drop to a crouch as a force propels itself at me, over me. Noah's lunging tackle misses me, worthy of a *SportsCenter* highlight, but as he sails over me, his knees connect with my shoulder and we fall awkwardly. Noah's momentum carries him to the corner, slamming him against the wall, while I land hard on my back, my head bouncing on hardwood, the gun no longer in my hand.

Everything is dancing, but there's no time. I get to my feet just as he does. He's like a shadow, in a fighter's stance in a dark room, the only illumination coming from the far corner, where the Maglite has rolled to rest and shines a wide yellow circle against the back wall.

My training comes to me by instinct, legs spread, knees bent, weight evenly balanced, fists raised. Noah makes a move toward me, but I jab with my left, connecting with his nose, straightening him up for a moment, then follow with my right hand, my knuckles catching on his teeth. His head snaps to the right, but he recovers quickly—more quickly than I would have thought—and lunges toward me, this time with his head down, not making the same mistake twice. My left leg shoots up for a kick, but I'm off my game, disoriented myself, and he's too fast, too athletic. His shoulder plunges into my midsection and sends me spiraling backward, he along with me. We land hard and I lose my wind.

"Who are you?" he spits, straddling me now, his palms pinning my shoulders. "What the hell are—wait—you're—you're that cop—"

In the moments it takes me to recover my breath, I bring up my right knee and find my backup piece on the ankle holster. I remove it and shove it into his rib cage.

"Get off me now," I say.

The pressure eases off my shoulders. My left arm free, I shove my palm against his chest and knock him backward, until I'm out from under him. I get to my feet with some effort, my gun trained on him, a tidal wave of adrenaline coursing through me.

"I didn't know you were a cop," Noah says, panting, touching the cuts on his face. "Aren't you supposed to announce who you are?"

But I'm not a cop tonight. Tonight, I'm a niece. The niece of a dear, sweet man who was shot five times in the extremities and speared with a hot poker.

"You okay?" he says to me. "I've never hit a woman in my—"

"Shut up!" I hiss. I move a step closer to him. "You killed all of them. Say it. Say it right this second, *right this second,* or I'll shoot."

As my eyes adjust in the semidarkness, I see Noah more clearly, a man in his boxers, crouched at the knees; I see the whites of his eyes.

"I didn't kill anybody," he says.

I drive my shoe into him like I'm kicking a field goal, catching arms and knees and maybe his chin. I see him fall to the floor. I see other things, too. *Uncle Lang, bobbing me up and down on his leg when I was a child. Tearing up at my cadet graduation, telling me how proud my father would have been—*

Tears fill my eyes, screams fill my head, adrenaline fills my chest. I struggle to keep control of my weapon. "Admit you attacked him," I say, "or die right now."

I want him to defy me. I want to kill him. I want to shoot him the same way he shot my uncle, in all the places it hurts, maximizing his suffering, making him beg for his life, before driving a red-hot stake through his kidney—

"I'm not going to admit something I didn't do," Noah says with control, with calm. "You can shoot me if you want. But I don't think you will. Because you're a fair person. And deep down, I think you know—"

"*Shut up!* You . . . you took him from me . . . you took him . . ."

My entire body quivering, my voice choking off, tears rolling down my face, my breath coming in tight gasps, I lower the gun, then raise it back up, the screams in my head drowning out everything else.

"What are you talking about?" he asks.

I shuffle toward him, only steps away from him, both hands desperately clutching my gun. "Say it!" I scream.

But it doesn't matter what he says anymore. *I'm going to do it. I'm going to pull this trigger.*

"I didn't kill anybody," he says.

My breath held tight in my lungs, I pull the trigger once, a single bullet, and then drop the weapon to my side.

Chapter 21

I STAND OVER the grave, the outlines of the freshly dug earth a tangible reminder of the funeral yesterday. It was a nice affair, with the police force in formal dress, a gun salute, the works. It was the very opposite of a private family ceremony, in part because Lang didn't *have* any family besides me, but appropriate, too, because Lang was such a public figure, a giant in this community, the chief law enforcement officer for almost two decades. Lang died in surgery that night at the hospital. The hemorrhaging was too massive, the doctor said. Too many wounds. Too much blood lost for too long.

Chloe Danchisin—Aunt Chloe—slides her arm inside mine and perches her chin on my shoulder. "He always loved this cemetery," she says. "He bought these plots for us when we were first married."

I blow my nose and take a breath. My throat aches from all the crying I've done over the past several days. "I . . . still can't believe he's gone."

Chloe rubs her hand on my back, tiny circles. "It's not fair to you, honey. It seems like just yesterday that Lydia died."

Almost three years to the day, actually, that my mother gave in to the cancer.

"You know how much Lang loved you, don't you?"

I nod but don't speak. My throat is so strained that I don't even sound like myself. My head is filled with a constant ringing.

"Oh, when he hired you to work here—he was so excited. He called me. We hadn't spoken in over a year, but he called me to give me the news. He was like a giddy schoolboy."

Despite the fact that I've shed enough tears over the last few days to fill a small lake, my eyes well up again. "I questioned his judgment," I say. "I doubted his investigation of the Ocean Drive murders. I actually—I actually suggested that Noah Walker might be innocent." I scoff at the notion in hindsight. It's so clear to me now. Noah killed Lang so he couldn't testify, and in much the same way he killed Zach and Melanie, and the prostitute in the woods. Different methods, but the same sociopathic brutality—maximizing their suffering, making sure they would bleed out in painful deaths.

Chloe directs my shoulders away from the grave, south toward the beach, and moves me along. "You were doing your job. I'm sure he was proud of you. Don't confuse his stubbornness with disappointment."

We walk toward the beach. Chloe looks good, notwithstanding the circumstances. Now single again for two years, she has lost about twenty pounds, cut her hair in a stylish bob, and dresses like she doesn't mind being noticed. Sixty is the new forty, and all that.

My head is finally clearing of the hangover, from the extra bottle of wine after I left Chloe last night and went home. The nightly drinking is weighing me down, leaving me off balance and foggy. But right now, foggy feels like the best I can do.

Ocean Drive is teeming with joggers and bicyclists and people heading, like us, toward the beach. The activity, the smell of the ocean—this is precisely what I remember as a kid.

"Chloe," I say, "why did we stop coming here when I was a kid?"

She keeps her head down, strolling along with me.

"Lang said there was a story."

"You don't know?" she asks.

"No."

"If *you* don't know, *I* don't know." She looks up at our surroundings, half-built structures and carved-out foundations. "That's the house, isn't it?"

I focus my eyes and realize that we're passing 7 Ocean Drive, the Murder House. The crime-scene tape has been removed, but the Gothic monstrosity has no trouble looking creepy all by itself. It brings back everything in a rush, my meddling at the crime scene, my argument with Lang, resulting in my thirty-day suspension.

We were never the same after he dinged me. I was sent off to the narcotics task force assignment, and I saw him only sparingly after that. I turned down several offers to get together, for dinner or drinks or an afternoon at the beach. I was resentful. I wanted to punish him. And now he's gone, and I'd do anything to have those weeks back. I'd tell him how much I love him, how he saved my life so many times, in so many different ways.

We arrive at the beach. Chloe lets out a satisfied sigh. Behind her, the beachfront homes stand in marked contrast to the cedar-shingled houses along Ocean Drive. They are gigantic, modern, concrete structures with oversize windows and sharp angles.

"Can I say something to you, sweetheart?"

I take her hand. "Anything."

The breeze plays with the bangs on Chloe's forehead. "Have you thought about going back to Manhattan now?"

I squat down, scoop up a handful of sand, weigh it in my hand. There is an inch-long scar on the palm of my hand that I got—according to my mother—trying to chop a tomato when I was a little girl.

Little things like that, small memories that sting the most.

"Lang called me a couple of weeks ago," she continues. "He said you were having nightmares every night. That you were drinking a lot, too, probably as a coping mechanism."

I look up at her. "He said that?"

"He did. He was concerned. He was glad to have you close, of course. But he wasn't sure this was the right thing for you anymore, working here."

I pick up a shell and send it flying into the ocean. I squint into the wind, the wet mist.

Chloe squats down next to me. "All your life, you've taken care of everyone else," she says. "When your father and Ryan died, your mother . . . Lydia was devastated. I know you were, too, but it always seemed like you were the one doing the consoling. And you were so young. You were, what, twelve?"

"Yes." It was less than a month before my thirteenth birthday.

"I remember just a couple of days after they died, you were supposed to be in bed, and Lydia was crying and Lang was holding her. We were all on the couch. And you walked in. You'd been sleeping. Your hair was all matted and your eyes were sleepy and you were in your pajamas. You opened your arms as wide as they could go and you said, 'Don't worry, Mommy, I have enough love for all of them.' Do you remember that?"

I wipe away a tear. I remember. I remember my mother looking like there was nothing left in the world for her.

"Well." Chloe rubs my arm. "Maybe it's time you took better care of yourself. Go home, Jenna. Your best friends are there. Matty's there. What's left here?"

I stand straight as the wind off the ocean kicks up. I look back at the oceanfront housing, at the endless stretch of beach. This isn't my home. It never will be. But it holds one thing for me that no other place in the world does.

"This is the only place I can be a cop," I say.

Chapter 22

THE ROOM LOOKS more like a maximum-security prison than a court of law. The number of sheriff's deputies has doubled, virtually lining the walls of the courtroom, beefy security guards with jumpy eyes, armed with handguns and cuffs and Tasers. The tension in the room has raised the temperature to something between stuffy and downright unbearable.

As we wait for the judge, I scroll through photos on my iPhone. Nearly all of the recent ones include Lang: in his ridiculous polka-dot swimsuit at the beach; flipping burgers on his Smokey Joe in his backyard, chomping on a cigar; asleep on his lawn chair, his wife-beater T-shirt creeping up to reveal his added poundage (a photo I often used when arguing about his diet). Silly shots, all of them, but so dear to me now, those little things, those frivolous moments that mean so much in hindsight.

And then, amid these pictures, the one from the lawn on 7 Ocean Drive, that crest with that hook-beaked bird, that insipid creature that has taken up permanent residence in my daily nightmares. What's with that stupid bird?

We all rise; then a collective hush falls over the room as the Honorable Robert Barnett, a handsome and deadly serious judge, assumes the bench. "We are back on the record in *People versus Noah Lee Walker,*" he says dryly. "For the record, the court has stood in recess for the last week. Six days ago, the next witness scheduled to testify, Southampton Town Police Department chief Langdon James, was attacked in his home and later died of his injuries. The court granted a recess at the prosecution's request."

I shift in the courtroom pew, a front-row seat granted me by the prosecution. Noah Walker denied any involvement in Lang's murder, but Judge Barnett revoked his bond anyway, out of an abundance of caution, so he's locked up again in Riverhead when he's not here in court.

"For the record, Mr. Akers is present today for the State, and Mr. Brody is present for the defense." The judge removes his glasses. "And of course, Mr. Walker, the defendant, is present as well."

My eyes move to Noah, sitting at the defense table with his hands folded and his eyes cast downward. His feet are crossed, raising the cuffs of his jeans slightly and revealing bare ankles. He didn't even bother to wear socks to the trial. He looks like a hippie islander.

I let you live, you little shit. You could at least show a little respect.

I replay that moment in his attic bedroom, feel the

surge of adrenaline returning. How close I came to doing it. How close I came to putting that bullet between his eyes, instead of firing it over his head.

As if he senses me, Noah turns his head ninety degrees and catches my eyes. He still has the shiner I gave him that night, though it's now a dull-yellow bruise. The split lip has healed and the swelling dissipated. His jaw probably still hurts, but nothing was broken.

As far as I know, Noah hasn't publicly complained about how I treated him that night, sneaking into his house, punching and kicking him, not to mention firing a bullet within inches of his scalp. That should be coming any time now, a police brutality lawsuit, probably a request for ten million dollars for his pain and suffering.

But for now, it's just his eyes locked on mine. Something flutters through my chest as I stare back at him, that nagging feeling that I can't read him, that I don't know him. He is neither antagonistic nor smug in his stare. He is neither enjoying himself nor resentful. He just stares at me as if somehow, in some way, we are discovering each other, we are connecting with each other, something is happening between us.

I snap my head away, breaking eye contact, sweat popping at my hairline. I take a deep breath and brush the hair off my face.

He is the worst kind of creep. He's the kind who can suck you in, the sociopath who can smile at you tenderly while he's devising monstrous ways to torture you. Well, not me, pal. Not anymore. You may have fooled me initially, but no longer.

I turn back, looking in his direction again. He hasn't moved. His eyes are still on me, his long dark hair hanging over his unshaven face. My heartbeat kicks into a higher gear. I uncross my legs and play with my hands. I shake my head slowly, discreetly, unsure of the meaning of what I'm doing, answering no to a question that has not been asked. His eyes narrow to a squint. His jaw rises slightly and his lips part, as if he's going to speak, but surely he won't, not in the middle of a court session while the judge is talking.

He will never speak to me again. And I will never speak to him.

I get to my feet and walk down the courtroom aisle toward the exit, which is guarded by two sheriff's deputies. I'm done with Noah Walker. The next time I see him, it will be at his sentencing, after the judge informs him he'll spend the rest of his life behind bars. *Yeah, let's make eye contact then, pal. Let's see the look on your face then.*

"Mr. Brody," says the judge, "you have a motion?"

"Yes, Judge, I do."

Defense lawyers always have motions. They always have bullshit arguments, smoke and mirrors, misdirection. But the next words coming from the mouth of Noah Walker's lawyer freeze me in my tracks, only a few paces from the courtroom door.

"Your Honor," he says, "the defense moves for a dismissal of all charges."

Chapter 23

THE COURTROOM, ALREADY respectfully silent, is sucked dry of all sound as Joshua Brody, Noah Walker's lawyer, makes his pitch for his client's release.

"There is no competent evidence tying the murder weapon to my client," he says. "There was never a fingerprint on the weapon. And the only evidence that the knife was found at my client's house would have come from Chief James—who obviously cannot testify now."

"Your Honor!" Sebastian Akers jumps to his feet, his perfect-cool persona shaken for the first time. "We will call Detective Isaac Marks—I'm sorry, Acting Chief Isaac Marks—who will testify that the chief showed him the knife after he discovered it under the heating duct in the defendant's kitchen."

"But Mr. Marks didn't *see* it under the heating duct. Only the chief did, allegedly," says Noah's lawyer. "The defense's theory is that Chief James planted that knife. But now we can't cross-examine him to establish that.

The prosecution shouldn't be allowed to suggest that the knife was found in my client's house when we can't cross-examine the person who supposedly 'found' it."

The judge looks at the prosecutor. "Mr. Akers, the defense makes a valid point here. If the defense can't cross-examine the chief about a frame-up, how can I let you put the knife in the defendant's house?"

"Everyone in this courtroom knows the reason why Chief James isn't here to testify," says Akers, his voice wobbling. "Everyone knows who made that happen." He turns and looks at Noah Walker.

"If the State believes my client killed Chief James, they are free to charge him," says the defense lawyer, Brody. "The last I heard, they found no physical evidence at that crime scene. They have no leads on the chief's death, just supposition. And more importantly, Judge, this trial is not about Chief James's murder. This trial is about Zach Stern and Melanie Phillips, and there is no evidence tying my client to the murder weapon, with the chief's untimely passing. And the chief obviously can't testify that my client confessed to him, either." He opens his hands. "So what do they have, without the murder weapon and without a confession to the chief of police? Without any physical evidence whatsoever? They have evidence that my client argued with Melanie Phillips at Tasty's Diner, and they have this ridiculous testimony from a jailhouse snitch that my client confessed to him."

"The jailhouse informant's testimony isn't evidence?" the judge asks.

"It is, Judge, but c'mon. The unreliability of jailhouse snitch testimony is well documented. He got a sweetheart deal in exchange for making up these ridiculous claims against my client. I mean, Judge, really." Brody takes a step toward the bench. "Can any of us say that a man should be convicted of two counts of first-degree murder based on no eyewitnesses, no physical evidence, no forensic evidence, no confession—nothing more than the word of a convicted felon looking to cut a deal? And keep in mind, Judge, that it's our theory that Chief James coerced the snitch into testifying. But now I can't cross-examine him on *that* issue, either. For the same reason the knife shouldn't be considered against my client, neither should the testimony of Dio Cornwall, the snitch."

"My God," I whisper to myself. He's making this sound credible. And the judge—he looks like he's actually considering this. How could this—this couldn't possibly—

No. No, no, no.

"Mr. Akers," says the judge, "I agree with the defense on the murder weapon. The prosecution cannot introduce evidence that the murder weapon was found at the defendant's house. And the testimony of the jailhouse informant is not exactly something you base an entire case around, now, is it?"

The judge puts out a hand. He seems troubled by this, too, as if he doesn't want to toss the charges and is looking for help. "But . . . aside from the knife, there was the defendant's confession to Chief James. Obviously, the chief can't tell us about that now. Is there—I don't suppose anyone else was present at that confession who could testify about it?"

"I . . ." Sebastian Akers shrugs and shakes his head absently.

"My memory, Mr. Akers, is that the chief was going to testify that he was alone with Noah Walker during the alleged confession."

"That may be—it—but Judge, it would be grossly unfair to the administration of justice for Noah Walker to *profit* by murdering the star witness—"

"Mr. Akers," the judge booms. "I know you have your suspicions about Mr. Walker's involvement in the chief's death. But it's been six days and you haven't arrested him, much less sought an indictment. Do you, or do you not, have evidence—*evidence*—that Noah Walker killed Chief James?"

Akers raises his hands helplessly. "As far as I know, the investigation is still in its infancy—"

"I will take that as a no." Now the judge shakes his head. "So I will ask you again, Counsel, am I correct that Chief James was the only one who could testify to Mr. Walker's confession?"

"Judge, I would have to—"

"Mr. Akers, you know your case. Don't stonewall me. Was Chief James the only person present with Noah Walker when he confessed to the murder?"

Sebastian Akers flips through some papers, stalling for time, but he knows the answer as surely as Noah's lawyer does, as surely as I do. The chief was alone with Noah during the confession.

A single thread in the weave has been pulled by the defense, and the entire fabric of the prosecution's case has come apart. Without Uncle Lang to testify, the State can't tie the murder weapon to Noah's house. The State can't say that Noah confessed to a decorated veteran of the Southampton Town Police Department. All Akers can say is that a jailhouse snitch claimed to hear a confession—if the judge doesn't toss out that testimony, too.

The case is over. I can't believe this. The case is over. He killed my uncle and is going to walk away from two other murders because of it.

And I passed on the chance to put a bullet between his eyes.

"We're going to take a thirty-minute recess," says the judge. "Mr. Akers, I'd advise you to use that half hour well. If you can't think of some reason between now and then, this case is over."

Chapter 24

I PUSH SEBASTIAN Akers into the witness room adjacent to the courtroom and close the door. "This can't happen," I say.

"Detective, I know you're upset, but right now I have to—"

"There's a police report," I say. "Lang filled out a report when Noah confessed. Can't you introduce that as evidence?"

Akers, on the verge of coming unglued, lets out a pained sigh. "A police report is hearsay. You can't use it unless the defense can cross-examine the cop who wrote it."

"And Noah *killed* that cop," I protest.

"But we can't prove that, Detective! You know as well as I do that we haven't been able to come up with a hint of physical evidence. His motive is all we have."

I look up at the ceiling, searching for answers in the peeling white paint.

"He told me Noah confessed," I say. "Lang told me."

"Well, sure!" Akers waves his hand, exasperated. "He probably told a lot of people. Hell, he told newspaper reporters. But guess what that is?"

I drop my head. "Hearsay."

"Hearsay. Inadmissible in a court of law."

A long moment passes. I steady myself by placing my hands on the small table. But I sense something in the silence. I look up at Akers, who is studying me carefully.

"Unless," he says.

I straighten up. "Unless what?"

"There are exceptions to every rule," he says carefully. "Including the rule against hearsay."

He gives me a long hard look. Sebastian Akers is a very ambitious man. Undoubtedly, he considers this high-profile case a launching pad for bigger and better things. Or, conversely, a crash landing if he blows it. And five minutes ago, standing before the judge, Akers was on the verge of seeing his case implode before a national audience.

And I was on the verge of watching the man who killed my uncle, and three other people, skip out of court a free man.

"Tell me about the exceptions," I say.

Akers watches me very carefully, wondering if we're on the same page. I'm wondering that myself.

"One exception in particular," he says. "It has to do with when the chief told you about the confession. If he just mentioned it to you casually later that day or something like that, we're out of luck."

"But," I say.

"But if he told you *just after* the confession

happened—let's say, if he walked out of the jail cell, stunned that Noah had confessed, and told you at just that moment, still in a state of excitement and shock—the law considers that statement to be sufficiently reliable to be admissible. It's called an excited utterance."

I sit down in the chair. "An excited utterance."

"Right. If he said it while he was still in the moment."

"Still in a state of excitement and surprise."

"That's right, Detective."

Akers's eyes are wide and intense. He's holding his breath.

"Whether Noah Walker gets justice, or whether he laughs his way out of court, and probably kills again," he says to me evenly, "is riding on your answer."

It's not the only thing riding on my answer. My sworn oath as a police officer is, too. Because I remember now. I remember when Lang told me about Noah's confession. It was on his back porch in the early afternoon; he told me Noah had confessed to him that morning, hours earlier.

I clear my throat, adrenaline buzzing through me. "So if I testify that the chief told me about Noah's confession immediately after it happened—"

"While he was still in a state of excitement . . ."

Time passes. Memories flood through my mind. My stomach churns like the gears of a locomotive. What does it mean to be a cop? Is it about rules, or is it about justice? In the end, what do I stand for?

What would my uncle do for me, if our roles were reversed?

Finally, Sebastian Akers takes the seat across from

me. "We only have a few minutes," he says. "So, Detective Murphy, I have a question for you."

My eyes rise up to meet his.

"When was it, exactly, that the chief told you that Noah Walker confessed?"

A hush falls over the courtroom as Judge Barnett resumes his seat on the bench. There are even more sheriff's deputies present now than earlier, ready to calm the crowd should it be necessary. The energy in the room is suffocating. Or maybe that's just the shortness of breath I'm experiencing, seated in the front row of the courtroom.

The judge looks over his glasses at the prosecution. "Mr. Akers, does the prosecution have any additional evidence to present?" he asks.

The room goes still. Sebastian Akers rises slowly and buttons his coat. He turns and looks in my direction but does not make eye contact.

"The State calls Detective Jenna Murphy," he says.

Chapter 25

THE JUDGE GAVELS the courtroom to order after the lunch break. The morning was spent arguing over the admissibility of my testimony, a bunch of lawyer-speak about the rules of evidence that nobody else in the courtroom understood.

Then I testified for an hour. I told the truth—that my uncle told me that Noah had confessed to him—and then I told a lie. I lied about *when* he told me. Does it really matter if he told me immediately after the confession or several hours later?

That's what I've been telling myself over and over, anyway, that a handful of hours should not be the difference between a killer going to prison and his walking free to kill again.

Joshua Brody gets to his feet eagerly for cross-examination. My adrenaline starts to pump. I know what's coming, and it's something I have to willingly accept, the price I have to pay for testifying.

"Detective Murphy," says Brody, "you once worked

for the New York City Police Department, correct?"

He's not wasting any time. "Yes. I resigned about a year ago."

"At the time you resigned, you were under investigation by the Internal Affairs Division, isn't that true?"

"Yes," I say, the heat rising to my face.

"You were under investigation for skimming money and drugs during the arrest of a drug dealer, true?"

"I was investigated for it. But I was never charged."

"You were never charged because you resigned from the force," he says. "The department couldn't discipline someone who no longer worked for them."

"I was never charged," I reply evenly, "because I did nothing wrong."

"Oh, *I* see." Brody looks away from me toward the jury, then turns his stare back to me. "You just coincidentally decided that it was a good time to move on, at the same time that you were under investigation."

"As a matter of fact, yes," I say. "And I would add—"

"There's no need to *add,*" he says, patting the air. "You answered my—"

"*I would add* that the district attorney's office was free to charge me, whether I worked for the NYPD or not. But they didn't."

There is so much more I could say, everything that happened that led up to that bogus charge. But I don't have the energy to fight.

Brody smirks. He's gotten all he can here.

"Detective, you weren't present for this alleged . . . 'conversation' between Chief James and Noah Walker."

"Correct. I was down the hall from the jail cell."

"You have no firsthand knowledge of what was said between them."

"Firsthand? No."

"You took the chief's word for it."

"Yes."

"And this jury," says Brody, gesturing toward the jury box, "they have to take not only the chief's word for it, but yours as well."

"I'm not sure I take your point, Counselor."

"This jury has to believe that *you're* telling the truth about what the chief said, *and* that the chief told the truth about what my client said."

I nod. "I suppose that's right."

"They have to believe you, who resigned while under investigation for being a dirty cop—"

"Objection," says Sebastian Akers, jumping to his feet.

"Sustained."

Brody doesn't break stride. "—and they have to believe the chief, whom they don't get to hear from at all."

I pause a beat, anger surging to the surface. "That's right, they don't get to hear from the chief, Mr. Brody. Because your client killed him before he could testify."

I brace myself for an objection, for Brody to go crazy, for the judge to excuse the jury and give me a thorough dressing-down.

But to my surprise, Brody doesn't object.

"My client hasn't been arrested for that murder, has he?"

"Not yet."

"As far as you know, there is no physical evidence implicating my client?"

"Not yet."

"Very good, Detective." I have no idea why he's letting my statement slide. Presumably, he's calculated that every juror—every human being in the Hamptons—has heard about the chief's murder, and most believe that Noah killed him. He must figure it's easier to acknowledge it, so he can make his points about the lack of any arrest or evidence thus far.

Or does he have some other reason?

"Can you tell the jury what happened to you the day after this alleged confession?"

"The . . . following day?"

"Yes, Detective," he says, approaching me, a spark in his eyes. "Isn't it true that the following day, you were *suspended* for one month from active duty?"

The spectators react sufficiently for the judge to call for silence.

"Yes, I guess that was the following day, now that you mention it."

"Why were you suspended?"

Because I doubted the guilt of Noah Walker. Because I thought the murder of the prostitute might be connected to the Ocean Drive murders. But I can't say that. It would be a gift-wrapped present to the defense. And it's not what Lang said in the report he wrote up. That would be the last thing he'd write down.

"Insubordination," I say. "I let our personal relationship intrude on our professional relationship. I was disrespectful and I was wrong."

"You were disrespectful to him?"

"I was," I answer, feeling a lump in my throat, recalling the moment.

"You and your uncle, you were upset with each other?"

I feel the first hints of emotion creeping in. I'm not going to break down in front of this jury.

"He was certainly upset with me," I say. "And he was right to be."

"You feel . . . I can see that you feel guilty about that."

I don't answer. I don't need to.

"Looking back, it bothers you, doesn't it? That just before his death, you were disrespectful to your uncle."

I know what my answer should be. It should be *Yes, but that doesn't mean I would lie for him.* But that is precisely what I'm doing here today.

"It bothers me," I answer.

"You wish you could make it up to him."

Again, I don't answer. He doesn't wait very long.

"You think my client killed your uncle, correct?"

I nod. "Yes."

"But you'd agree with me that, with the full resources of the STPD on the case for almost a week, there's been no proof thus far to back up your suspicion."

"Not yet."

"So this case here," he says, pointing to the floor, "this case might be your *only chance* to get Noah Walker."

"Objection," says Akers, but the judge overrules him.

"And with the chief unable to testify about this

supposed confession from my client, and with the judge on the verge of dismissing the charges against my client, you now *suddenly* come forth to claim that the chief told you about this confession immediately"—he snaps his finger—"immediately after it happened."

I don't reply. My eyes move along the floor, then upward to the defense attorney.

"What a convenient and unexpected coincidence!" Brody says, waving his hands.

I look at Noah Walker, his chin resting on his fists. He watches me intently, his eyebrows pitched, as if—as if he pities me.

"No further questions," says Brody.

Chapter 26

NOAH WALKER PLACES his head gently against the bars of his holding cell, barely touching Paige Sulzman's head on the other side. His hands come through the bars and interlock with hers.

"I don't like you coming here," he says. "I don't like you seeing me like this."

"I know, baby. Good thing I'm stubborn."

"It's not a good idea. How would John—"

"John's in Europe. Copenhagen, this week, I think. I told you. He'll be gone for another two weeks."

Despite his protests, Noah looks forward to the fifteen-minute visits Paige is allowed every night in lockup. Riverhead is a dank, dark, miserable cesspool, purgatory for the accused in Suffolk County, short on hope and long on desperation and bitterness. Paige, with her freshly cut hair and generous smile, her sympathetic eyes and gentle demeanor, is like a rose sprouting in a swamp of manure.

"You could use a shave and a haircut," she says, trying to keep it light.

He acknowledges the attempt at humor, but it's hard to find anything funny right now. The trial is at its apex. Difficult decisions need to be made.

"Your lawyer did a good job today." The hope in Paige's expression, the tears shimmering in her eyes, reveal her lack of objectivity, but Noah doesn't totally disagree.

"Yeah, he did. But still, babe. The jury heard a cop say I confessed to the murders. What's the jury supposed to think when they hear I confessed?"

"That she made it up," Paige replies. "That she's trying to make it up to her uncle out of guilt. I thought that came through very clearly."

"Yeah, I know." He doesn't sound like he's convinced, because he's not. Yes, his lawyer did a good job cross-examining Detective Murphy, but the jurors seemed to like her regardless, and their opinions are the only ones that matter.

"She just lied," Paige says, spitting out the words. "She just *lied*."

Noah purses his lips. "She thinks I'm guilty. I could see it that night, when she broke into my house. She thinks I killed her uncle, and she thinks I killed Zach and Melanie, too. She thinks she's doing the right thing."

Paige draws back. "You're *defending* her? You must be joking."

Noah almost laughs at the paradox, the fact that he's sticking up for the cop who lied on the witness stand to put him away. "I just . . . understand why she did it."

He wants to be upset with Murphy. She's surely no friend of his. But there's something in the way she handles herself, like she's trying to prove something to somebody but isn't sure what she's proving, or to whom. He feels like he understands her. And regardless of what she did to him today, he can't shake the feeling that . . .

. . . that they understand each other. That she doesn't really believe, deep in her heart, that he's guilty.

"Oh, why is this happening?" Paige says softly.

There's no answer to that question. Noah feels like he's caught in a tornado, unmoored from any reality, whisked away with brutal force and carried through the air against his will. He has lost all control. Forces beyond his reach—the sensationalist media, ambitious prosecutors, crooked cops—have aligned to deem him guilty and deny him any chance of fighting back.

He must focus on this one fact: It doesn't really matter what anybody else thinks. It only matters what twelve jurors believe. He's seen the looks on their faces, their disgusted expressions, their averted eyes. He knows he has an uphill battle. He can only hope that their minds are still open, however slightly, to what he has to say.

He has to testify. His lawyer doesn't want him to. But he has no choice. He has to find some way to convince those jurors that he's not the killer they think he is.

If he fails, his life is over.

Chapter 27

JOSHUA BRODY LETS out a sigh. Almost three hours have passed, Noah testifying in response to Brody's questions, and now it's coming to an end. A pregnant pause by the lawyer, to emphasize these final questions—questions already asked and answered, but important enough to be repeated.

"Let me ask you one last time, Noah," says Joshua Brody. "Did you kill Melanie Phillips?"

Noah leans forward into the microphone on the witness stand. "No, I did not."

"Did you kill Zach Stern?"

"No, I did not."

Joshua Brody casts a glance at the jury. "No further questions."

Noah takes some deep breaths. Halfway done. The easy half, and it wasn't that easy. *It has to feel natural, not rehearsed,* his lawyer kept telling him as they prepared for today, and Noah feels like, all in all, it was convincing. From time to time during Joshua Brody's questioning, he glanced over at the jury. Did he see reasonable doubt on their faces? He doesn't know. This isn't what he does for a living. And he's in the moment, tense and focused. He wouldn't trust his instincts, anyway.

But he can't suppress the surge of hope he feels. He has a chance.

"Cross-examination?" Judge Barnett asks.

The prosecutor, Sebastian Akers, drops a notepad on the lectern between the prosecution and defense tables. This is the kind of moment a guy like Akers lives for. The packed courtroom, the big trial, the cross-examination that will make or break this case.

Keep your composure, his defense attorney told Noah. *Akers wants to paint you as someone who committed murder in a blind rage. He wants you to show the jury that rage. He's going to try to bring it out, get you upset.*

"Mr. Walker," Akers begins, "you have no alibi for the night of the murder, correct?"

Noah clears his throat. "As I told Mr. Brody, I stayed in that night."

Akers makes a face. "What I meant was, nobody can *corroborate* your alibi, correct?"

"Correct."

"The jury has to take your word, and only your word, for it."

"Yeah, I guess so."

"And you admit you were once given a key to the front door of 7 Ocean Drive, correct?"

"Yes. I've done work on that mansion for years. At some point, it made sense for the contractor who used me to just give me my own key."

"And that key has now magically disappeared."

"I don't know about 'magically'—but I don't know where it is."

There was no evidence of forced entry at the mansion on the night of the murders. The fact that Noah had his own key isn't a good fact for him.

"You deny that you confessed to this crime to Chief James. You deny that, right?"

"Yes."

"So when he said you did, he wasn't telling the truth."

"He wasn't."

"And when Detective Murphy testified to what the chief told her about your confession, she wasn't telling the truth, either."

"I don't know if she was or not. Maybe the chief said that to her. Maybe he didn't."

"If he did, then he was lying to her, too."

"Right."

"Or maybe Detective Murphy just made the whole thing up! Right, Mr. Walker?"

Noah feels perspiration on his forehead, his neck. "Could be."

"So maybe she was also lying. Right, Mr. Walker?"

"Maybe."

"Sure," Akers says with no shortage of sarcasm, flipping a hand. "And Dio Cornwall, who shared a cell with you in lockup, who testified that you confessed to killing Melanie, that you said you 'cut her up good' and that she 'couldn't be no movie star now'—Mr. Cornwall was *also* lying. Right, Mr. Walker?"

"He was lying. I never said anything like that to him. I never talked to him about my case at all."

"I see." Akers looks at the jury. "Any idea how Mr. Cornwall would have known the name Melanie, or that she'd wanted to be a movie star, if you didn't tell him anything about your case at all?"

"I—I don't know. Maybe he read it in the newspaper."

"The newspaper? Mr. Walker, Dio Cornwall was in lockup with you. Do you recall ever being given a copy of any newspapers while you were in lockup?"

Noah pauses. He casts his eyes downward.

"If you like, we can bring in the sheriff's deputies who controlled lockup while you were—"

"No, we never got newspapers," Noah concedes. "I don't know how Dio got that information. Maybe Chief James told him."

"Chief James? So now you're saying not only that Chief James lied about your confession, but that he helped Dio Cornwall make up a story, too?"

"I don't know."

"And Chief James isn't here to testify, is he, Mr. Walker? So we'll never be able to ask him, will we?"

Noah fixes a glare on the prosecutor. He feels his blood go cold.

"During your direct testimony, you admitted that you confronted Melanie at her job—at Tasty's Diner—asking her to take you back. You admit that, correct?"

Noah shakes his head, focuses on the change of subject. "Yes, I admit that we argued, and I grabbed her arm, but Remy has the date wrong. He said it happened two days before Melanie was killed. June second. But that's wrong. Melanie broke up with me in April. About seven weeks before she died. *That's* when I talked to her at Tasty's."

He met Paige a week after Melanie dumped him, in April. He'd moved on from Melanie. But he's never told anyone that. He's never publicly acknowledged his affair with Paige. And he won't now. No matter how many times Paige has told him to do so. He won't bring Paige into this.

Akers nods along, his eyes alight. "Pretty big difference between April—seven weeks before the murder—and two *days* before the murder."

"Yes, it is."

"So Remy's lying, too."

"I don't know if he's lying—"

"But he's not telling the truth."

"That's right. He's not."

"So, to summarize," Akers says, strolling along the edge of the jury box, "Chief James, Detective Jenna Murphy, Dio Cornwall, and Remy Handleman—none of them are telling the truth. But you, Mr. Walker, on trial for your life, whom Melanie broke up with so she could start dating Zach Stern—*you* are telling the truth."

Noah feels his pulse ratchet up. The way Akers is stacking up all the evidence . . . nobody's going to believe Noah. It hits him hard, for the first time. *They won't believe me. They're going to convict me.*

"I'm telling the truth," he pleads. "I swear I am. I would never hurt somebody else."

"You'd never hurt anybody?" Akers asks, with mock

innocence. "Well, Mr. Walker, isn't it true that, in 1995, you brought a rifle to Bridgehampton School and opened fire on a number of your classmates?"

Chapter 28

THE COURTROOM ERUPTS at Sebastian Akers's question. Noah's defense lawyer, Joshua Brody, is on his feet, arguing. Judge Barnett stands down from the bench and walks to the far end of the courtroom, away from the jury, for a sidebar with the lawyers. The spectators are all abuzz.

I wasn't in Bridgehampton back in 1995, but I have a memory of Uncle Lang mentioning that someone had brought a BB gun to school and shot a bunch of the kids on their way into school. He never mentioned a name; no reason he would have. This was before Columbine, before zero-tolerance policies cropped up around the country and kids were expelled from school for even bringing toy replicas in their backpacks.

If this was in 1995, Noah would have been young. Eleven, twelve, thirteen, something like that. It would have been a juvie beef. And if it was in juvenile court, it would have been confidential. I wonder if the town even knew who it was who did it. There would be rumors, sure, but I wonder if there was ever an official announcement. Judging from the reaction of the spectators—many of whom are presumably lifelong Bridgehampton residents—it seems like they're hearing this news for the first time.

The lawyers and court reporter and judge resume their positions, and the room goes quiet again.

Noah's lawyer, Joshua Brody, objects. "This is a juvenile offense," he says.

"Your Honor," Sebastian Akers replies, "he just testified he'd never hurt anybody. He opened the door. I'm entitled to impeach him."

"Overruled," says the judge. "Proceed, Mr. Akers."

And the prosecutor does just that, with a vengeance, a gleam in his eye. "You were arrested on Halloween, 1995, for shooting a number of schoolchildren on the south playground of Bridgehampton School, correct, Mr. Walker?"

"I was . . . I was arrested, yes. It was a BB gun."

"Fifteen schoolkids were shot that day, weren't they?"

"I believe . . . that's right."

"One child was hit in the eye, wasn't he?"

Noah nods but doesn't speak.

"That boy was *nine,*" says Akers. "He had to have two surgeries to repair the damage, isn't that true?"

Noah's eyes are fixed on the floor now. "That happened, yes."

"Yes, that 'happened.' That *'happened'* because you shot him with a BB gun, correct?"

Noah doesn't speak. Still staring at the floor.

"Is that a yes, Mr. Walker?"

"I didn't shoot him," Noah says, almost in a whisper, though the microphone gives it sufficient volume.

"No? You didn't shoot that boy? You were wrongfully accused then, too, is that it?"

"I didn't shoot him."

"I see. So when school officials said you did, they weren't telling the truth, either, were they?"

Noah's shoulders close in on him, like he's trying to shelter himself from a storm. "I don't want to talk about that anymore," he says.

"Oh." Akers lets out a chuckle. "Well, what do you wanna talk about? The Yankees' chances in the postseason?"

That gets a roar from the spectators. I thought it was clever, too, but I'm watching Noah. His face is turning red. He's practically curled up into a ball. Akers, if he's half the trial lawyer he thinks he is, senses it, too.

By the time the laughter has subsided and the judge has gaveled the room to order, Akers has slowly approached Walker, a tiger stalking prey.

"You shot fifteen people that day, Mr. Walker."

"I—no—I'm not going to—I don't want—"

"But you claim the school officials lied."

"I said I don't—"

"Just like you claim a decorated police chief, Langdon James, lied."

Noah shakes his head.

"Just like Detective Murphy lied."

It's clear now Noah's not going to answer, and that seems to be fine with Akers. He's watching—we're all watching—a defendant smoldering on the witness stand, and Akers is hoping he'll erupt.

"Just like Dio Cornwall lied. Just like Remy Handleman lied."

Noah turns his head away, as if he's done with this examination.

"All of them lied," says Akers. "It's a grand conspiracy, isn't it, Mr. Walker? The whole world against you."

Noah says something, but he's turned away from the mike and it's inaudible.

"Mr. Walker—"

"Yes!" Noah hisses, spinning around, nearly knocking over the microphone. Akers jumps back. The judge reacts, too. Several of the jurors recoil, seeing a new side of Noah Walker.

"Everyone's lying! The chief, that detective, the prison snitch, Remy, who couldn't tie his own shoes without help—they're all lying! They set me up!"

Noah surges to his feet, sweeping his hand, this time knocking the microphone to the floor. "They all set me up! They framed me! They're all liars!"

"Sit down, Mr. Walker, or I'll have you restrained!" the judge commands. "Deputies?" he calls out, and quickly two sheriff's deputies approach Noah.

When Noah doesn't immediately take his seat, one of the deputies grabs his arm. He yanks it free. Both bailiffs reach for their batons, but Noah drops himself back into his chair. The judge calls for order and admonishes Noah. His face has lost all hope now; it's distorted with bitterness.

But when he looks up, his expression breaks, the

scowl changing to despair, and for the briefest of moments, I think he's looking at me. Then I realize he's looking past me. I glance over my shoulder and see the woman he was with when I arrested him—Paige, I think her name was. She's mouthing something to him from across the courtroom, but I can't make out what she's saying.

I look back at Noah, who shakes his head and breaks eye contact.

"Your Honor, I have no further questions," says Sebastian Akers.

Chapter 29

THE FIRST DAY, Noah didn't think much of it. It had been a long trial. There was a lot of information to review. It could just be the simple matter of plowing through all the material, wanting to be thorough.

The second day, he began to wonder. He had no experience with this kind of thing, so he tried not to think too much about it.

The third day of jury deliberations, he began to have hope. Somebody on that jury was doing some heavy thinking about his guilt. *Don't read too much into it*, his lawyer advised him during a visit. *A lot of people have lost a lot of bets trying to guess what a jury is thinking.*

At a quarter after one on the fourth day of jury deliberations, Noah is summoned by the sheriff's deputy. He is heading, as always, toward the side door of the county courthouse, reserved for prisoner transfers, but the transport vehicle slows a block from the courthouse. The crowd has swelled beyond the sidewalks into the street. There are blockades, but they are hopeless against the swarm of onlookers. The transport vehicle moves slowly, and people grudgingly open a path, shouting at the vehicle as it passes, some of them even slapping the hood or one of the side windows.

When the vehicle turns toward the transfer door, Noah sees the trucks from all the national media lined up, faces of reporters he'd seen on television before the trial began and with whom he's now practically on a first-name basis, plus countless other reporters who couldn't get inside the courtroom but are always here, every morning, ready to shoot video footage or snap his picture.

The thousands of locals are here for various reasons, geriatric trial-watchers, concerned citizens, people just interested in the spectacle of it all, friends or family of Melanie Phillips. From time to time in the courtroom or standing outside here by the prisoner transfer, he has seen people who vaguely resemble Melanie and wondered if they were cousins or aunts or uncles. Melanie had a big family, though Noah never met any of them. They were only together for two months before Melanie ended things.

He remembers that day well, the day Melanie broke up with him, her resolve, the firmness of her words. *I'm sorry, but I've made my decision.* That was it. She wouldn't hear his protests. She just made the statement, a second time to be clear, and that was that. Noah always wondered if she'd discussed it with her friends or family ahead of time. He imagines someone advising her, *It's best to do it clean, just break it off, no long explanations or debate.* It bothered him to think that others knew about their breakup before he did.

He lets these thoughts occupy him so he won't think about what's coming as he passes down a long corridor lined with armed deputies, as he enters the courtroom from the side and dozens of heads turn in his direction. The law enforcement presence in this room is also heavy; the wall space is occupied by sheriff's deputies ready to keep order when the verdict is read.

And then it's as if everything is under water, almost dreamlike. His lawyer says something to him, but Noah doesn't really listen; he's gone to another place now, readying himself for what's about to come. Judge Barnett walks in and calls for the jury. The jurors file in and take their seats, one by one. You're supposed to watch them as they come in, looking for clues—*If they make eye contact, they're going to acquit you; if they don't, they're going to convict.* That never made sense to him, why you'd look for clues in the first place, when you're about to find out in a few seconds.

Instead, he turns around and finds Paige in the fourth row by the aisle. She moves her head so they can see each other between the other spectators. She mouths the words *I love you.* He wants to stay there, looking at her, but his lawyer takes his arm and he gets to his feet for the reading of the verdict.

He turns to face forward but doesn't look at the jury. He finds a blank spot on the wall and stares at it, thinking through everything that has happened and wondering, *How did it come to this?*

He hears a woman's voice. It turns out the foreperson of the jury is the single mother of two who has her own graphic design business, the one who sits in the front row of the jury box, three people from the left end. Is it a good thing that a woman is the leader? Another question that doesn't make any difference. All that matters is what she's going to say next.

"On count one, murder in the first degree with special circumstances, to wit the murder of Melanie Phillips, we find the defendant, Noah Lee Walker, guilty."

Noah sucks in his breath.

"On count two, murder in the first degree with special circumstances, to wit the murder of Zachary Stern, we find the defendant, Noah Lee Walker, guilty."

Noah turns and sees Paige. He starts toward her and she runs up the aisle toward him. There are bailiffs covering the gate that cordons off the spectators, and there are other bailiffs assigned specifically to Noah. Both sets of deputies do their jobs. Paige nearly makes it through, coming within a few feet of the defense table. The deputies grasp Noah firmly, gripping his arms, holding down his neck. He goes limp, compliant, before surprising them by breaking free and reaching Paige.

It won't last, but he just wants to touch her one more time. "Oh, baby," she says to him, her face wet.

He puts his hand gently on the back of her neck and kisses her quickly. Then he moves his mouth to her ear. "Don't give up on me," he says as the deputies recover their leverage, pulling him back. When he refuses to go down, they shove a Taser against his neck, electrical current surging through him. His legs and arms go limp just before his mind does. He falls to the floor in a heap, his last memory of this courtroom.

Book II

BRIDGEHAMPTON, 2007–08

Chapter 30

DEDE PARIS AND Annie Church have disappeared. They were last seen leaving their last final exam at Yale on May 9, completing their sophomore years. They said something vague to their friends about backpacking through Europe with the cash they've saved up while waitressing. They told their parents they were going to stay in New Haven for summer school and rent an apartment with their waitressing money. Neither set of parents made any attempt to verify their stories. Since May 9, over three weeks ago, no known acquaintance or family member has seen either woman.

Which is exactly how they want it.

Dede and Annie rush out of the ocean, holding hands, and find their towels and bags and umbrella. They slip into their flip-flops and don their shades. They are two beautiful, tanned twenty-year-olds, euphoric with love, with very few answers in life yet but, fortunately, very few questions, either. They will have the rest of their lives to discover their calling, to do their internships, apply to grad school, and brace for a hard world. This summer, they're going to discover each other, and nothing else.

By the time they reach the place where they're staying, their skin has long dried, and the withering oven-hot sun beats down on them. Fortunately, they don't have to go far. Their place is just a two-minute walk from the beach. They're staying at 7 Ocean Drive.

Well, it's not their place, exactly. But nobody else is staying here, and it would be a shame for it to stay empty all summer, wouldn't it?

"I love how freak-show this house is," Dede says, looking up at the scowling Gothic structure. She is tall and lanky, with bleached-blond hair cropped like a boy's that practically glows against her suntan. "I keep waiting for Elvira to pop out or something."

They turn east, walking along the southern border of the estate, covered by thick shrubbery that is taller than they are. Dede, the more athletic and adventurous of the two, was the first to explore the shrubbery, looking for a point of entry. The coiled-wire fence hidden within the shrubbery was formidable but nothing that a good set of shears couldn't handle, if you had time and patience, and they have plenty of both this summer. Besides, it didn't have to be pretty, just a large enough hole for them to slip through, the slipping made easier by the thick pieces of rubber they've tied over the jagged edges of fence to avoid cuts and scratches during ingress and egress. Sure, they have to squat down and turn sideways to make it through, but it's worth it—rent free and a ten-thousand-square-foot mansion all to themselves.

As they slide through the opening, Annie looks up at the mansion, the faded multicolored limestone, the stained glass and sharply pitched roofs and medieval-style adornments. She remembers the week she spent in the Hamptons as a girl, when she and her sister heard all about this place.

"No one ever leaves alive / The house at 7 Ocean Drive," she says in her best ghoulish horror-movie voice, repeating the poem she'd heard. *"Not friend or foe, not man or mouse / Can e'er survive the Murder House."*

"That creeps me out," Dede says.

They head toward the rear of the house. The ten-foot shrubbery provides good cover on the grounds, but the mansion itself is perched on a hill, and they've decided their entries and exits should be as covert as possible. In the rear there is a door that, once upon a time, was probably reserved for the servants. The door doesn't have a knob, just a latch held closed by a chain, another victim of Dede's shears.

The smell of disinfectant and soap greets them when they open the door. They scrubbed down the rear entrance the first time they came in, clearing out the cobwebs, mopping the floor, scrubbing the walls. The first thing they see is the door to the basement, which is likewise chained. Sure, they thought it was a little odd that an interior door would be locked in such a way, but they haven't bothered to investigate. There's enough house without it, and their tolerance for *creepy* has just about hit its limit. The basement will remain a mystery.

They pass through the foyer, ignoring the museum-like rooms on each side, and climb the winding, creaky stairs. A veranda off a bedroom on the third floor that they found last week has a panoramic view of the ocean.

Annie leans against the railing, sighing with satisfaction. Her hair, up in a ponytail, is the color of cinnamon but has lightened in the sun. Dede comes up behind her and kisses her long bronzed neck. She runs her hands along the outline of Annie's figure. Annie leans back into Dede's arms, gently humming as Dede cups her breasts, caresses the skin on her flat belly. "That tickles," says Annie as she turns to face Dede. They kiss deeply and lie down together on the blanket they've spread out, their legs intertwined.

And then they hear a noise. The hollow *clink* of metal tapping metal, and footsteps, and then a man whistling. Staying low, they inch toward the side of the veranda and peek through the wooden supports.

A man approaches the side of the house with a long ladder held at his side. He is shirtless and looks pretty damn good that way, a V-shaped physique, rippled abs. His curly dark hair falls from a Yankees cap, turned backward.

"Hot tool-belt guy," Annie whispers. "If I liked boys . . ."

The hot tool-belt guy drops the ladder against the side of the house and quickly climbs up. The women don't move, holding their breath, as he reaches their level on the third floor.

"Just behave yourselves, ladies," he says without looking in their direction. "Deal?"

Busted! Neither woman says anything. Neither woman moves.

"Deal?" he repeats.

Dede stands up, leans on the railing. "We have to behave? That's no fun."

Annie stands up, too. "So what's your story, guy?"

The man gestures upward with his chin. "Me, I'm just patching up the flat roof. Not having as much fun as you, looks like."

"That's not fair," Annie says, which sounds close to an invitation. She gets an elbow from Dede. "So what's your name?"

"Noah," he says.

"Are you going to turn us in, Noah?" Dede asks.

He considers them a moment. "Well, that wouldn't be very nice, would it?"

"It sure wouldn't."

"Just don't make a mess while you're here," he says. "I'll have to clean it up."

He starts to climb. Both girls can't help but enjoy the view. Straight or gay, this guy is hard not to admire.

"And one more thing," he says as he reaches the flat roof. "Don't go in the basement."

"Why's that, Noah?"

"Didn't you hear? This house is haunted." The man hauls himself up on the roof and disappears.

Chapter 31

ANNIE'S BEATER VW Bug pulls up to the gate of 7 Ocean Drive. The sun has fallen now at nine o'clock, so all is clear. When they use their car, which isn't very often, they prefer to enter and exit under the cover of darkness.

Dede gets out to push open the massive gate, using all her weight to do so. Once it's open, she turns back, squinting into the car's headlights.

Beyond the beams, across the street, she sees someone, standing flat-footed, looking at her. She does a double take, shields her eyes with a hand—which doesn't really help—and moves away from the blinding beams to get a better look. It seems as if . . . the figure moves along with her, and then disappears—maybe into the shrubbery?—leaving Dede with spots in her vision from the car lights.

Dede rushes back to the car and gets in.

"What's the matter?" Annie asks.

"I thought I . . . saw someone. Across the street. Staring at us. Watching us."

Annie strains to look behind her. "I didn't see anyone when we drove up."

"I know. Me either."

"What did he look like?"

Dede lets out a shudder. "Couldn't really see. A man, looked like. Kind of—you're gonna laugh—like a scarecrow, sort of? Like, his hair was all stringy and sticking out. He had a hat on, too, I think."

"A scarecrow?" Annie looks at Dede with mock horror. "You don't think . . . the Tin Man might be out there, too?"

"Stop."

"Not the Cowardly Lion!" Annie brings a hand to her mouth.

"Just drive the car."

Annie pats Dede's leg. "You're paranoid, girl. We're not supposed to be here, so you think everyone's looking to bust us. I mean, someone walking down Ocean Drive in the summer isn't exactly unusual." She puts the car into gear and drives through the gate. Dede closes the gate behind them, taking another look across the street and seeing nothing.

"That's the thing, though," she says when she reenters the car. "He wasn't walking. He was just watching us. I mean, I think. With the headlights, I couldn't really see. It could just be my eyes playing tricks."

Annie pulls the Beetle onto the grass next to the massive detached garage, hidden from sight. She lets out a sigh. "Good to be home," she says. "There's no place like home. There's no place like—"

"Would you shut up?"

As they walk toward the back entrance, they see the ladder the hot tool-belt guy used yesterday, broken down and lying in the grass. "Noah was cute," Annie says.

"Was he? Was he *cute?*" Dede throws another elbow.

"Now, now, dearest, I only have eyes for you."

Inside, they unpack their groceries. They've found a place in Montauk that sells lobster tails and oysters at nontourist prices, and Dede apparently looks old enough to buy champagne—the cheapest they had. Tonight is an anniversary of sorts, exactly six months from the day they met on campus.

Annie gets the food ready while whistling that *Wizard of Oz* song "If I Only Had a Brain." Dede keeps punching her playfully in the arm, but it only emboldens Annie. As much as it gets under her skin, it's one of the reasons Dede loves her.

Yes, she thinks, *I do love her*. Dede has no trouble opening her heart to Annie. She's accepted her sexual orientation for years now. She came out in high school, and she grew up in Santa Monica, where they practically throw you a parade for doing so. Annie, though, had never been with a woman before meeting Dede. Of course, she *knew,* on some level, but growing up in rural Michigan, she didn't acknowledge her sexual preference to her friends or her devout Catholic parents, or even to herself. You'd think, by 2007, people would have loosened up enough, but Dede knows as well as anyone that discrimination doesn't evaporate overnight but slowly fades over time.

Dinner is great. The dining room is over-the-top ornate, full of all kinds of detail on the walls, little statuettes perched around the room, tall windows with ornamental trim, an enormous chandelier hovering over a big five-sided dark oak table that's surrounded by high-backed chairs with leather cushions. It's like Henry VIII meets Count Dracula.

On their jam box, they play some symphonic music that Annie, the violinist, chose; she plays maestro, conducting the music with her fork. And the lobster and oysters are delicious. The cheap champagne is like Pop Rocks in Dede's mouth. It goes to her head quickly, enhancing her euphoria. *Annie is it*, she thinks. *She is my one and only.*

The window rattles and Dede turns to it. The wind, surely. But still, she walks over and cups her hand over the glass to block the interior reflection, looking out onto Ocean Drive.

"Is the Scarecrow still out there? I'd be more worried about him, if he only had a brain."

"You've been waiting to say that, haven't you?" Dede looks back and finds Annie sitting on the windowsill on the opposite side of the dining room. "What are you doing?"

Annie has her Swiss Army knife open, carving into the wood.

"Annie, you can't do that! This place is, like, three hundred years old. And it's not like you can just erase that."

Dede walks over to get a look at what Annie is doing. As Dede suspected, she is carving their initials in jagged letters:

DP + AC

"I don't want to erase it," Annie says. "I want it to be here forever."

Dede puts her arm around Annie and draws her close, breathing in her shampoo. "Forever?" she says tentatively. Her heart is pounding. This is one of those moments when she feels so vulnerable, her heart laid bare to be embraced or trampled.

"Forever." Annie looks up at Dede. The champagne tastes even better to Dede the second time, on Annie's tongue.

Chapter 32

THE GIRLS STAYING at 7 Ocean Drive are now on the second floor of the mansion, the southwest bedroom. The purple-and-gold bedroom, with the canopy bed and the velvet. The master bedroom where, over two hundred years ago, Winston Dahlquist once slept.

They are naked, and they are doing very fun things to each other. Their young bodies are shapely and athletic and limber, fueled by lust and maybe love—who can say?—and helped mightily by the two bottles of champagne they've drunk. The alcohol has undoubtedly lowered their inhibitions, and also impaired their judgment a bit—which is probably why they've forgotten to pull the bedroom drapes.

Now, to be fair, the bedroom window looks south, toward the beach and ocean, with only one house in between, which is not nearly as tall. A reasonable person would thus believe that, even with the drapes open wide as they are, she would not be visible to anyone.

But a reasonable person might not expect a man to be standing on the beach, peering northward with a pair of binoculars.

The man who thinks of himself as Holden lowers the binoculars and lets them hang around his neck. Wait—no—no, no. He removes the binoculars and throws them into his bag, which he calls his Fun Bag. This time of night, having binoculars is a dead giveaway—no chance of bird-watching or any other legitimate reason for using them, at ten in the evening. You might just as well wear a sign that says PEEPING TOM.

Be more careful, Holden! He likes calling himself that name. It gets him in the mood, in much the same way the alcohol gets those girls feeling more sexually adventurous. He rolls his neck. Stretches his arms. Cracks his knuckles. Jogs in place a moment, some sand kicking up.

He picks up his Fun Bag and climbs the beach onto Ocean Drive. He is happy, almost giddy. The sky is a deep purple and a soft wind plays with his hair. He is healthy and prepared. Tonight, he is Holden, and he can do anything.

He wonders how long they'll stay up in the bedroom. Could be they'll fall asleep, exhausted from the alcohol and sex. It won't matter. He'll be prepared either way.

They probably have the doors locked. They certainly should—there are scary people out there! Not that a lock will stop him.

He has a key to the place, after all.

But the front door isn't an option—too creaky and

noisy. No, he'll use his private entry, his secret way into the house, reserved for special occasions.

Because this has all the makings of a special occasion.

Chapter 33

HOLDEN RESTS IN the room that Winston Dahlquist once called the guest parlor, a waiting room of sorts off the ground-floor living room. It is ridiculously ornate, like all the rooms—candelabra and chandeliers and custom molding, a fireplace and a marble mantel, a Persian area rug.

They are almost directly above him. He closes his eyes and listens to their laughter upstairs. They are in love, he thinks, or at least they sound like it. His heart is pounding. He is here, and they don't know it. That is special all by itself—they think they're sharing something intimate, but he gets to be a part of it.

He opens up a small compact and checks himself over. His hair is smartly combed. His shirt is pressed. His beige trousers are new. His erection is at full mast, pushing against his trousers.

There's no way to describe this. One part forbidden, one part intimate, one part sexual, and one part full of possibilities unknown even to him—he's not sure what he's going to do yet. There should be a word for how he feels.

He thinks of how they'd react if they saw him. What they would say. What they would do. The snappy dialogue that would ensue. The flirtation. They'd be attracted to him, wouldn't they? Of course they would. Maybe a . . . a threesome? Wow. Maybe.

Footsteps overhead. Holden shakes out of his fantasy and listens closely. The footsteps are heading . . . where? Down the hallway toward the staircase?

No. No, she's just walking into the master bedroom. He hears the water turn on now.

He sighs. This is not good enough, not real enough. He thought this was going to be special. This is kind of fun, but not *special*. He's too far away from them, too remote. Should he go up the stairs? No, that would be too risky.

The kitchen, maybe. There will be glasses and dishes they touched. Maybe an article of clothing they left behind? That would help. That would really help.

He has to take a piss. But he can't do that. Even if he used the bathroom near the back, and even if he sat down like a girl to cut down on the noise, he'd either have to flush—which they'd hear—or leave evidence behind. He's not stupid. He's not stupid at all. Stupid? He's the opposite of stupid. He's really smart.

Oh, maybe he should just leave.

But tonight I'm Holden.

Okay. He removes his shoes to minimize his footfalls and drops them in the Fun Bag. He picks it up and pushes through the French doors quietly, into the living room. From there, he walks through the foyer. He stops at the staircase, where he hears them upstairs singing in unison to Justin Timberlake:

"I'll let you whip me if I misbehaaaave!"

He smiles to himself, feels himself relax. Feeling better, he walks into the dining room, where two empty bottles of champagne, an empty bottle of Evian, a bottle of Tabasco, two plates of discarded lobster tails and oyster shells, and a dish of horseradish rest on the pentagonal table beneath a grand chandelier. Winston Dahlquist used to bring the girls in here. They'd feast on duck and lobster and dates and olives. They'd drink the finest French wines. He probably viewed it as fattening them up before the slaughter.

He hikes the Fun Bag over his shoulder, carefully picks up one of the empty champagne bottles and one of the plates, and heads into the kitchen.

He's never liked the kitchen much because it's not original. Back when Winston built this place, the kitchen was for servants only, tiny and functional. Winston's descendants remodeled the kitchen in the seventies, tripling the size, installing cherrywood cabinets, marble countertops, and stainless steel appliances. It just looks like a boring kitchen, no character. But it's safe, and it will have to do.

He opens up the Fun Bag just to be safe, just to be sure, just to be prepared. He thinks of the girls having sex upstairs, and then singing "SexyBack," and it helps him. They'd like him. He's sure of it. They could share so much.

He smells the champagne bottle. Nothing special.

Then he sees lipstick on it, so he touches it with his lips. Not cherry ChapStick, but red and sticky and sweet. Yes. Good. This is getting better now. This was a good idea—

And then it happens in an instant, sneaking up on him, how, *how* it could have happened he isn't sure, because he's so cautious and careful, but he hears footsteps bounding down the stairs and suddenly those footsteps are in the dining room, adjacent to the kitchen, where he is. He moves very quietly toward the opening, hoping, *praying* that nobody heard him, and peeks into the dining room.

It's the blonde, the taller one with the short hair. She's unplugging the stereo resting on the windowsill. She looks good bending over, just wearing a bra and panties. So firm and lean. So . . . so special.

Oh, God, if I could just . . .

He ducks back, just on the off chance that she might cast a glance in his direction. His heartbeat is drumming so loudly that he can't hear, he can't think straight, but he prepares just in case, he's had it planned out just in case, and he recites it to himself now. *I'm the owner. This is my house.* Just in case.

And he reaches into the Fun Bag, also just in case.

He slowly steps back into the recesses of the kitchen and holds his breath.

It'll be okay, he thinks. *This will be better. It will enhance the whole experience, make it more real, more vivid.*

That's what he's telling himself when the blond girl walks into the kitchen.

Chapter 34

THE BLOND GIRL doesn't see him at first. Her head is down and she's balancing the remnants of the meal—the champagne and water bottles, the plates of food and the Tabasco—and turns toward the counter in the center of the kitchen to plop it all down before she even realizes she's not alone.

She recoils in an instant, her breath whisked away in surprise, her hands rising up defensively, everything she'd been holding crashing to the tile floor. Glass shatters everywhere. The sound only amplifies her shock.

Be indignant. This is your house. She's the intruder. Say that. Say that!

"I'm the . . . owner," he manages. He raises a hand in peace.

The girl is too stunned for a moment, but Holden planned this out well. The words did the trick. She doesn't turn and run, not immediately.

"Oh—oh. I—you're the own—"

"Dede? Is everything okay?" It's the other girl. *"Dede?"*

The blonde looks back toward the living room, then back at Holden.

"How . . . many of you are . . . here?" he asks. *Excellent! Just what an indignant owner would say.*

"Just two of—oh. Oh." Her eyes dart downward just as Holden feels the warm stain spreading across his crotch. He just pissed himself. He looks down, and then back up at her.

"We'll leave right now, mister. I'm really sorry."

She spins on her heels to leave. Holden closes the distance between them in an instant. She senses his approach and starts to run and is nearly out the door when he reaches her, stabbing the Taser into the back of her neck. She goes down hard, her body suddenly limp and unable to break her fall, her face smacking against the kitchen wall and landing hard on the ceramic tile.

"Dede?" comes the voice from upstairs.

Holden drags the blond girl—Dede—into the kitchen, away from the view of the dining room, a trail of blood smearing in her wake. Is she . . . dead? The fall was nasty. She's bleeding from the nose and forehead.

What has he done? What's he *going* to do? He's thinking fast, but the adrenaline is catching up with him now and he can't let it paralyze him, he's got to think-think-think—

Hearing the urgent footfalls in the living room, Holden grabs a frying pan from the overhead rack and raises it above his head. The brunette gasps before she's even entered—seeing the bloodstain first, no doubt—and when she rushes in, her eyes are already cast downward at her lover. She lets out a horrific scream as she looks up to meet Holden's eyes, but by then the frying pan is already crashing down on the crown of her skull.

The pan almost bounces out of Holden's hand from the harsh impact. He's never hit anything so hard. The brunette is stunned, reaching for support but unable to find any. She sinks to her knees, still upright but precariously so, and before she falls like a tower tumbling over, Holden raises the pan and cracks it against her skull a second time. When she crumples to the floor, she is lifeless, like a balloon figurine that the air has been let out of. Her eyes are open but still.

Is *she* dead?

Holden bounces on his toes, looking at each of them. The blonde is still breathing. The brunette is not.

"It was a . . . accident," he says. "I didn't . . . I just wanted . . ."

What does he do now? Panic sweeps over him. *Run*, he thinks, but *No, too many clues left behind.* The blonde knows what he looks like.

She moans. Her shoulders move. She's trying to turn over.

Holden watches her. Watches her struggle. Watches her suffer.

But this is their fault. They shouldn't have surprised him. They made him do this.

"No . . . no . . ." The blonde is making noise on the floor. He taps her with his foot. She groans in response. He bends down and rolls her over on her back. Turns her bloodied face to the left, so she can see her girlfriend.

"Look at her," he says. "Look."

Her eyes widen in horror. She manages a low, guttural, garbled wail.

It's the most beautiful sound he's ever heard.

Chapter 35

HOLDEN PUTS A hand on his stomach. It causes a physical pain, a rumble in his stomach like hunger for food, a growl that resembles the angry hum of the motorcycle on which he's riding at the moment.

He needs it again. He needs the thrill of the chase, the anticipation, the climax itself. It's been over a year since Dede and Annie, and he can't decide what was most invigorating: the initial approach, sneaking into the mansion; the physical act; the pain and suffering . . .

. . . so much to choose from. It's kind of like deciding what you like best about pizza, the cheese or the sauce or the toppings; they are inseparable ingredients of a delicious experience. But if he had to choose, it was none of those things. No, it was the aftermath, what's happened every day since, the feeling of invincibility that comes with knowing he got away with it, that he can do whatever he pleases and nobody can catch him, nobody can stop him.

Oh, there was an investigation. Apparently the girls,

Dede Paris and Annie Church, hadn't told anyone where they were spending the summer. They had told their friends one lie, their parents another, but nobody the truth. It was only through cell phone records that authorities were able to place them in the Hamptons at all. But it was over two weeks after he'd killed them that a search even began, and it wasn't much of a search. Nobody had any idea where the girls were staying in the Hamptons. They never even focused on Bridgehampton, much less the house at 7 Ocean Drive. The best guess was that the girls were staying in Montauk, because that was where they found Annie's car, in a tow yard after it had been parked illegally in a church parking lot, stripped of its license plates. (Yes, Holden has congratulated himself for moving her car.) It was when the authorities found the car that they officially determined . . . *drumroll, please* . . . that "foul play" was involved.

Ta-da! They don't have a clue. The lesson: *You can do whatever you want. If you're smart. If you're disciplined. If you take care in choosing your victims. If you don't get greedy.*

He drives by the nightclub again, passing the alley where they congregate in the shadows, waiting for any car that might pull over. He slows his motorcycle to an idle and looks to his right, directly where he knows they are. Several of them step out from the shadows into the light of the streetlamp in their skintight dresses, hiked up to show plenty of leg, their hair teased up, their boobs pushed out, hoping to make eye contact with potential customers. There are a half dozen of them, a nice variety of busty and petite, white and black and Hispanic. A smorgasbord of potential victims.

Victims. It's fun to think of them that way. Not women but prey.

He immediately crosses the tall, leggy blonde off the list, because she is too much like Dede—though Dede ended up being great fun in the end. Still, variety is the spice of life, and, more to the point, an intelligent man like Holden realizes that he cannot leave a pattern of any kind in his wake.

He quickly narrows it down to a busty black woman and a petite blonde.

The blond one it is! Smaller, probably no more than a hundred pounds, and therefore easier to subdue, should any difficulty arise.

But why should any difficulty arise? He has his Fun Bag back at the motel. And unlike last time, when Dede and Annie surprised him, this time he'll have the chance to show off his charm, to gain her trust, lure her in.

She'll have no idea what's coming. She'll probably think the corkscrew is for a bottle of champagne. She'll think the handcuffs are just a kinky sex thing.

She might wonder about the handheld kitchen torch, though.

It's past midnight and there is a healthy stream of people coming and going from the club nearby. Witnesses, potentially—a careful man like Holden thinks of such things—but most are drunk and, in the end, what could they say about him? He's wearing a helmet with a tinted face shield, and he's removed the license plate. All anyone could possibly describe is a guy in a leather jacket wearing a helmet on a black motorcycle.

Anyway, if it was entirely risk-free, it wouldn't be any fun.

Yet he feels a pang of doubt, even as he nods toward the petite blonde. Can he go through with it? He's rusty; it's been over a year. As much as he's been romanticizing it since then, he now remembers how scared he was at the time. Exhilarated, yes, but scared, too.

On his nod, the blonde saunters up to him, wearing a black outfit that covers little more than a bikini would. Her belly is flat, with a piercing through her navel. She has the body of a twenty-year-old, the face of someone older, more seasoned, more worked over. Her heels make her two inches taller, but she's a little thing.

"Hi, handsome. You want some company?"

"I want . . . all night," he says, keeping his helmet on, the face shield down.

"I'm by the hour, hon."

"I want . . . all night." That's Holden being smart. If she's leaving for the night, nobody will expect her back in an hour. Nobody will think to look for her at least until tomorrow. Assuming anybody looks for her, period.

"The whole night? That's two thousand." She runs her hand over his arm, the leather of his jacket. "It's worth it."

"No," he says. See, that's Holden being smart again—make her think this is a real negotiation, that he actually plans on paying her something. "Five hundred."

"Five hundred for this?" she says, running her hands over the outline of her body, moving to the music coming from the nightclub. “C’mon, lover, fifteen hundred. For a night you’ll never forget.”

He doesn’t know what a streetwalker makes in a night, but it can’t be anywhere near that. “A . . . thousand,” he says.

“Awww, baby. Hang on.” The girl walks back to her friends and says something. *See, you were right—she’s telling them she’s done for the night, not to expect her back. Smart, Holden.*

“Do I need a helmet?” she asks when she hops on the bike.

He turns back to her as she wraps her arms around his waist.

“No,” he says. “You’re safe with me.”

Chapter 36

HOLDEN AND THE blond hooker drive to a motel off Sunrise Highway. He rented the room two days ago, paying in cash and asking for a room in the back away from traffic. He parks within ten feet of the door and brings the girl inside. The room isn't much to look at. The carpet is torn up, the wallpaper is peeling, the lighting is dim, and the mattress is about as thick as a slice of cheese. But it's clean and it doesn't smell. He's seen worse. And he's certain she has, too.

He sets his helmet on the small table where the television sits. He spots the Fun Bag in the corner, just where he left it. He looks in the mirror and fixes his hair.

"We need to take care of business first."

He turns and gets his first look at her in normal lighting. She has a round face, her eyes set slightly too far apart, with a crooked smile that is probably supposed to be sexy. Her dirty-blond hair is teased up in some kind of bun on top of her head. She is very slender, and her skin is pale and freckly. Her breasts are small and her butt is tiny and round.

"Okay." He has a thousand in cash. He peels it out and hands it to her. She stuffs it in her purse. Is that her idea of safekeeping? It must be. Though it's not that safe. She's in a room with a stranger, after all. It's not safe at all. *She's* not safe at all. But that's an occupational hazard. Everything she does is full of risk. That must be hard, having to make a living by meeting strange men and—

Stop it. Stop thinking like that.

"I'm gonna freshen up," she says, and then she spins on her heels and heads to the bathroom, her red purse slung over her shoulder.

He looks at himself in the mirror. *Don't start thinking about her life. Think about what you want. Think about what you're going to do. Think about the handcuffs and the corkscrew and the torch. Don't fuck this up. You've been waiting a year for this—*

She returns looking a little more chipper, her eyes glassy.

She's high. She took something in the bathroom.

He looks over her arms. No signs of needle marks. Cocaine, probably. That's probably how she gets through this job, high as a kite.

Stop it. You don't give a shit about her or how she copes with life.

You don't care.

"So what's your pleasure, guy?" Her tone is less

flirtatious than it was on the street. More businesslike.

"My . . . ?"

"What do you want me to do?" Her eyes bug out, like she's impatient.

"I just . . . can we . . . can we just . . . talk?"

He's trembling. She looks at his hands. She sees it, too.

"Okay, we can talk." She sits down on the bed and looks up at him. "What do you wanna talk about?"

"I . . ." He swallows hard. *What the hell is wrong with you?* "What's your name?"

She shrugs. "What do you want it to be?"

He shakes his head. "No . . . no."

"Okay, my name's Barbie."

Her name isn't Barbie. That's her street name.

"Do you . . . wanna know . . . *my* name?"

"Sure, mister. Lots of guys don't want to tell me their name. It's your money."

He stares at her, unsure of himself.

"Okay, what's your name, guy?"

She's so hardened. Deadened. Drugged out. She'll spread her legs for him or suck him off, she'll twist and turn her body however he asks, but she won't really be here. This isn't real.

It's not supposed to be like this. Dede and Annie, they were real. He thought the one thing missing was that he didn't know them first, didn't get intimate with them, killed them almost at first sight. But that was better. That was better than this—

"Got anything to drink, mister?"

He shakes his head, unable to speak. He should've

thought of that. He should've had a bottle of whiskey or something.

"Got any music?"

Shit. He shakes his head again. He feels everything slipping away, every turn a wrong one . . .

"I . . . can't," he whispers.

"Can't what?"

Sweat has broken out on his forehead. His pulse is racing. He doesn't feel right.

"I can't . . . kill you," he says. His eyes slowly rise to meet hers.

She studies him a moment, lips parted, fear beginning to spread across her face. He feels himself getting hard. He feels the energy suddenly fueling him.

And then her eyes grow big again, when she sees the look on his face.

There. There it is!

She bounces off the bed, rushing for the door.

Yes.

"No!" she cries as he grabs her arm. "No, please!"

He pins her up against the wall, bringing a hand over her mouth. She bites down on his hand, causing a glorious pain, but he pushes back hard, slamming her head against the wall with all the force he can summon. Her eyes roll back and she begins to slide down the wall, unconscious.

He lowers himself, sliding down with her. He drags her over near the bed and lays her out properly.

"Thank you, Barbie," he whispers.

He handled this wrong, but she salvaged it for him, a last-minute save.

He learned something. He won't make this mistake again.

He walks to the corner to get his Fun Bag.

Book III

BRIDGEHAMPTON AND SING SING, 2012

Chapter 37

SING SING CORRECTIONAL Facility, thirty miles north of New York City on the east bank of the Hudson River, houses nearly two thousand inmates over fifty-five acres of property. Up the hill from the lower-level secured facilities is Cell Block A—"Maximum A"—one of the largest max-security cell blocks in the world, with over six hundred inmates packed into six-by-nine-foot cells. They are murderers and rapists and sex traffickers and mob bosses and major drug dealers, divided into fierce factions predominantly by race—the Bloods and the Crips, the Latin Kings and *Trinitarios*, the Aryan Brotherhood. If you belong to one of the gangs, they have your back—you're protected—but even then you're not *really* protected, because the sins of the individual are the sins of the gang, and retaliation in Cell Block A is as common as census counts four times a day. In the last eight days, Cell Block A has been on lock-down four times, as the Latin Kings and the Bloods have worked out their differences the only way they know how. Guns are uncommon; it's by shanks and razors, anything that can be pried loose and sharpened into a weapon, that most of the injuries are inflicted.

The first time Noah Walker walked into Cell Block A, he was overwhelmed. Overwhelmed by the sheer enormity, the cell block extending four stories high and so far from right to left that there seems to be no beginning or end, just an endless wall of steel and chain-link barriers. Overwhelmed by the noise, a deafening clamor of hundreds of caged men shouting, radios playing, gates slamming.

This is his home now, on the top tier of A-Block, Gallery L, seventh cell. He will live in L-7 for the rest of his life. He will live amid a massive series of cages, covered by a concrete-and-brick dome with windows that miraculously let in very little light, sunshine filtered through filth. The polluted air, the noise, the solitude of hour upon hour spent in a cell no bigger than a normal person's closet—in the seventy-three days that Noah has spent here, they have had the effect of deadening him, killing his hope, erasing his dreams, leaving him numb.

Outside the cell—the mess hall, the showers, the machine shop, and the prison yard—it's a different story. Noah is alert at all times, his eyes constantly moving about. Noah is not affiliated. The only real option for a white guy is the Aryan Brotherhood, and he's not going anywhere near those racist morons. That makes him fair game to everyone. Stick a shank into Noah's back, or accost him in the shower, or jump him in the yard, and nobody will retaliate. Noah is alone in every sense of the word.

And with every day that passes, he finds that he cares less and less. There is nothing for him here but the passage of time. He is simply waiting for time to move along until he dies.

His tiny cell is barren of personal effects. He hasn't built up enough in the commissary for a radio, and no television is allowed. He has only two personal items, a photograph of Paige and a copy of his favorite novel, *The Catcher in the Rye*.

In the photograph, Paige is in Noah's attic bedroom, her hand up to shield her face from his camera, a look of embarrassed amusement on her face. Strands of her hair curl around her cheek. He likes this photograph because it touches all of his senses. He hears Paige's voice—*Don't take my picture!* He smells her the way he liked her best, sweaty after sex. He feels her hand on his arm while she tries to keep him from snapping the photo with his phone.

Paige. He will never see her again. He told her not to come here, and to drive the point home, he told her he wouldn't see her if she came. They have no future now, and it's better she remembers him when life was good, to hold that sweet memory close to herself, rather than having her image of him deteriorate slowly over the years as he grows harder, more bitter.

He met yesterday with his lawyer, who told him there would be a one-month delay in getting his appeal on file. Noah told him that was okay. He doesn't have a chance. He knows that. He's in no hurry to find out that his appeal has been rejected.

That's the worst part, worse than the fear in the

prison yard, or the loneliness, or the shame of being convicted of a double homicide. The lack of any hope, of any future, of any meaning to his life, will kill him—if a shank in the neck doesn't.

Which of those will come first, he has no idea.

Chapter 38

THE MACHINE SHOP in Sing Sing is in the former "death room," where the electric chair, "Old Sparky," killed more than six hundred people, including the spies Julius and Ethel Rosenberg, over the course of seventy years. "Old Sparky" has been moved to a museum, and the death penalty has been abolished in New York—Noah now often wishes it hadn't—so instead, Noah works in that space assembling chairs for toddlers, to be used, he assumes, in either an elementary school or a hospital.

If there have been any moments of enjoyment in his two and a half months in Sing Sing, they have come while he's been doing this work, taking care and pride in putting together these chairs. He's always enjoyed working with his hands, knowing that there is something tangible to show for his effort. Someone will sit in this chair. Someone will learn something in this chair. Someone will laugh in this chair.

"On the count!" One of the COs walks in for the

census, taken four times a day to make sure all prisoners are accounted for. The correctional officers cannot, as a practical matter, follow around every inmate all the time, so they move them in groups through the narrow hallways, always staying to the right of the yellow stripe down the center, and even let them walk on their own when going to the yard or the gym.

At the CO's call, Noah stands and keeps his hands at his sides. The CO counts off the inmates aloud. There are eleven in the machine shop, divided among the various rooms for printing, woodwork, and welding. There are only three, Noah included, here in woodworking.

Noah gets back to work, squatting down on one knee. Behind him, he hears the other two inmates—both of them African American, Al and Rafer—abruptly put down their tools and walk out of woodworking. Noah senses something.

He gets to his feet just as three men enter the room. Unlike Al and Rafer, these men aren't black. They are white. He recognizes one of them as Eric Wheaton, the leader of the Aryan Brotherhood here at Sing Sing. His two friends are massive, with shaved heads and skin ink up and down their tree-trunk arms.

Wheaton, himself above average in size but dwarfed by his companions, is the elder statesman of his clan, probably fifty. He shows Noah his teeth. "Well, Noah. Seems like you been avoiding us. My friends have offered to be your friends."

"I don't need friends like you," says Noah. He wishes he had something in hand, like the hammer on the floor.

"You don't need friends? You're the only guy in A don't need friends? How's a guy like you gonna get along in here with all the mongrels?"

The men on each side of Wheaton fan out, forming a semicircle around Noah. Two more men, nearly as big as the first set of goons, also proud members of the Brotherhood, enter the room. Now it's five on one.

"So I'm askin' nice," says Wheaton. "For the last time."

Noah takes a breath, steels himself. "I don't need you or your white-trash racist asshole buddies."

Wheaton's smile widens, showing stained, crooked teeth. "He's too good for us, friends. He's Jesus. Didn't you hear? Surfer Boy Jesus. Someone help me remember, now—what happened to Jesus?"

With that, they close in from both sides. Noah keeps his fist in tight and pops one of the goons in the mouth, snapping his head back, and then spins to his right and connects with a roundhouse left to the jaw of the thug from the other side. It's enough to throw the man off balance but not enough to knock him over. Noah will still have to deal with him and with the other two. He turns back to his left for the oncoming rush, but he's not fast enough; the biggest of the goons barrels into him, three hundred pounds of force, knocking him to the floor. He kicks out his legs and tries to bench-press the man off him before a boot connects with his temple, sending a shock of lightning across his eyes. Then the man on top of him rises up and slams down a fist. Just in time, Noah ducks his head, and the man's fist hits the floor instead of Noah's face. He cries out in pain. Noah lunges up at the midsection like a bucking bronco to topple the man off him.

But they are too many, and too big. After the initial burst of action, it simply comes down to numbers. Five on one. Five men kicking and punching Noah, who is pinned down. Blood flies from his mouth and nose with each kick, each punch, until he can no longer hold his head up. Now he is nothing more than a punching bag. He feels his ribs crack with successive kicks, but he can't offer any response. He is getting the life beaten out of him, and if they want to kill him, he can no longer stop them.

After a while, the pressure comes off his chest, and he is being tugged by all four limbs. Then he is lifted off the ground and thrown down onto one of the large woodworking tables.

"Keep his arms out, boys," one of them says. Noah is hardly conscious as his arms are spread out, palms up. Men climb onto the table and sit on each of his forearms, while two others sit on his shins. He is completely pinned down.

By the time he feels the prick of the nail on the palm of his hand, he is unable to even cry out. He looks through the fog, through the tiny slits of his eyes, and sees Eric Wheaton poising the nail over his right hand, a hammer raised above his head.

When the hammer comes down on the nail, it's like a drilling rig finding oil, blood spurting into the air. Noah lets out an animal cry and his eyes go to the ceiling. They do quick work of it, nailing both hands to the wooden tabletop, while Noah focuses on a single thought.

Let me die, he prays.

Chapter 39

"ALMOST READY, BABE?"

I flip the page, then flip back, reading through police reports and investigation summaries and cross-referencing trial transcripts.

"Babe?"

"Um. Yeah. Almost ready."

Well, not so much. I'm sitting on the bed, feet up, doing work. But I can get ready fast.

Matty pokes his head into the room. He's wearing a new Hugo Boss sport coat and cologne of the same label. His hair is freshly slicked back from his shower.

"What are you doing? You haven't even showered?"

"No, I—sorry," I say. "Just reading."

"Reading what? Christ, Murphy, do you ever stop working? And that comes from someone who works on Wall Street." He walks over to the bed, where I'm sitting with the transcript on my lap. Matty reaches for the stack of paper I'm reading, revealing the solid-gold cuff links on his sleeves.

"This is the guy who killed your uncle? The 'Surfer Jesus' guy?"

"Yeah." I look up at him. "Just checking something."

"Checking what? That guy went down, what, four months ago? What is there to check?"

I shrug. "There was a shooting at Bridgehampton School a long time ago. Halloween of ninety-five."

"And that has what to do with what?"

"Noah was arrested for it."

"Noah," he says. "Now you're on a first-name basis with the guy."

"I pulled the file yesterday," I say. "Let me run this by you, okay?"

"Hurry." Now he's at the bedroom mirror above the dresser, checking himself over, fixing the collar of his new shirt.

"Fifteen people were shot that day in the southern playground," I say. "Noah was on the east end of the yard, by the trees. Of the fifteen shot, about eight of them were hit within thirty feet of where he was standing with his BB gun."

"Uh-huh."

"Another seven were walking up to the school but farther away, farther west."

"Oh. Okay." He smoothes his hair, looks himself over once more, and reaches a favorable conclusion.

"They were more like sixty, seventy feet away. One of the kids on the farther west end, a kid named Darryl Friese, took a BB in his eye."

"Yeah? Wow."

"His *left* eye."

Matty doesn't answer. He walks into the bathroom and runs the water. When he walks back out, wiping his face with a hand towel, he nods at me.

"You still aren't in the shower," he says.

"You're not listening to me."

"Sure I am."

I'm tempted to ask him what I said. But that would embarrass both of us.

"If Darryl Friese was walking north up to the school, and Noah was shooting from the east, how did he hit Darryl on the left side of the face?"

Matty tosses his shoulders. He doesn't know. He doesn't care, either. He finishes with the towel and gives me a sideways glance. "I've seen this guy Noah on TV," he says. "Handsome dude. Should I be jealous?"

"Matty—"

"Who's better-looking, him or me?" he asks.

"Are you kidding me?"

He points at me. "That's a nonanswer. You think that guy's got something on me? He doesn't make seven figures, does he? C'mon, Murphy, give it up," he says, grabbing my ankle. "You like that guy more than me?"

I move my leg, forcing his hand off my ankle. I get off the bed and walk out of the room. He follows me down the hallway.

"What? I was listening. But Murphy, what's your deal? That thing was a lifetime ago. I mean, I know you miss your uncle, and I'm sorry and all that—"

"That's very sweet of you," I deadpan.

"—but seriously, you gotta snap out of this. You're turning into a real drag."

I stop and spin on him. "Am I?"

"Yeah, you wanna know the truth. You are."

I take a step toward him. "This is the guy who killed my uncle. I'm trying to understand him."

"Why? You trying to get closure or something?"

"I don't know. Maybe."

"Well, can you get 'closure' when we don't have reservations at Quist in . . . now it's twenty-four minutes," he says, checking his watch.

"I can still get ready," I say.

"Yeah, you'll wash your hair and tie it into a ponytail and throw on something too casual for where we're going. God forbid you try to look hot when I'm in town. God forbid you put on some makeup and spend more than two minutes on your hair. You're this . . . you're the hottest woman I know, but it's like you don't give a shit about that."

I narrow my eyes to get a better look at this man named Matt Queenan. "I *don't* give a shit about that," I say. "Did you just figure that out?"

"Y'know, I'm gonna let you in on a little secret, princess." He wags a finger at me. "A lot of women would *want* to look hot for me. You think I don't get overtures all the time? Every day? You think there aren't a dozen women who'd jump at the chance to date me?"

"Oh, I'm sure there are *hundreds*," I say, not hiding my sarcasm. "You're the great Matty Queenan! You make *seven figures* a year! Why don't you go find one of those women tonight?"

I return to the bedroom. As I pass him, he grabs my

arm. "You know what, I think I will," he says through his teeth.

I yank my arm free and give him a forearm shiver to the chest. "Don't grab my arm."

"Don't fucking push me," he says, knocking me back into the wall.

My Irish up now, I lean in and punch him right in the kisser, connecting with his teeth and feeling his jaw crunch. "Is that better?"

He stumbles backward, unprepared, touching his mouth and then checking his fingers, finding blood. "You fucking *bitch*. Nobody hits me."

I shrug. "Hit the road, Matty," I say. "Or I'll hit you again, a lot harder."

"Yeah?"

He moves at me, but I feint toward him and he backs off. He's a lightweight. He knows I could take him. He couldn't handle the embarrassment.

"Have a nice life in this shithole town with your shithole job," he says, turning to leave. "I'll have another date by the time I get back to Manhattan."

Chapter 40

AFTER MATTY DRIVES away, I throw on a baseball cap and head to my car. I don't feel like being around here, smelling his lingering cologne, thinking of him. My nerves are still rattled, but I know, in my heart, that I wasn't going anywhere with him. It was going to happen sooner or later.

I try to avoid the knowledge, also buried deep within, that I'm probably not going anywhere with *any* guy, that I'm not cut out for a relationship. I always rolled my eyes at the cliché of the cop who's married to the job, but now I can see the merits of the stereotype. It's not that I don't care about anything besides my job—it's that the job doesn't let you leave. You see death and misery and suffering, and you don't just click that off when you go home; it doesn't wash off in the shower or vanish with a lover's embrace. You are polluted, toxic, and so you hold back so you don't infect someone else with the poison. You keep part of yourself segregated, hidden.

And as long as I'm being brutally honest with myself:

The truth is I've *always* felt alone, long before I was a cop. Always different. The "red sheep" of my family, I always called myself, because of my shiny red hair contrasted with the blond hair of Ryan and my parents. (I'm told my red locks came from a great-grandmother I never knew; I've only seen a black-and-white photo of her.) I was tall and athletic, while Ryan was stout and bookish. I was a restless troublemaker, while Ryan was calm and content. I was a rebel without a clue, in a loving, happy family, as if I somehow missed out on the one gene that allowed me to just fit in like everyone else.

I drive to Uncle Lang's cottage on North Sea Road. The shrubbery remains well maintained, courtesy of the Realtor who's listing it. The door is locked, but I have a key. The house has been cleaned, the rugs shampooed, the kitchen scrubbed, the fridge emptied of perishables. It feels weird being here without the clothes strewn about, the smell of dirty socks and fried food—the house as it became after Chloe left Lang.

Chloe, Lang said to me, when I saw him before he was wheeled into surgery. *Look up Chloe.* One of his last thoughts was the love of his life. But even *they* couldn't maintain a relationship. What chance do I have?

This is the question I pose as I unscrew the bottle of Beefeater gin. I decide to be an optimist and view the bottle as half full, and thus available for my consumption.

Oh, look at me. I'm a cop with an attitude on her last chance, in a town that gives her sweaty, breathless nightmares almost every night, who drinks too much and can't connect with members of the male species, and with an acting police chief who's no fan of mine, who's probably hoping to run me out by boring me to death with lousy assignments. I'm surprised Matty only *walked* out on me, instead of sprinting.

I find a stray coffee cup in the cupboard, pour myself some gin, and head into Lang's second bedroom, where his remaining effects have been boxed up. A roomful of boxes is so lonely. His desktop computer still sits on a simple wood desk, with the keyboard on a lower shelf that slides out. I boot up the computer and stare at the screen as it requests a password. I feel a pang in my heart as I type the password—JENNAROSE—and watch the computer come to life.

Lang kept copies of his "murder books"—police reports, investigators' notes, crime-scene photos, autopsy reports, interview summaries for a given case—in his home office; they're packed up now and sitting in his garage. He also wrote up summaries of each of these cases in individual word-processing documents, narrative versions of the events from crime to conviction. He'd talked for years about writing his memoirs when he retired, hoping for a boost to his nest egg and also a way of looking back on his tenure, recording it for posterity. *If they made it into a TV series, I could live with that, too,* he used to joke.

There are over fifty files in his CASES folder, going back decades. I look for the one from 1995, the BB gun shooting at Bridgehampton School, but there's no entry for it. I don't know why I want to understand what happened there. Matty, asshole that he is, did have a point. But that's me in a nutshell, the kind of cop I am—I have to fit every piece of the puzzle together. And no matter how minor a detail a school shooting from almost seventeen years ago may have been, it's still a piece that doesn't fit.

I stare at the home screen of the computer, the icons for the antivirus and the recycle bin, the Microsoft Word file folder. One small file sits in the corner, not in any folder, a Word document entitled CHLOE.

Look up Chloe, Lang said to me in the trauma center before he died. "Look up" Chloe? I assumed he meant contact her, let her know what had happened, ask her to come to the hospital.

Look up . . . Chloe, the document?

I double-click on the icon and wait for the document to pop up. A handful of seconds later, it appears. It's a letter, dated two days before his death.

My dearest Chloe, it begins. *I have to tell someone, and even now, with you gone from me forever, I want that someone to be you.*

"Oh my God," I say to the empty room as I read the letter. "Oh my God."

Chapter 41

"L-7." THE GUARD taps on the cell door with his pen. He gets no answer. "L-7," he says again. "I'm doing the go-round."

Noah raises his head out of his hands, blinks into the light.

"Where you gonna be after lunch, L-7?"

Noah shakes his head. He's been back in A-Block for three weeks now, after spending over a month in the prison hospital and having multiple surgeries at Phelps Memorial, where he was kept under heavy security and cuffed at the ankles to his bed. Since returning to A-Block, Gallery L, cell number 7, he has only left his cell for required trips—the mess hall, classes, and the occasional psych visit. He doesn't have a job, still not having regained a sufficient range of motion in his hands to do much of anything, and won't go to the prison yard or the gym. So even though inmates are allowed out of their cells in the afternoon, after lunch, he has stayed within this cramped, dreary space, staring at the walls, for almost the entire day. He sleeps, he supposes, but in the zombie-like daze in which he finds himself, it's hard to distinguish between sleep and wakefulness, between dream and reality. His life has become a meaningless fog. There is no hope or despair, no fear or happiness.

"L-7?" It's one of the "white shirts," the senior correctional officers, joining the other CO. "You in pain, L-7? You know we have meds for you. All you have to do is tell us who did this to you."

The warden cut off pain medication as soon as Noah was released from the prison hospital, trying to get Noah to implicate the Aryan Brotherhood in the attack. Everyone knows who attacked Noah, but they can't prosecute them or even write up a disciplinary ticket without Noah's cooperation.

Noah's no snitch. He'd like nothing more than to stick it to Eric Wheaton and his buddies, but it's just not in him to rat someone out. Growing up with his buddies, that was the one rule you didn't break. You might bend the law or outright fracture it; you might fail to do unto others as you would have them do unto you—but you never snitched.

"That's your choice, L-7." The lieutenant and the other CO leave.

Time passes in slow motion. Noah goes to the mess hall for lunch but doesn't touch his food; he's lost almost twenty pounds since the attack.

Later in the afternoon, another CO shows up at his cell. "Mail, L-7," he says, and he reaches through the bars and drops a single envelope into the small bucket reserved for such things. "Sorry for your troubles."

He's sorry? Noah looks up at the CO, who gives a grim shake of the head and moves down to the next cell. They read the inmates' mail in Sing Sing, unless it bears the seal of an attorney-client communication, so the *sorry* must pertain to the mail he just received.

How, he thinks, *could things possibly get worse?*

Noah's limbs are stiff when he gets up; he's sat in the same position for almost three hours straight. He reaches into the bucket and grabs the envelope, perforated at the top by whoever read it. When he opens it, there is a Post-it that simply says *Sorry* and then a newspaper article, folded up. He unfolds it with a knot in his stomach and reads the headline: MANHATTAN SOCIALITE'S DROWNING RULED SUICIDE. Along with the article is a photo of Paige Sulzman in a sundress at some fancy gala.

"No!" he cries out. "No!" He forces himself to read a bit of the article, enough to know that Paige was found dead in her pool, before he grabs hold of the prison bars and shakes them. "No!" His bandaged hands start to bleed through the gauze and pads, but he doesn't care, doesn't even feel the pain. He screams until he has no voice, hundreds of other inmates hearing his cries and joining in with shouts and catcalls of their own.

Finally, exhausted, Noah crumples to the floor, leaning against the cell door. "Not her," he whispers. "Not Paige." She was supposed to move on. She was supposed to forget about him and get on with her life. She was supposed to leave John Sulzman and start the interior design business she'd always dreamed of having. She was supposed to have a life. She promised him. He made her *promise* she'd do that.

He cries, for the first time that he can remember. The tears pour out until he is gasping for air, coughing and gagging.

And then he has nothing left. He lies flat on his cell floor, oblivious to the dust, to the insect that crawls past his face. He stares into nothingness. He finds consolation in one and only one thing.

That the first chance he gets, he'll see Paige again, this time in another world.

"L-7?" a CO calls out. "Everything okay?"

Noah raises his head, turns to the guard.

"Hey, CO," he says. "I want to go into the yard."

"There's less than an hour left of yard time," the CO replies.

But that's okay. Noah won't need longer than that.

Chapter 42

THE PRISON YARD for A-block is a large swath of concrete and dead grass, plus a full basketball court, all of it surrounded by fence and razor wire. It is unseasonably mild in late February, but most of the inmates still wear the allotted jacket and cap.

Noah Walker moves into the yard with a purpose, turning in the direction of the basketball court. He is not wearing either the jacket or the cap, because he doesn't plan to be out here very long.

Beyond the basketball court, on a set of low wooden bleachers, Eric Wheaton and four of his Aryan brothers sit, smoking cigarettes and engaging in animated banter. They snap to attention when they see Noah Walker heading their way. For a moment, they look amused, even pleased, but the closer Noah gets, his body tensed, his fists closed tightly, the more they sense this is not a social call.

Two of the biggest Aryans—the bodyguards, they call themselves—jump to their feet and approach Noah.

They aren't looking for a fight, but they won't back down from one, either.

"Well, well," says Eric Wheaton, getting to his feet as well.

"How are the hands?" calls out one of the bodyguards.

Noah slows. His hands are not fully healed. A couple of the tendons were damaged badly, and a couple of the fingers on his left hand do not fully close into a grip.

Luckily, Noah is right-handed.

Noah looks to his right, then spins left and lands his right fist on the jaw of one of the bodyguards, feeling a satisfying crunch. The other two goons with Wheaton, plus the other bodyguard, converge on Noah, but he lowers his head and plows through the center of them like a halfback running for daylight. Prepared for a fist-fight, and not expecting his evasive move, the Aryan brothers are unable to stop him.

"No!" Eric Wheaton calls out, raising his arms and trying in vain to move along the bleachers to avoid Noah's charge. Noah bears down on Wheaton and leaves his feet, tackling Wheaton in midair and knocking him over the back of the wood supports. They both fall hard to the ground, but Wheaton gets the worst of it, hitting his head with a wicked thud. Noah turns him over on his back and puts his hands on Wheaton's neck, pressing his thumbs on his throat with all his might. He hears the calls of the other Aryans; the roar of the other inmates enjoying the show; the whistles of the COs; the voice over the loudspeaker calling for the inmates to retreat to the far corner, like a referee moving a boxer during a ten-count.

Someone knocks him off Wheaton with a force that feels like a truck. It could be an Aryan. Could be a CO. He doesn't care. Several bodies fall on top of him. He hears utter chaos around him and closes his eyes and his mind to it. He takes several hits to the back of the head, and then his hands are zip-tied behind his back and he is lifted off his feet, facedown, blood dripping from his nose and mouth. He doesn't care about this, either. He doesn't care if he killed Eric Wheaton or just gave him a very, very sore throat. Either way, the ultimate result will be the same for Noah.

"You're going to the Box, tough guy," one of the COs grunts at him. The Box, officially the Special Housing Unit—solitary confinement—is a short, wide building separated from A-Block. The upper floors are reserved for inmates in protective custody because they are rats or because they are believed to be on the verge of violence, usually attack victims expected to retaliate when they return to general pop. But the bottom floor is where Noah will be sent. In a prison known to house the worst of the worst criminals, the lower level of the Box is for the worst of the worst of the worst—humans by designation, but closer to animals, violent predators, locked in small cells with tiny windows and low ceilings.

Noah is thrown inside one of those cells, the floor sticky and reeking of urine and feces. His fellow inmates howl like hyenas and scratch and claw at their cell bars. Noah's zip-ties are cut, the COs make a hasty retreat, and the door slams him into darkness.

It will come now. It won't take long. A correctional officer, probably, aligned with the Brotherhood. The saying in Sing Sing is *The only difference between an inmate and a CO is the color of the uniform.* But it doesn't matter to Noah. It doesn't matter if it's a shank in the mess hall or an assault in the yard, or a visit from a CO late in the night. It will come soon now.

Time passes. He can't measure it, doesn't even try. But at some point, the outside door to the Box opens, and then he hears footsteps. One, two, three COs, wearing full inmate-extraction gear—hats and bats, they call it: helmets with face shields, heavy boots and gloves, vests, pads on their knees and elbows, thick batons. In the darkness of his cell, he can't see their faces, only their silhouettes from the light streaming in behind them: The men are as big as houses, more muscular than the Aryan bodyguards, and prepared for action.

"On your feet, hands backward through the bars," one of them says. "You give us any trouble and we'll beat you down."

He complies. He won't give them any trouble. They walk him through the open air and he lifts his face up to the stars, feeling the cool air on his skin for the last time, as he takes his final walk—the waltz, they used to call it, when there was an electric chair, the walk from Death Row to the execution chamber.

They take him through another door, walk him down a hall, footsteps echoing on the hard surface. He is disoriented, thinking of Paige, humming symphonic music fit for a waltz, ready now, however it will come.

Then his feet are on carpet, a surface they have not touched for many months. He doesn't understand. He looks up at a door that says WARDEN'S OFFICE.

Two COs see Noah and give him a smirk. Then they open the double doors, and Noah is pushed into the warden's office. So this is how it happens? Right here in the warden's office?

Then he sees the warden, a lean, aging black man. Standing next to him is . . .

No.

"What . . . what is this?" he says.

Detective Jenna Murphy says, "I'm having you transferred, Noah. We're sending you back to Suffolk County Jail, pending a post-conviction hearing."

"A . . . hearing on what?"

"You were framed, Noah," she says. "And I can prove it."

Chapter 43

THE COURTROOM IS wall-to-wall with spectators and media, cops and prosecutors, people from the community, standing room only once again. The room is so quiet that you can actually hear that ringing sound that absolute silence produces, everyone craning forward, eagerly awaiting the next words that will come from the mouth of this witness—even the judge, peering over his glasses at the witness stand, his brow furrowed, his lips pursed.

The news leaked out yesterday—CNN picked it up first—but not the details. The details are for today. For this hearing. For this moment.

Detective Jenna Murphy, dressed in a blue suit, has testified for over an hour thus far, setting the table for what will come next. Noah's defense lawyer, Joshua Brody, has proceeded methodically, establishing her credentials, her minor role in the investigation, and going through a lot of technical questions and answers that the court needs to establish the "authenticity" of the letter found on her uncle's computer. Ultimately, the judge decided that the letter could be admitted into evidence, which paved the way for Brody to cut to the heart of this hearing.

"My uncle was the chief, so he could take over any crime scene he wanted," says Detective Murphy. "He took over the investigation of the crime scene at 7 Ocean Drive, and he removed the bloody knife and Melanie's charm necklace before any investigators arrived. Then he controlled the search of Mr. Walker's house after his arrest." She shrugs. "He could do whatever he wanted. Nobody would know."

Joshua Brody nods. "So you're telling us—"

"I'm telling you that my uncle taped the knife and necklace under the heating duct and pretended to 'discover' them there," she says. "I'm telling you that my uncle planted the evidence in Noah Walker's kitchen."

A release throughout the courtroom, a collective gasp. Behind him, footsteps—reporters, prohibited from using smartphones in the courtroom, rushing out to send off a text message, a tweet, a quick phone call. That courtroom exit is probably like a revolving door right now, journalists stepping out for the breaking news, then returning to hear if there's anything more.

But Noah Walker won't turn back to look. His eyes are forward, on Jenna Murphy. The woman who spin-kicked him in the face the first time they met, who broke into his house and fired a bullet only inches from his head the second time, who provided the crucial testimony, the testimony that led to his conviction, the third. And who now, after reading a letter from her uncle on his computer, is coming forward to stand up for Noah.

"There was testimony at trial," says Brody, "that my client confessed to the murders of Melanie Phillips and Zach Stern."

Murphy nods, blinking slowly, her expression blank. If she is enjoying this, she doesn't show it; if she's conflicted, she hides that as well. Something tells Noah she's good at that, at concealing her thoughts, her feelings.

"That's what the chief told me," Murphy says. "But it was a lie. He lied to me, and I repeated the lie to the jury without realizing it was false."

Another audible reaction from the spectators, another banging of the gavel from the judge. "Anyone who is unable to sit quietly," says the judge, "will be removed."

"Noah didn't confess to Dio Cornwall," Murphy says. "I talked to Dio after I found this letter on my uncle's computer. Chief James told him he would get a better sentence if he lied about Noah confessing to him—and a worse sentence if he didn't. He gave Dio information so Dio could tell a convincing lie to the prosecutors. Everything my uncle admitted to in this letter, Dio confirmed to me."

"I see." Brody nods. "And what about Noah's so-called confession to the chief himself?"

"It never happened." Murphy shakes her head. "He lied to everyone about that. He lied to his lieutenants. He lied to prosecutors. He . . ."

She pauses, clears her throat, the first sign of any emotion at all from her.

"He lied to me," she says.

A thrill courses through Noah, tears filling his eyes. He wouldn't let himself believe it. This roller coaster, this sensation of free-falling through the air, this entire terrifying journey through a system with murky rules and mysterious procedures—he's never been able to trust it. Not even coming here today. He wouldn't allow his hopes to rise, only to crash to the ground again.

But now. Now it's happening.

"If I may ask, Detective," says Brody. "Why did you come forward? This man was your uncle. You could have easily brushed this aside."

Jenna Murphy, eyes cast downward, shakes her head. "Because it's not supposed to be like this," she says. "It's supposed to be about justice, not winning. Because deep down, even my uncle understood that, which is why he wrote that letter."

Noah begins to tremble uncontrollably, the tears streaming down his face. So many times he gave up hope, so often he wanted to die. He thinks of Paige, who can't be here to see this, and squeezes his eyes shut, crying harder than he ever remembers crying.

His lawyer's arm comes around him, while Noah hears the voice of the prosecutor, Sebastian Akers, reminding the court that the prosecution, through Detective Murphy, brought this information to light, that the prosecutor is just as concerned with the proper administration of justice as anyone.

And then someone else is talking. The judge, the

Honorable Robert Barnett, known as one of the county's toughest judges.

"Listen, Noah," his lawyer whispers to him.

Noah raises his eyes, his vision blurred by the tears, the catch in his throat leaving him speechless.

"Based on the material that's been submitted to the court, as well as the testimony today," says the judge, "and the lack of any objection from the State, there is only one conclusion this court can reach. The defendant has been the victim of a blatant miscarriage of justice. The defendant's Article 440 motion is well taken."

The judge removes his glasses and looks at Noah, pausing first, considering his next words.

"Mr. Walker, the State of New York owes you an apology. You have spent nearly a year of your life under this cloud. And I understand you have suffered greatly while incarcerated—incarcerated for a crime that, it is now clear to me, you did not commit. I only hope that you won't let this ordeal consume you with bitterness and anger, that you can find something positive out of this experience. If I could give you back the last year of your life, I would. But I can't. All I can do now is find, as a matter of law, that your convictions cannot stand."

Noah, emotionally overloaded, shaking, manages to nod in response.

"The defendant's motion is granted," says the judge, banging the gavel. "The defendant's convictions for the murders of Melanie Phillips and Zachary Stern are hereby vacated. The defendant shall be discharged from custody immediately."

Chapter 44

THE GATE OPENS, and Noah Walker strides through it, looking around as if he's entering a new world. It may feel that way to him. Prison, from my experience on the other side of the bars, at least, is a universe unto itself, especially for the lifers. The loss of hope is a powerful toxin, like being dead while alive.

I've sent a lot of people to Sing Sing, murderers and rapists and even some drug dealers, but there's nothing fun about doing it. If I could run the world, I'd find another way to treat most of these criminals—most of them, not all of them—but we find widespread solutions to widespread problems in this country, so we just build big prisons and stick everyone inside them and, for the most part, forget about them once they're gone.

Noah stops short when his eyes come to rest on me where I'm leaning against my car. He looks different—not just the short prison haircut, which makes him look younger, but also something in his eyes, more relaxed, even refreshed.

"They said I had a ride," he says.

"That's me."

He looks at me, considering.

"Don't look so happy," I say.

He raises an eyebrow.

"Hey, I'm not putting a gun to your head."

"No, you did that once already." He has a small bag with him, things he brought into the prison. He walks over and gets into the car.

I walk around to the other side and climb in. My ten-year-old Chevy isn't exactly a limousine, but it beats the hell out of a prison transport bus.

"Your own personal copy," I say, dropping a *New York Post* on his lap, the front-page headline NEW YORK OWES YOU AN APOLOGY—quoting the judge—with the text underneath, *Officer's Emotional Testimony Clears "Surfer Jesus" of Murder Charges*.

Noah reads a little of the article, then exhales and gazes out the window. "I didn't think your testimony was emotional," he says. "I couldn't tell *how* you felt."

"That makes two of us."

He looks over at me but doesn't say anything. Pure heat radiates off him, the source of which I can't place. Maybe anger, aggression, bottled-up rage. I kick on the air-conditioning. Must be the unseasonably warm March weather. That must be it. Yeah.

Not a word passes between us as I turn onto the Long Island Expressway. I focus on the road and flip through the radio channels; no kind of music seems right, so I go to talk radio, all about spring training for the Yankees and Mets. It's been so warm in New York this March, I'm not sure the Yankees even needed to travel to Tampa to practice.

All the while, Noah says nothing, just stares at me. Once again, I turn the AC down—or up, whatever, I make it colder—and pull my shirt off my sticky chest. Something flutters through me, some sense of foreboding, danger, anxiety.

"You wanna stop staring at me?" I say.

"Are you gonna arrest me?"

I look over at him, his prison haircut—high and tight—accentuating his thick neck and shoulders, concealed previously by his long hair. The beard is gone, too, but he hasn't shaved in a couple of days.

"You're sweating," he says.

"No, I'm not."

"My mistake." But he's still turned toward me, as if, at any moment, he might lunge at me or something. That wouldn't be a smart move for a guy who's finally tasting freedom again. But maybe he likes doing that, living on the edge, pushing his luck. Or maybe he just wants to make me nervous.

We drive like that for a while. I turn up the radio, as if hearing the speculation over Mariano Rivera—will 2012 be his last year?—at a higher volume will somehow shield me from Noah's stare.

As we're driving through Queens, he breaks the silence. "Do you expect me to thank you?"

"No," I say. "I don't need your gratitude."

"Good. Because you don't have it. You lied at the trial. You're the reason I got locked up to begin with."

I whip the car to the right, swerving across a lane of

traffic, just making the exit for Little Neck Parkway. I find a small park by Horace Harding and pull the car over.

"Get out," I say as I push the car door open. I walk into the park and wait for him to meet me there. He walks toward me briskly. For a moment, I think he's not going to stop, that he's going to knock right into me, or put his hands on my throat. He stops just short of me, close enough that I can see a tiny nick above his lip, that I can smell him, that prison smell of sweat and rage.

"Did you kill them?" I ask.

His eyes narrow and his head tilts slightly, like he doesn't get the question.

"You have double jeopardy now," I say. "No one can ever prosecute you again for Melanie and Zach. So now it's just you and me. Did you kill them?"

He smiles, bemused. "You gotta be kidding."

"You were framed, yes, but that doesn't mean you're innocent. Lang thought you were guilty. He just didn't think he could prove it. You can frame a guilty—"

"No," he spits. "I didn't kill them."

My heart banging against my chest, choking my throat, my hands balling into fists, I ask my next question. "What about my uncle?"

He shakes his head. "You're unbelievable."

"Tell me," I say.

He regards me for a moment. He takes another step forward, leaning into me so close, it's as if he's about to make a pass at me. I hold my breath and steel myself.

"I . . . don't think I have double jeopardy for that murder, now do I, Detective?"

"You might as well," I say. "You're a media darling. We'd look vindictive if we prosecuted you again. Sebastian Akers would sooner swallow his own tongue. So what's it gonna be, cowboy?"

His nose almost touching mine, his breath on my face, his eyes searching mine, that heat radiating off him. "Okay," he says. "I'll answer your question."

His face moves around mine, his razor stubble against my cheek, his lips touching my ear.

"I didn't kill your uncle," he whispers. He draws back, turns, and walks to the car.

Chapter 45

WHEN I ARRIVE at work the next morning, I get a lot of stares, a lot of whispers as I pass. These days at Southampton Town Police Department, I'm about as welcome as a venereal disease. I've given the department a black eye. Oh, there are probably a few people who would admit, if pressed, that I did the right thing, that I prevented a miscarriage of justice, even if I had to tarnish the department, and the memory of a beloved chief, in the process.

But most people just seem to remember that last part—that I've brought shame on the department, that I crossed the thin blue line.

"Chief wants to see you," says one of the assistants, passing me.

More good news: My old partner, Isaac Marks, is now running the show. The town supervisor took the *Acting* off his title two weeks ago, making Isaac the new, permanent chief. You might think I'd benefit from that, that my former partner would look kindly on me, but you'd be wrong. Isaac was at Noah Walker's house during the search, when my uncle planted the incriminating evidence, and since my testimony, Isaac has had to answer questions from reporters and the town supervisor. He's denied any wrongdoing, of course—he had no idea, he says, that Lang planted the knife and necklace—but nobody is completely convinced, so he's beginning his tenure under a dark cloud—thanks to me!

He should feel lucky they gave him the job before all of this came out about Lang; if the decision were made today, he surely wouldn't have received the promotion.

But when I walk into his office, Isaac doesn't look like he feels lucky.

"Morning," I say.

"Sit, Murphy." He throws something across the desk. A folder full of something, with the words SAFE IN SCHOOL INITIATIVE across the top. I have a pretty good idea what's coming.

"After that school shooting in Ohio in February," he says, "the school board here has been anxious to review the safety procedures for the school. Evacuation, prevention, that kind of thing. You're going to run it. You'll be reassigned to Bridgehampton School for a couple of months. It's all in the folder."

I stare at the folder in my hand, dumbfounded. This is not an assignment for a veteran detective. Both of us know it. Isaac can't fire me, because I'm too protected right now—the media would pick up on it, and it would look like exactly what it was, that the STPD was retaliating against me for coming forward with the evidence against Lang—but there are other ways to punish a rogue cop like me, the best of which is to give me shitty assignments, to bore me to death until I quit in disgust.

"Isaac," I say.

"What did you call me?" His head snaps up.

"I'm sorry, *Chief*—Chief, I've been doing some looking into the murders at 7 Ocean Drive, now that they're 'unsolved' again—"

"They're not unsolved. We know who killed them. We let the killer walk free, didn't we, Detective?" A bit of color to those plump cheeks of his.

"I . . . understand," I say. "Could I just tell you what I'm thinking?"

"Tell me what you're thinking, Murphy. I can't wait." He throws up his hand, like he'd rather have a needle stuck in his eye, and leans back in his chair.

"Besides those murders, there's my uncle's murder. And that murder that you and I were looking at, the prostitute in the woods, impaled on the tree stump."

"Yeah?" He scratches his neck. "So?"

"Well, all four of these have one thing in common—they resulted in slow, torturous deaths," I say. "But especially my uncle and the prostitute in the woods. Both of them were impaled. I think that could have meaning. I think they're connected."

"Noah Walker killed Zach and Melanie. He probably killed Lang, too, but now that you've gone and made Noah untouchable, you couldn't get the DA to prosecute him if God came down from heaven and declared Noah guilty. And the prostitute? Who the fuck knows who killed her? Let Sag Harbor worry about that."

Just another hooker adiosed *in the Hamptons,* Uncle Lang had said.

"I don't want you investigating those murders," Isaac says. "I want you at the school. Effective immediately. If you go near those cases, you'll be disciplined. That's all." He flicks his hand at me, a shooing gesture.

Looks like I'm going to have to eat this shit for a while. I return to my desk and start to gather my things.

A woman's voice calls out to me. I turn and see a uniform, a rookie, the only female patrol officer working Bridgehampton, all of six weeks on the force.

"Haven't had the chance to introduce myself," she says. "Officer Ricketts."

We shake hands. Ricketts is probably in her mid-twenties but looks more like she's in her midteens, big wondering eyes and cropped blond hair.

"Nice to meet you, Ricketts. Call me Murphy. Let me know if I can ever help."

"Well," she says as I begin to turn away from her.

"Well, what?"

"I was wondering if I could be any help to *you,*" she says. "I've heard a lot about you. I'd like the chance to work with you."

I remember being that young, being green, being a woman on a male-dominated force. Being hungry. Looking for a chance to prove myself.

And, actually, there is something . . . .

"This would have to be on your own time," I say. "Off the record."

"Sure, no problem," she says, not hiding her eagerness.

Well, what the hell? "Okay, Ricketts," I say. "Get me a list of all unsolved murders on the South Shore over the last decade. Focus on victims of knife attacks, or some spearing instrument."

"Knife . . . or spearing," she repeats, writing it down on a notepad.

"Stabbed, impaled, sliced, diced, whatever," I say. "This guy likes to cut people."

Chapter 46

WHEN I ENTER Bridgehampton School, red brick and white pillars on Main Street—Montauk Highway, if you prefer—I am directed to the school principal, a woman named Paulina Jacoby. She looks like a school principal, conservatively dressed, her gray hair neatly combed, a humorless way about her. Her office is simply decorated, with a nice view of the massive school grounds to the south. Behind her, yearbooks going back to the seventies line an entire bookcase.

We spend a few minutes with small talk—they had a good relationship with the former chief, she tells me; she knows I'm his niece, pretty much everybody knows that by now. "We were . . . pleasantly surprised to hear from Chief Marks," she says.

Chief Marks. It will take a long time before I'm used to hearing that.

"But we're always happy to hear from the STPD. There is no such thing as a school that has too much security."

True—but what she's saying is, we called her, not the other way around. That isn't surprising. Isaac was trying to find the least desirable assignment he possibly could for me, without being too obvious about it. If he assigned me to parking meter duty, it would be blatantly clear that he was punishing me. A school assignment is just perfect, from his perspective. Who can be against school security in this day and age? But that doesn't change the fact that this is an assignment for a much younger cop than me. He's a devious one, Isaac, that little fuck.

"We've been lucky," the principal says, knocking on her wooden desk. "We haven't had a school shooting for sixteen—well, now I guess it's seventeen years."

Right. That's right. "The BB gun shooting in 1995," I say. I point out the window. "Out there on the south grounds."

She nods, looks through thé window. "That was Halloween. We banned costumes at the school for over a decade after that."

"It was Noah Walker," I say. "Noah shot those kids with the BB gun."

She looks at me, unsure of how to answer. Because Noah was a juvenile at the time, the criminal proceedings against him would have been sealed. The school would have been prohibited from publicly announcing his name.

"Well," she says, "I guess it's not much of a secret, after it came out last year during his trial."

Not a secret at all. But she's getting a little squirmy, so I don't push the point.

"Well, let me introduce you to our security

personnel," she says, getting out of her chair. "Is there anything else you'll need from me?"

"Maybe just one thing," I say. "Could I take a look at the school yearbook from 1995?"

Once I have some time alone, after meeting with the school security personnel, and once I'm shown to a small office, cramped and windowless, that probably was once a janitor's closet, I crack open the yearbook, heading to the index in the back and finding the name *Walker, Noah.*

I flip to the page and run along the names on the right column until I come to his. Noah would have been, what, twelve or thirteen back then. I admit to a curiosity—and maybe more than curiosity—about how a guy with a ripped physique and rugged good looks would have appeared as an adolescent.

I find his name, but when I look across to the corresponding picture, there is no face staring back, just a NOT PICTURED graphic. Okay, that probably makes sense; he was suspended from school after the Halloween shooting that year, so he probably was gone by the time they were taking yearbook photos. I let out a sigh, disappointed, but then catch myself—why am I disappointed? And why am I thinking about Noah Walker's muscles?

Next to the graphic for Noah: a weaselly-looking kid with straw hair parted down the middle, a skinny face, and eyes too close together. He isn't smiling or frowning; he looks confused, actually, like the invention of the camera was a revelation at that moment.

But I know this guy. I look at the name on the side

and square it up. This is Aiden Willis. Right. Aiden Willis, the raccoon eyes, the squirrelly guy who works at the cemetery—I saw him at Melanie's funeral, then again at the Dive Bar, when I bought him a beer and he disappeared.

Small town. You forget that. The locals all grew up together, know one another.

I flip to the index, then find the page for Isaac Marks. Isaac, my former partner and new boss, asswipe that he may be, was the same age as Noah and Aiden. In his photo, he is wearing a stern expression, like he's trying to look tough. That feels about right. Isaac, back then, probably dreamed of being important, of having the respect he probably didn't receive in school. All speculation, of course, but it fits with the kind of guy he is now—and we don't really change that much, do we?

I look up. Noah, Aiden Willis, and Isaac Marks. Isaac and Noah, the same age, the same class; Aiden, one year older. They all would have known one another back then. A tiny school. Everyone knew everyone.

I pick up my phone and dial the extension for the school principal. After a moment, they put me through.

"Ms. Jacoby?"

"Please, it's Paulina," she says.

"Paulina," I say. "Do you have anyone on staff who was here during that school shooting in 1995?"

Chapter 47

THE SOUTH SIDE of Bridgehampton School is over an acre of open grass, with a baseball diamond closer to the school and a playground next to it for the younger kids. To my right, but a healthy distance away, are the woods, a thick layer of trees providing the eastern border of the school grounds. As I move closer to the school, to my left—northwest—I see the parking lot that bends around from Main Street.

"Here," says Darryl Friese, walking with me. "I was right here. I didn't even know what happened at first. I mean, my first thought? I thought, like, an insect had flown into my eye or something. Dumb, right?"

I shake my head. "There's no such thing as dumb in a situation like that."

Darryl turns to me. He was nine in 1995, which makes him twenty-six, maybe twenty-seven now, but these seventeen years have not been kind to him, his hair receding badly, an unhealthy gut hanging over his slacks. His left eye looks odd because of the color, grayer than his other eye, which is solid blue, but otherwise there's no lingering trace of the BB injury.

"Okay, so let's get this exactly right," I say. "Stand at exactly the same angle, the same position."

He adjusts himself. "It was just like this. I remember because this girl, Angela Krannert—God, haven't thought about her for a long time—anyway, Angie was standing by the back entrance of the school, and I was walking toward her. I remember—the last thing I was thinking, before the BB hit me—I was trying to think of something that would make Angie laugh."

He is facing directly north. If he walked straight forward from this angle, he'd eventually walk right into the school's back door.

He points over by the woods. "You see that little alcove there?" he says. "Kids used to go there to make out or smoke cigarettes. Because you were technically still on school property, but you were hidden."

I nod. I see it. A tree stump, a small clearing. "That's where Noah was set up?"

"Yeah."

I line it up. Noah, from his position, would have been almost directly to Darryl's right.

"So how did he shoot me in the left eye?" Darryl laughs. "Believe me, I've always asked that. They just chalked it up to the pandemonium. I mean, it was chaos. I was out of commission, basically. I was on the ground screaming. But nobody could hear me because they were all screaming, too. Nobody knew it was a BB gun, not at first."

"They said you must have spun around, giving him a clear shot at you."

He laughs. "That's *exactly* what they said. And I get it, I was just a punk kid, nobody believed me. I have a seven-year-old now, and the things that come out of his mouth?" He shakes his head with conviction. "But I'm telling you, I got hit with the BB before anybody knew what was going on. There was no screaming, no chaos, nobody scattering in different directions. I was probably the first one shot. No," he says, "I was walking straight for Angie at the back door."

I survey the place again. The woods, Noah's perch, directly east, to my right.

And to the northwest, the school parking lot.

With a healthy row of shrubbery separating the parking lot from the south grounds. A perfect place to hide.

"Is this part of some investigation?" Darryl asks me. "Are you investigating the Halloween shooting again?"

"No," I tell him. "Nothing like that."

Which is technically true. I'm not investigating the 1995 Halloween shooting per se. I'm just trying to learn more about Noah Walker, and by extension the people with whom he associated. I don't know, yet, who ran with Noah back then, back when they were preteen punks.

But I do know this much: One of them was the second shooter that day.

Chapter 48

"YOU JUST TRY to find something that interests them," says the phys ed teacher, a man named Arnie Cooper, an aging African American man. He's tall and well-built, age adding a few inches to his midsection, but you can still see the remnants of an athlete—the high hurdles, from what I've heard, and what I've seen in glass cases near the gym, in framed photos on the walls. Born and raised in Bridgehampton—"south of Main Street," he is quick to say—state champion in the high hurdles in 1978, a member of the US Olympic team that didn't compete in the 1980 games in Moscow because of the US boycott.

Behind us, the south grounds of the school are littered with multicolored foam archery targets, the bull's-eye yellow, the next ring orange, then powder blue and black. Half of the fourth graders are missing the target altogether, the rubber-suction-cupped arrows sailing in the air and falling harmlessly to the grass.

"Hard to get kids to run around and play anymore," the teacher says. "They got their faces buried in those phones and contraptions. That's all I did when I was a kid. I always remember running." He gestures to an older student out on the yard, some kind of teacher's assistant. "Brendan, I'm gonna be a few minutes, okay?"

Coop, as he demands everyone call him, walks with a limp these days, the years of clearing hurdles and pounding his feet having taken a toll. "I was running okay in my thirties, though," he tells me as we walk along the yard. "And I was definitely running okay the day of the shooting."

He stops and gestures toward the back door of the school. "I was in the gym shooting hoops when I heard the screaming," he says. "At first, it didn't mean anything to me. Just kids shouting, y'know? But then it did. I think it was . . . hearing an adult voice. Some of the parents walk the little kids up to the school. When I heard a parent yelling, I knew something was wrong. So I came out that door."

"And what did you do?" I ask.

"Well, soon as I came out—I mean, it was all wrong. There were kids lying on the ground, there were parents covering up their kids, people were scattering like cockroaches, y'know what I mean? I'm thinking, *These kids have been shot. I mean, really shot. With bullets.* But there wasn't really any blood I could see, so it was confusing." He stops, puts his hands on his hips, shakes his head. "Man, it had been a long time since I was that scared."

"So you—"

"So someone was pointing over by the east side of the school, and someone was saying, 'He went that way, he went that way,' and someone else was saying, 'He's dressed as Spider-Man, he's Spider-Man,' so I started running around the side of the school toward the front, toward Main Street, looking for Spider-Man."

We start following that same route, walking east and then turning north, moving along the immaculately landscaped grass and trees, toward the paved drive off Main Street.

"I practically ran right into the street," he says. "I didn't know where he was." I follow him until we're standing just along the curb on Main Street.

He gestures to his right, down the street to the east. "That's where I found him," he says. "Right next to Small Potato."

A little shack of a nursery stand, painted red with white supports, covered in chicken wire, empty this time of year, its quaint green sign proclaiming it the OLDEST FARM STAND IN THE HAMPTONS. I bought my Christmas tree here after Thanksgiving.

"Back then, they were selling pumpkins," he says. "But they'd pretty much packed up by then. There wasn't anyone there. But Noah, he was sitting on a bench just past the nursery, in a Spider-Man costume with the head part removed. He wasn't moving. He was wearing headphones. He looked—I mean, I know how this sounds—but he looked like he was waiting for a bus."

"Well—was the rifle nearby?"

He raises his shoulders. "I didn't see it. They found it later. He tossed it in the bushes behind him. I just told him he had to come with me, and I gripped him pretty tight and hauled him back toward the school, but he didn't resist me. He didn't fight. All he said was 'What did I do?'"

What did I do? "So," I say, "this kid shoots a couple dozen people with a BB air rifle, runs around to the front of the school, and sits down on a bench like he's . . . like he's waiting for a bus. Like nothing's wrong."

Coop shakes his head, laughs in agreement. "I know. I hear what you're saying. I figure it's one of two things."

I turn and face him.

"Either he didn't do anything wrong," he says, "or he's one cold-blooded son of a bitch. The kind who doesn't feel anything. Who could slice someone open while he's smiling at them, and then look you in the eye and deny it. You know what I mean?"

"I think maybe I do," I say. I drop my eyes and nod slowly. "I think maybe I do."

Chapter 49

I TURN OFF Sag Harbor Turnpike onto the gravel drive, my car crunching over the rocks. I pull up to a small shingled shack with a tent over the entrance and an old, beat-up wooden sign with a single word—TASTY'S—carved into it.

The parking lot is full, and so is the restaurant, when I walk in to the scent of delicious seafood. I love places like this, no-frills dives, simple tables with paper tablecloths, random photos and signs hanging on the walls, food served in paper trays. The menu is on a chalkboard on the wall—both kinds of clam chowder, steamers, shrimp two ways, scallops two ways, oysters on the half shell, mussels, fried clam strips, about four versions of lobster, and hand-cut French fries.

Ricketts, the rookie cop who's off duty today, has a table for us. She's already nursing a bottle of Miller High Life. There's a second bottle on the table, either for her or for me. Either way, I decide I like this kid.

"Hey, rookie."

"I love this place," she says. "Best seafood on the South Fork, and the cheapest. They haven't raised prices in a decade." She's a little looser than the first time I met her, when she was in uniform at the station. She's wearing a sweater and jeans and her short blond hair is tousled.

A man appears with a Mets cap on backward and a gray shirt. Ricketts orders the scallops, so I do the same, along with a couple of waters, and we'll split a cone of fries.

Ricketts reaches down to her purse and removes a file folder. "Your list of unsolved murders over the last decade on the South Shore," she says. "Anything involving a knife or cutting."

I nod. "How many?"

"Eight," she says.

"Eight?" I reach out my hand for it. "Gimme."

She pauses. "You, uh . . . might want to eat first. You might not have an appetite afterward."

"That bad, huh?" Okay, fair enough. "But eight?"

"Well, I counted Melanie and Zach as unsolved."

"As you should."

"The prostitute found impaled on the tree trunk last summer, too."

"Definitely." Bonnie Stamos. Some images will never leave your mind, and one of them is that poor girl, her body split in half over that tree stump.

"And I'm including . . . you know—"

"Chief James." I nod. "As you should."

She finishes a swig of beer. "Then that's eight." She

gestures around the place. "You know, this is where Melanie Phillips worked."

I partake of the alcoholic beverage she's offered me, because I don't want to seem rude, or make her feel lonely.

"Oh, you knew that. Of course you did. Sorry. I'm—maybe I'm—"

"Relax, Ricketts. I'm hard to offend."

She takes a deep breath. "I was kind of nervous to meet you, actually. I saw you one other time in the station, but I was intimidated, actually."

"By me?" The beer is tasting good. "You shouldn't be. We girls have to stick together."

"I know, but you're like, this—pretty much everyone's intimidated by you. Y'know, coming from Manhattan, and you're smart and tough and . . . well, beautiful. Most of the men don't know how to handle you. Most of them want to sleep with you, from listening to them. But they also want to see you fall on your face."

That sounds about right, that last part. "Keep your head down and do a good job," I say. "The acclaim will come, if it's deserved. You have to prove yourself to these cavemen by your actions. Let the rest of that stuff slide—the sexist comments, all that crap. It will all fall away if you do a good job as a cop."

"Okay," she says, nodding compliantly like a student.

"Don't sleep with other cops," I say. "Because then it won't matter how good you are. You'll just be the girl that fucks."

She takes a deep breath.

"I didn't say it was fair, rookie. I'm just trying to help

you avoid headaches. You'll be subjected to double standards all over the place. You'll have to be better than the men to be considered equal to them."

"Okay." She nods. "Okay."

"There's a lot of good men on the force. I'm only talking about a few bad apples here. Unfortunately, some of those bad apples are the ones calling the shots. So keep your head down and work your ass off. Always have your partner's back. And call me, anytime, day or night, if you need anything."

Her face lights up. "Yeah?"

"Of course."

"Here you go, guys. Scallops and a cone of fries." A different man, wearing a button-down shirt and blue jeans. Tall and trim, bronzed skin, a nice smile, thick brown hair swept to one side. The kind of guy your parents would want you to bring home. And I thought the scallops looked yummy.

"Hey, Justin, this is Jenna Murphy. Jenna, this is Justin Rivers. This is his place," Ricketts says.

"Here every day," he says. "Great to meet you." He wipes his hand on his jeans and offers it to me, a strong grip when I shake it.

"Likewise," I say. "So you're the guy who hasn't raised prices in a decade."

"Yep, yeah, that's right." He makes eye contact with me, holds it for maybe one meaningful beat longer than normal, but then breaks it off. A shy one. Not a slickster. I like the shy, awkward ones. Why do I always pick the jerks to date instead?

No ring on his finger, either. A girl always looks.

"Well," he says, clapping his hands, "nice meeting you, and enjoy your food."

"I will," I say as he walks away. "I will."

"I know, right?" Ricketts laughs. "Now you know why it's my favorite place."

The scallops are the best I've ever had, cooked just perfectly, a touch of butter and lemon but not overplaying it, letting the seafood speak for itself. The fries are nicely seasoned and the creamy garlic sauce accompanying them is enough to make me change religions. We top it all off with a second round of beer, but I'll stop there.

"Okay," I say, now that we've gotten a peek at the hunky owner of this place, I've dispensed my advice, and I've had some of the best seafood I've ever eaten. "Now it's time to ruin my appetite."

"It will," she says. "It definitely will."

Chapter 50

"OKAY, HERE." RICKETTS removes a piece of paper from her file folder. "Eight victims over the last decade. All unsolved."

"I know about the ones last year, summer of 2011," I say. "Zach and Melanie, Bonnie Stamos, my uncle. Let's start with the older ones, before I came here."

"Good," she says. "That's what I did."

"Dede Paris," I say, reading the first name. "Last seen May 9, 2007."

"The first two go together," says Ricketts. "Dede Paris and Annie Church. Yale sophomores. May ninth was when they left New Haven that summer. They lied to their friends and family about how they were spending their summer. They came here to the Hamptons. That was discovered later, through cell phone records and then their car, which was ultimately found in Montauk after a lengthy search."

She removes two photos from her file folder and

hands them to me. "Dede is the blonde, Annie the brunette."

Dede's photograph is from a volleyball game. She's tall and athletic, with blond hair cropped tight against her head. The photo of Annie is a school photo, probably from high school, a bright smile and warm eyes, her hair past her shoulders, reddish brown.

"So they were killed in Montauk?" I ask.

Ricketts shrugs. "Nobody knows. That's where their car was found. Their bodies were never found. Or, I should say, most of their bodies was never found."

I look at the document she typed, organized and professional. "Her finger," I say, reading her one-line summary for Dede.

"Yeah, they found one of Dede's fingers in the woods near Montauk, two years after they disappeared. We always assumed foul play but didn't know it until somebody's dog found the finger. Then they got a DNA match."

So they were killed in 2007, and a single finger was found in 2009. Two years, and nobody found it. Well, that's possible, sure, but . . .

"Tell me about the finger," I say. "Was it decomposed? Was there anything distinctive about it?"

"No and yes." She opens her folder again and shows me a photograph of the finger. "Not decomposed much at all, well preserved, with a ring on it—a class ring from . . . Santa Monica High School, if I'm reading that right."

"Okay," I say, handing her back the photo. She slides it into her folder. "So after that, we have the third one . . . Brittany Halsted," I say. "July 2008."

"Prostitute," says Ricketts. She hands me another photo. A mug shot. Oh, she's young, not more than eighteen or nineteen in this photo. She is thin, blond, attractive but with a beat-up look about her that most working girls have.

"She used the name Barbie on the street," says Ricketts. "Last seen alive getting on the back of a motorcycle outside a nightclub in Shirley. She told her friends she was going to be gone for the night."

The whole night. Smart of him. Nobody would be expecting her back. It would give the offender some time before anyone would be looking for her.

"Last seen *alive*," I say. "So they found her."

"They found Brittany." She hands me another photograph. "A couple of miles down Sunrise Highway from where she was picked up on the motorcycle."

She is lying facedown in a bed of leaves, her head turned toward the camera, her eyes shut. She has the ghostly mannequin look of a corpse dead for at least a couple of days. A pool of blood surrounds the lower half of her body.

"This photo doesn't show it," says Ricketts. "But he carved her up. He disemboweled her. The ME thought he used a corkscrew."

"Oh, God, a corkscrew?" I say, as if there were a nice way of disemboweling someone.

I look at the remainder of the sheet. "So then, in 2010, we have Sally Pfiester. And then we move up to 2011, to Melanie and Zach, Bonnie Stamos, and my uncle. That's interesting."

"Why's that interesting?"

I look at Ricketts, who is watching me carefully. She's a pup, looking to learn a thing or two, so I explain my thoughts. "We don't know if this is the same offender," I say. "But if it is, look at the timing. He kills in 2007. Then, in 2008, he kills again. Then he doesn't kill again until 2010, with Sally Pfiester."

"So—what does that mean? He didn't do anything in 2009."

"Well, he *did* do something in 2009," I correct. "He planted Dede Paris's finger for us to find. Clearly, he'd preserved that finger, or it would have been badly decomposed. And just in case we had trouble identifying it, he made sure her high school class ring was on it. He might as well have posted a sign saying, 'Look, everyone, this is Dede's finger!'"

"He wanted us to know," she says. "Why?" Ricketts sits quietly, her eyes moving around the room, her mental machinery fully in gear.

"He was struggling," I say. "He didn't want to kill anybody else. But you know what else was bothering him?"

"What?"

"He wasn't getting any attention," I say.

She draws back. "Attention? You think he wants to get caught?"

"Oh, no. This guy does *not* want to get caught. Quite the opposite—this guy gets off on the thrill of getting away with it. Of doing something so terrible and walking away scot-free. I'm sure the stories about Annie and Dede were all over the South Shore papers in 2007. Two Yale undergrads gone missing? It was probably huge news on the South Shore. And the murder of the prostitute in 2008? Well, not as big, but still a gruesome murder, right? So once again, he's getting attention, he's reminded of how powerful he is. Big, newsworthy crimes, crimes that *he* committed, and he's reading about them in his bathrobe with a cup of coffee."

"But his conscience was bothering him," she says.

"Right." I point to her. "So in 2009, he's struggling. He doesn't want to kill again. But he needs the adulation, the feeling of power. So what does he do?"

"He reminds everyone of what he did in 2007."

"Exactly. He plants Dede's finger with the class ring, and *voilà!* There were probably a ton of stories, all over again, this time assuming the Yale students are dead, how tragic, how horrible, how mystified the police are—"

"And how powerful he is."

"How powerful and impressive he is." I sweep a hand. "He gets the thrill of it without the bloodshed or the risk."

"That's fascinating," she says, leaning her head on one hand. "How your mind works."

I wave it off. "I could be all wrong. Might not even be the same person."

Her eyebrow rises slightly. "Well, it makes sense to me. Especially when you see what he did to Sally Pfiester in 2010."

Book IV

THE HAMPTONS, 2010

Chapter 51

HE IS COLD, though the sun beats down on him at this beach café, the temperature nearing ninety degrees.

He has to piss, though he just went twenty minutes ago.

His stomach churns like rusty grinding gears, though he's just eaten.

He sees her through his sunglasses, basking in the white-bright sunlight, a bronzed, lithe body, the backpack over both shoulders, a white tank top and denim shorts, sunglasses perched atop her white-blond hair, as she takes a photo of herself on her smartphone with the Atlantic Ocean in the background.

He watched her. Watched her as she ate at this very café—vegetables and hummus, a glass of Chardonnay—and texted on her smartphone, and told the waitress what she's doing this summer, and got a recommendation for a good beach to "crash on" tonight. She and the server even talked music briefly—she likes the modern pop stuff but prefers classical, cello music mostly, of course Yo-Yo Ma and du Pré but also a newer crop, like Alisa Weilerstein, whoever that is.

He likes the name Alisa. It would be cool to have a girlfriend named Alisa.

He wrote down everything she said. The beach where she will sleep, her musical preferences. And this, too: *Sally*. She told the waitress her name was Sally.

Not quite as exciting a name as Alisa.

He reaches for the check the waitress has left and notices the tremble in his hand. His fingernails chewed down to the point of bloodiness. He shouldn't chew his nails. He knows that. His mother would say it makes him look "unrefined."

But he's got lots of . . . refinement. Is that a word? He'll look it up later.

He feels the pressure building in his bladder, a dam on the verge of bursting.

Sally is exiting the beach now, walking up onto the asphalt parking lot, her hands gripping the shoulder straps of the backpack. The muscles in her legs straining, well defined. Her arms are hard, too—long thin slivers of muscle.

But his favorite part is the backpack. It means she's passing through. Not a native. A loner.

No friend or spouse or lover expecting her home tonight.

Holden is smart. Maybe not school-smart. But he isn't dumb.

And he knows his history well:

A peasant, any peasant will do, and better still a stranger;
Whosoever shall not be missed is welcome in my chamber.

He walks over to his motorcycle and throws on his helmet but keeps the shield up. Climbs onto the bike. Looks over at Sally as she passes. Nods to her.

Too nervous to speak, though. And probably best that he doesn't. His voice might shake. He's still a little nervous. A little rusty.

He drives off, lets time pass, the sun disappearing in a burst of color to the west.

He uses his secret entrance into 7 Ocean Drive, the one specially for him. The one he used when Annie and Dede were staying there. The one he uses when he wants to sleep there himself, which he does from time to time.

It's his house, after all. Even if nobody else knows it.

Once he's inside, down in the basement, he drops his Fun Bag and gets to work. He lays down the tarp, tests the chain's connection to the ceiling, locks and unlocks the handcuffs.

Tonight he's going to feast on duck and pheasant, on grapes and cheese.

And then he's going to find the girl named Sally and bring her back to the chamber.

Chapter 52

SALLY PFIESTER STRETCHES her legs in the cushy sand and rests her head against her soft pack, the water crashing to the shore only ten yards away. She looks up into a purple sky and lets out a satisfied breath. This is just what she needed, this summer. After a soul-killing desk job for two years and a ridiculous decision to accept that marriage proposal, she was starting down a road from which she would not be able to turn aside. Oh, he was a nice enough guy, and he had a terrific smile, a good sense of humor, but he didn't ignite that pilot light inside her.

Isn't life supposed to be exciting? Aren't you supposed to love, not merely tolerate, your job? Aren't you supposed to commit to a man not because it's "time," or because you want kids, or because he'd be a good provider—but because he makes your heart go pitter-pat?

Of course. Yes to all of that. It seems so obvious now. It didn't when she was stuck in that rut, like a hamster on a wheel. But once she opened her eyes and broke off the engagement, quit her shitty job and gathered up her savings for a year of travel, it revealed itself to her so clearly. She wants to explore. She wants to meet people and experience new things. She wants a man who's adventurous, nonjudgmental, not materialistic. She wants a man who is patient and at ease with himself. She wants a man who transports her to a world she's never known. Or fuck it, she'll do without a man altogether.

The decision to travel alone—deemed by her mother insane, by her envious friends awesome—was the best she could have made. She's only nine weeks in thus far, traveling the beaches of Long Island this summer by foot before heading to the West Coast and then Europe, but she's learned so much about herself, about what she wants and needs and expects from life.

And damn, all this walking has restored her triathlon physique from two years ago. She feels like herself again.

She's reaching for her smartphone—because solitude has its limits; she still posts regularly on Facebook and texts with her friends—when she sees something out of the corner of her eye, a figure emerging from the ocean in a wet suit, the glow of moonlight on him. She's a night swimmer, too, but it's a bit chilly this evening, so she took a pass.

The man trudges up the beach in her general direction, but then stops. For the first time, she notices that he's staked out a spot on the beach just like her, about twenty yards to her left. There aren't that many people sleeping on the beach tonight, but then again, she chose this remote beach for that very reason.

A light comes on by the man's spot—a flashlight? No, a battery-charged lantern—and he seems to be settling in for the night. She watches him for a time and then returns her gaze to the sky.

Sometimes she likes company and seeks it out, hangs out at bonfires, shares a bottle of wine or a joint, but other nights, like this, she prefers the quiet of her own company. It's her choice. That's the best part. It's her decision entirely.

And then: Faint at first, and then her hearing adjusts to it, over the sound of rolling waves—music. The soft whine, the dramatic upward lilt to the impossibly high notes, so sweet and despairing.

Cello music, she thinks. *He's listening to cello music.*

Chapter 53

HE CAN SEE why Sally likes this music. It's really good. It can be really loud and it can be really quiet, really fast and really slow. It can be violent. It can be chaotic. And it can be like a lullaby, almost. It makes him feel happy and sad within the same song—except they don't call it a song, they call it a *concerto*. He already knew that. He knew they were called *concertos* before he looked up the cello stuff this afternoon.

This music can do one other thing, too, at least tonight: It can get Sally's attention, up the beach a ways.

"Excuse me."

He pretends to be startled at Sally's voice. It's actually not that hard to pretend, because he's nervous, anyway. So it kinda works double like that.

"Sorry to bother you. Is this—is this Weilerstein?"

"Oh, um . . . is the music too . . . too loud?"

"No, not at all—"

"Sorry."

"No, I love this music. You're a fan?"

"Yeah." He shrugs. "I don't know much about it. I just . . . like it."

See, he planned this out. He knew that if he pretended like he knew all sorts of stuff about the cello, she'd ask him questions he couldn't answer. That's an example that he's maybe not so smart in school, but smart in planning stuff.

She laughs. "That's all you *need* to know. People get so caught up in all the pretentious bullshit."

"Yeah. It's just so . . ." He leans forward. "Like you feel happy and sad at the same time, kinda."

"I totally know what you mean. It can be so emotional, right?"

He can hardly see Sally's face as she stands over him, but he can smell her. Fruit. She smells like fruit.

"I have . . . wine," he says. "If you . . ."

"Yeah, I mean . . . if that's cool."

"Okay, yeah." Still nervous. But that's okay, because it makes him seem harmless to her.

She sits down next to him on the blanket he's laid out, next to the Fun Bag with the wine bottle sticking out.

Through the speaker on his iPod, the cellist bursts out of a lull with a crisp flourish.

Holden pours some wine into a plastic glass and hands it to Sally. "It's not . . . fancy or anything," he says.

"No, that's cool, whatever."

He hopes she doesn't notice his fingernails, all chewed up. But it's dark.

They listen to the music. The smell of the ocean, the

gentle rush of the waves, the berry scent of Sally's shampoo . . .

"Now, *this* is paradise," Sally says. "I mean, what's better than listening to music like this with the waves crashing out here, the stars in the sky, and a glass of wine?"

The wind kicks up, plays with Sally's hair. She has on a sweatshirt, but her legs are bare. He considers offering her a blanket—but better to stay low-key.

One concerto ends, Sally making a comment about the fluidity of the cellist's bow strokes, and before long she has drained her glass. That should be enough.

"I'm Sally, by the way."

"Holden," he says.

She looks over at him. "That's a nice name. Unique. Like *The Catch*—oh. Oh, wow." She puts her hand on her chest, sits upright.

A new concerto. The cellist hits a climax early on, joined by other strings and some percussion.

"I think . . . I think something . . ." Sally lets out a low moan.

He lifts his face to the sky, feels the gentle breeze. "I think . . . it's time," he says.

"I—I feel funny." Sally lets out a moan. She tries to push herself up, but it's like the signals aren't reaching her limbs. She can't make her arms or legs work.

"I finally . . . get it," he says. Warmth spreads through him, like a cup of hot cocoa.

There is a monster inside me. It can sleep for days, for months. But it will never go away.

"Help . . . help me." Sally turns to him, her face tight

with fear, her eyes searching his. He watches her face closely, the trembling lips, the wide eyes, the flaring nostrils, pure horror. So pure. So real.

She's losing her motor functions. She can't move her arms or legs anymore. She'll have trouble speaking, too. But she can still breathe.

"I . . . pl-please . . ." Just a whisper now. Her arms give out and she falls prone on the blanket, the music dropping to a low point. Lots of highs and lows with this cello music. Like a roller coaster. Like his stomach feels sometimes.

Her lips are quivering and her eyes move frantically about. That's going to be the extent of her physical movements until the drug wears off. By then, it will be too late.

He puts himself over her, lowers his face to hers. "Don't be afraid," he whispers, his voice feeling stronger now. "You can't . . . move, but . . . you'll still feel."

Her trembling lips try to form a word.

"You'll feel . . . everything," he says.

Chapter 54

HE RESTS HIS cheek against the concrete wall, sniffing the faint smell of bleach. The chamber is all concrete—floor, walls, ceiling. The acoustics are poor and the lighting is dim; there is no electricity in here and zero sunlight, so he makes do with three kerosene lanterns he has placed strategically. The effect is haunting, the light constantly changing as the small torches flicker inside their containers.

Is this what it used to look like? He imagines it is. The walls were probably padded in some way back then, and of course there were a cage and a long chain—but otherwise, this seems right.

"Let me go, mister . . . I promise I won't say anything. . . ."

Sally: straining in a backward position, suspended in the air like a roasting pig over a fire. Her back arched painfully, her hands cuffed behind her back, her legs bound together likewise, then the hands and feet joined together by yet a third set of cuffs, attached to the chain that loops through a hook in the ceiling and runs to the crank attached to the wall. A crude pulley system. Not so crude, really, in fact quite well constructed and in fair working order, despite decades of nonuse. They don't make 'em like they used to.

The metal pole, built into the floor, protruding upward five feet with a steel tip, only two or three feet below Sally's straining, suspended body, lined up almost precisely with the lowest point of her body, near her belly button, her intestines, allowing gravity to do its work when the time comes.

He turns the crank one full rotation. Sally's body free-falls downward a foot or so, the chain shaking but holding. Her head bobs from the impact, but her body hardly moves, bound up as tightly as it is. She lets out a squeal, more animal than human.

He walks over to her to measure things up, her terrified eyes, in the flickering light, like something primeval. She is so beautiful. Fear is so raw, so pure.

She tries to wiggle free. Admirable, but useless. She is basically hog-tied in midair, and even if she were somehow able to free herself of the various steel handcuffs—to pull a stunt beyond even Houdini—it would only mean a quicker and more violent death on the spear.

Maybe that's what she wants now. Maybe she's given up. Dede and Annie didn't. They fought. The prostitute, Barbie, though—she gave up. That was the best, watching her eyes surrender all hope, waiting, praying for the end to come.

He touches Sally's face and she snaps her head away violently.

That wasn't very nice.

"Let me down from here, mister, please! I have money!"

He can't let her go. He realizes that now.

I can no longer resist it, any more than I can resist my very existence.

Shaken, he returns to the wall and grabs hold of the crank.

There is a monster inside me. It can sleep for days, for months.

He turns the crank another full rotation.

But it will never go away.

It will feast on me, prey on me, until the day I die.

Book V

BRIDGEHAMPTON, 2012

Chapter 55

"YOU SHOULDN'T BE doing this," I say as I walk along the side of the road down Ocean Drive toward the Atlantic, the wind calm and the sun beating down on us.

"Roger that," says Ricketts, my rookie companion.

"I'm a dead-ender," I tell her. "You know what that is?"

"I think so. Your career's hit a wall?"

"Roger *that*." Without realizing it, I find that my stride has slowed as I near the end of the road, as I approach 7 Ocean Drive.

"Point being, I've got nothing to lose," I explain. "Chief's going to stick me in one dead end after another until I quit. So I figure I might as well solve a crime or two in my free time. But you, Ricketts? You've got a whole career ahead of you."

Ricketts is wearing a Red Sox T-shirt with running shorts and Nikes. She has the same build as me, lean and hard, but she gets it from genetics, not from working out like I do. "Dad always said I had an attitude problem."

"The Red Sox shirt being one example," I note.

I feel my heartbeat escalate, a banging drum against my chest. My breathing tightens up as well.

"Are you okay, Murphy?"

I stop and take a breath. Something about this damn house, every time I get close to it. Like my nightmares, only while awake. Put claustrophobia and panic in a bowl and stir for two minutes.

"I'm fine. Let's go." I trudge forward on shaky legs, not eager to share my sob story of scary dreams and panic attacks with the rookie.

"Why are we going to the house?" she asks me, a welcome question, allowing me to focus on the case, and not on this feeling overcoming me.

"The hooker, Brittany Halsted," I say. "He stuck a corkscrew so far inside her it almost came out the other side. Sally Pfiester, that backpacker? He used some kind of spear and drove it almost all the way through her midsection, right?"

"And somehow managed to drain all the blood out of her body," Ricketts says. "By the time they found her on an East Hampton beach, she was white as a bedsheet."

"Right. And last year, the other prostitute, Bonnie Stamos—impaled on a tree stump. And then my uncle Lang . . ."

I can't bring myself to finish the sentence, but she gets it. The killer drove a heated poker through Lang's kidney and into the kitchen floor.

"He likes to do more than just cut them," says Ricketts. "He likes to stick it in deep. You think maybe this is a sexual thing with him?"

We stop at the grand wrought-iron gates of 7 Ocean Drive. All at once, it's like the temperature has been turned up, the loss of breath, the pressure on my chest. I close my eyes and take a deep breath.

"Jesus, Murphy, are you having a heart attack or something?"

Something. I shake it off, slide between the gates, and look back at her through the bars. "Nobody invited us here," I say. "And we're cops."

"Right," she says.

"As in, we're not supposed to do this."

"Roger that."

"You can turn back now, Ricketts."

"I could."

"You *should* turn back now."

"I probably should." She slips through the small space between the gates, joining me on the other side. "But I'm not. I'm going where you're going. Tell me why we're at the Murder House."

I nod, take another breath, and move up the driveway until it curves off toward the carriage house up the hill. At that point, I take the stone path that, after a healthy hike, will lead to the front door of this grandiose monstrosity of a house.

"This place always gives me the creeps," says Ricketts. "It's like a multiheaded monster. All the different-color limestone, the different rooflines, all those gargoyles and ornamental spears pointed up at the sky."

"Yeah, it's a real fun place." I divert from the stone path onto the enormous expanse of grass before the slope upward toward the mansion. I stop at the stone fountain with the monument bearing the family crest and inscription. "This is why we're here," I say.

"Because of a fountain?"

I point at the small stone tablet, the crest featuring the bird with the hooked beak and long tail feather, the circle of tiny daggers surrounding it. "That," I say. "That fucking bird."

She doesn't get the context. She doesn't know that this miserable little winged creature has been haunting my dreams.

"Looks like an ordinary bird," she says, moving closer. "An ugly one. But it looks harmless. Why would you have a little bird like this on your family crest? You'd think it would be a falcon or an eagle or some scary, majestic bird."

I've spent the last two days researching that animal, trying to identify it among hundreds of species of birds in a catalog. When I matched it up, some things started to make more sense.

"It's a shrike," I say. "A small bird, yes. No large talons, no great wingspan. Not what you'd think of as a bird of prey. You're right, it looks harmless. But guess how it kills its food?"

Ricketts looks upward, thinking. "I'm going to use my powers of deductive reasoning and say . . . it spears them somehow."

"Close," I say. "It impales them."

She draws back. "Really?"

"Really. It scoops up insects, rodents, whatever, and carries them to the nearest sharp point—a thorn, the spikes of a barbed-wire fence, whatever it can find—and shish-kebabs them. Then it tears at them with that hooked beak."

Ricketts slowly nods. "Most of our victims suffered some version of impalement."

I wag my finger at that monument, the crest and the shrike. "This isn't a coincidence. Our psychopath has a real hard-on for this family, maybe for this house," I say. "So I want you to find out everything you can about 7 Ocean Drive. And this note under the crest—*Cecilia, O Cecilia / Life was death disguised* —find out what that means, too."

"I will," she says, not hiding her excitement. "Right away."

"Great. Now it's time for you to go home, Ricketts."

"Why? What are you gonna do?"

I nod toward the house. "I'm going inside."

"I'll come with you."

"No." I shake my head. "Walking into the yard is one thing. Breaking into the house is another. I don't want to be responsible for you."

"I'll take my chances."

"Get lost—that's an order," I say. "Besides, you have a lot of work to do."

Chapter 56

I HOLD MY breath and push open the front door. When I walk in, I immediately feel a weight pressing down on me, my movements slowing, an impossible wave of heat spreading through me.

Fight through it. You have work to do. So do it!

I stagger forward, feeling disoriented, light-headed, as if drugged.

So, so hot, like a fireplace inside my chest.

The dramatic Old Testament frescoes on the ceiling. The gold-framed portraits of men in formal eighteenth-century dress, mocking me.

Feeling my oxygen depleting, taking shallow breaths and keeping my chin up, my wits about me, as the childish cackling and taunting echo through my ears.

Please, don't make me go there

Please, don't do this

I wanna go home

The anteroom angling sideways, the lighting in front

of me spotty, but I'm not turning back, there's got to be something here and I'm going to find it—

Into the foyer, the staircase to the second floor before me, a parlor of some kind to my right, antique furniture and custom molding and chandeliers, an ornate fireplace. I turn toward the parlor but can't move toward it, as if a gravitational pull is drawing me in the opposite direction, and suddenly I'm staggering to my left instead, nearly losing my balance—

The dining room. Elaborate carvings on the walls, tall windows with fancy trim, a chandelier hanging over a pentagonal oak table with high-backed chairs. I reach for one of the chairs and grip it as if holding on for my life.

"I can't do this," I whisper, the childish taunts still banging between my ears, drowning out even my own voice. *I need to be here, but I can't be here.*

I push myself off the chair and start across the dining room, headed toward what must be the kitchen, my nerves scattered about, my vision unfocused, oxygen coming as if I'm taking breaths through a straw.

I draw my sidearm, for no reason that makes sense.

Get out of here

Stay and investigate

My legs finally give out, and I fall to my knees as if in prayer.

Let me go

Don't make me do this

Someone please help me

Let me out of here

I put my hand on the windowsill for support, push

myself up with my free hand, my Glock held forward with the other hand, trembling.

Then I look down.

On the windowsill, jagged letters carved into the wood.

DP + AC

Black spots before my eyes, my body turning, my legs like gelatin, moving in slow motion, like my feet are wading through thick sand, I can't breathe, I can't breathe—

Let me out of here

Bam-bam-bam

Let me out of here

Bam-bam-bam

The ornate patterned tile floor, then my hand on the door, pushing it, pushing it, why won't it—then turning the handle and *pulling,* fresh air on my face, sunlight—

I take a deep, greedy breath of fresh air and slam the door behind me.

I fall to a knee on the porch and gather myself. I don't know what just happened, why it always happens, why I'm having these dreams, why it all seems to be getting worse, and suddenly tears are falling off my cheeks, my body is trembling uncontrollably, my breath seizing, and I don't understand any of this, I don't know why something inside me seems to be breaking and I don't know how to stop it.

I only know one thing I didn't know before.

"They were here," I say to nobody.

Dede Paris and Annie Church were in this house.

Chapter 57

THE MOTORCYCLE TAKES a left off the turnpike onto the gravel drive, and I keep driving north, but the first chance I get, I turn left into a side street, do a quick U-turn, and head south. I pull into the parking lot a few minutes later, my car bouncing over the uneven gravel.

When I push the door open and walk into Tasty's, Noah Walker is at a corner table, just getting started on a beer. He's halfway to raising the bottle to his lips when he sees me. I see the hunky, clean-cut owner, Justin Rivers, behind the counter. He gives me a soldier's salute—kind of dorky; he's a looker but sort of a nerd—and I nod back.

"If it isn't Bridgehampton's finest," Noah says, taking a swig as I approach. He wears the grunge look well—T-shirt, cargo shorts, and sandals. Since his hair was cut tight while he was at Sing Sing, he looks less like Matthew McConaughey and more like a muscle-head weight lifter. A thick vein runs along his rippled biceps as he lowers the beer bottle to the table.

Not that I'm looking at his rippled biceps.

I stand near his table in the near-empty shack of a restaurant, hands on my hips. "Y'know something, Walker, I can't decide if you're the smartest criminal I've ever met, or a guy with a lot of really bad luck."

He sets down the bottle and finishes his swallow. "Good evening to you, too, Detective."

I look around the place. Only two other customers this time of night, past the dinner rush, and they're at the other end of the shack.

I drop two photographs on the table, next to his beer. "You know those women?"

Noah looks at the photos casually at first, then with what looks to me like a glint of recognition in his eyes, and he lifts the photos, peering at them. His eyes drift off them, like he's recalling something. After a long moment, he looks at me.

"Why?"

"It's a simple question, Noah. If you have nothing to hide, *why* shouldn't matter."

"They look familiar, but I don't know why." He drops the photos back on the table. "Okay?"

"You've worked for years at 7 Ocean Drive," I say.

He shakes his head, bemused. "That house again? Yeah, I think everyone in the world knows by now that I did work on that house."

"Those two girls," I say, "were staying in that house in 2007. They went missing afterward. They were Yale undergrads who came to the Hamptons and were never seen again. Nobody was even looking for them in Bridgehampton, and definitely not in that house. But now we know they were there. So that's two couples who stayed in that house, two couples dead—"

"So now you're accusing me of *that,* too?" He gets up from his chair, kicking it back violently. "You know something, Detective? I can't figure *you* out, either. First you ruin my life by lying on the witness stand and sending me to prison. Then you tell the judge I was framed, and I start to think you might be a human being. And now you're back accusing me of everything that's ever happened in this town. I mean, I can't even have dinner . . ."

I narrow my eyes, appraising him. The same read as always—I'm not getting *killer* from his vibe. I'm not sure what I'm getting.

He keeps his eyes on me, challenging me, a twinkle of a dare in his eyes. The smell of his sweat coming off him.

"There's a lot of coincidences involving you, Noah." I back away from the table. "But for now, I'll leave you to your dinner."

The other diners in the restaurant, getting a good eyeful, return to their meals as I pass them. I wave to Justin on my way out.

"Hey," Noah says as I'm ready to push through the door.

I turn, and he's walking up to me.

He looks me over, works his unshaven jaw.

Heat across my chest.

"Lemme ask you something," he says. "You're an experienced cop, right? You've stared down all sorts of bad people, cold-blooded killers?"

"I've seen my share."

"Do I really seem like a killer to you?" He opens his arms, as if to give me a clear view. The thick scarring on his palms, from the crucifixion at Sing Sing.

That's been my problem all along. Even when certain evidence points to him, when the facts line up against him—every time I look him in the eye, I just don't see it. There is anger behind his eyes, and he's lived rough, no doubt. But is there rage? The capacity for horrific sadism? That mental switch that flips on and allows him to turn into a monster?

I tell him the truth.

I say, "I'm not sure."

Chapter 58

MIDNIGHT. THE TEMPERATURE fallen to the low fifties, the wind coming hard off the ocean, less than a mile to the south, carrying some hint of the rain that just stopped an hour ago, with me unprepared in my short sleeves. I left the bar in a fog, not drunk exactly, not on alcohol at least, my emotions swirling, my thoughts consumed by the murders, by Uncle Lang, by my shipwreck of a life, and somehow instead of driving home I found myself at the cemetery on Main Street.

The lighting from the street is dim, casting the cemetery in almost complete darkness. I can't even read the tombstone, but I know it, of course, by heart.

LANGDON TRAVIS JAMES, it reads. HE KEPT US SAFE. That's what he told Chloe he wanted said about him, when it was all over, that he devoted his life to protecting people. And he did. Sure, he cut some corners with the Ocean Drive murders, but he thought Noah was his guy—he thought he was framing a killer whom he otherwise couldn't catch. Wrong methods, but right reasons.

And I, of all people, exposed him. I didn't have a choice. I hope he knows that. Aunt Chloe promised me that he does, wherever he is now. Aunt Chloe, whose blank tombstone rests next to Lang's. He bought these tombstones early in their marriage, Chloe said, so they'd be together forever.

He was broken when she left him. She surely had her reasons, but he lost the love of his life. He was never the same person again. My mother was never the same after my father and Ryan died in that car accident, either. Losing your soul mate, by death or divorce—is it better than never having one in the first place? Better to have loved and lost, as they say, than never to have loved at all?

I drop to my haunches, suddenly exhausted. Chloe's right. I have to leave this place. It's doing something to me. But that means I'll have to give up being a cop. Nobody will give me another chance. The job's my love, probably the only one I'll ever have. But I'll have to leave. I don't think I can survive many more of these night terrors, these panic attacks or whatever they are.

But first things first.

"I'm not leaving," I say to Lang's stone, "until I figure out who killed you."

The winds die down.

A noise. A shuffling movement.

I get to my feet and spin around. I look south into darkness, my eyes not fully adjusted.

A beam of light, twenty yards away, a small yellow circle on the ground.

I draw my sidearm.

"Who's there?" I call out.

The light swings in my direction until it passes across my face, then returning to me, blinding me.

"Town police!" I call out, shutting my eyes.

The light on my face disappears. I open my eyes, unable to see much of anything from the overload to my retinas; I squint and drop low.

"Identify yourself!" I yell.

I hear something, feet adjusting in wet grass, think maybe I see a figure moving. The flashlight beam has disappeared, nothing but spotty darkness. I break into a run, the gun at my side, my eyes still off-kilter after the blinding light, dodging tombstones as best I can. As I race farther south, some faint light off the side street helps me navigate.

The figure up ahead, in a full-out sprint.

"Stop! Town police!"

I pick up my pace, feeling like I'm closing the gap, a faint mist hitting my face, but it's not far from the street, and then the woods, plenty of places to hide. I'm running full-speed, but I'm running out of time.

I fire a round into the earth, the gunshot's echo piercing, and the sloshing sound of feet running on wet grass suddenly stops.

"Don't move! Town police!"

I shuffle forward, both hands on the gun trained ahead of me, though I can't really make out the figure yet. "Hands out where I can see them!" I order, as if I could possibly see them.

As I get closer and my eyes readjust, I make him. He has turned to face me. His arms are extended upward.

A mousy face, hair jutting out from beneath a baseball cap flipped backward.

"Who are you?" I ask, but I think I know the answer.

"Who are *you?*" he says.

"Detective Murphy, STPD. Tell me who you are, and don't move!"

"Aiden Willis."

I shuffle toward him, closing the gap, less than ten yards away. The wind picks a lousy time to kick back up, carrying mist and some stray leaves.

"You in the habit of running from cops, Aiden?"

"I didn't know you were a cop."

"I announced myself." Moving closer still. Gun still held high. Adrenaline still pumping.

"So? How do I know it's true?"

A fair point, I guess. This time of night, in a cemetery.

"Where's that flashlight?" I ask.

"In my hand."

"Shine it under your chin," I say. "And move slowly, Aiden. Don't make a cop with a gun nervous."

He complies. The light goes on, and there he is, illuminated by a haunting, ghost-story-around-the-campfire light under his face, those raccoon eyes that constantly flitter about.

"What are you doing here, Aiden?" Moving closer, under five yards now.

"What are *you* doin' here?"

"Hey, pal, you wanna stop asking me the same question I ask you?"

"I work here."

True enough, that. Isaac told me he did maintenance here.

"You're working at midnight, are you?"

"It rained. We got an open site for burial tomorrow. Sometimes the rain messes it up. I'm just checkin'."

"Who's getting buried?"

"How should *I* know?"

I feel my adrenaline decelerating. "You scared the shit out of me," I say.

"You scared the shit out of *me*."

What's with this guy repeating everything I say? But I have no basis to detain him, and now that my heart has stopped racing, and the wind's finding its way under my shirt and licking my sweat-covered face and neck—I'm reminded how freaking cold it is out here.

"I remember you now," he mumbles, or at least that's what I think he said.

"What?"

Did he say he *remembers me?*

He double-blinks. "Can I go now?"

I let out a breath. "Yeah."

The light goes off under Aiden's face.

Bathing him in darkness again.

Chapter 59

LET ME OUT

Bam-bam-bam

Let me out

Bam-bam-bam

I can't see can't breathe

Darkness, then penetrating light from above, a shadow blocking it

A face coming into focus, backlit by blinding yellow

A boy, long hair, a hand

Don't touch me, please don't touch—

I lurch forward in bed, sucking in air, my heartbeat rattling. The same nightmare, but different.

Closed in, dark, *let me out,* suffocating—

But a boy. This time, a boy.

I squeeze my eyes shut and try to re-create it, to make out a face, but it's like trying to grasp vapor in your hand. You can't pull back a dream from the netherworld of the subconscious.

It comes when it wants to, and it vanishes at will.

I climb out from under the covers, wipe thick sweat off my forehead, splash cold water on my face in the bathroom. A quarter to five. Slept for four hours.

I throw on a shirt and shorts, lace up my New Balance shoes, and hit the pavement for ten miles.

The Hamptons, at their most charming at sunrise, the tranquil bays and deserted beaches and open roads, the smell of recent rain. I run over sand and grass and asphalt, working out the kinks, exorcising the night demons.

Later, I'm in my car, heading toward the school, my thrilling assignment. I dial information on my cell phone and get the number for the church.

"Presbyterian church." An elderly woman's cheery voice.

"Hi," I say, "I was wondering if you could tell me if there's a burial today."

"Today? Hold on, sweetie." Muffled conversation in the background. "Today? No, ma'am. We don't have any burials scheduled for the rest of this week. What's the name of the deceased?"

No burials today. Aiden Willis lied to me.

"I must have the wrong cemetery, my apologies. Thank you very much."

Why would Aiden lie about his reason for being at the cemetery last night?

My cell phone buzzes in my hand. It's from the substation.

"Murphy," I say.

"Detective, it's Margaret at the substation. Chief Marks wants to see you."

"I'm on my way to my assignment," I say.

"He said right now."

I blow out air.

"He didn't say it very nicely, either," she adds in a quieter voice.

Chapter 60

I TURN MY car around and drive to the substation. What assignment is Chief Marks going to give me now—school crossing guard?

By the time I enter his office, I've worked up a little attitude. How much worse can it get for me here?

Isaac takes his time reading a report, making me wait—purposeful, a show of authority—and starts talking to me without looking up. "Detective Murphy," he says, "why are you asking people at the school about the Halloween BB gun shooting from seventeen years ago?"

I should have seen this coming. "I'm trying to figure out more about Noah Walker," I say. "Who he hung around with. Who helped him shoot all those kids."

"*Helped him* shoot those kids?" The chief drops his report. "Nobody helped Walker shoot those kids. He did it all by himself."

I shake my head. "There was a second shooter."

"No, there wasn't. I was there. I was the same age as Noah. Same school."

I'm well aware of that fact, Isaac.

"The angles of the shots fired," I say. "And why was Noah just sitting on a bench by the school, waiting to get caught?"

"Are you kidding me? Because he's a psychopath, Murphy. The kind that could slaughter a family and then sit next to you on a bus and engage in polite conversation. He had no remorse, no guilt, no sense that he'd even done anything wrong." He leans forward in his chair. "And why are we even having this conversation? Why are you looking into this?"

"Because if Noah didn't kill those people at 7 Ocean Drive, or my uncle, then someone sure made it look like he did."

"Someone set him up . . . and someone set him up seventeen years ago, the school shooting, too? You're actually trying to tie those two things together?"

I shrug. "Call it a hunch. But yeah. This is a really small town. It's possible. Look, I'm doing the assignment you gave me. I'm doing this other stuff on my free time."

"I don't want you doing it on *any* time," he says. "No more questions about a second shooter. No more investigations into 7 Ocean Drive or your uncle. Can I be any clearer?"

"No, you're very clear, Chief," I reply. "In fact, I'd like to compliment you on how clear you're being, *Chief*. May I be excused, *Chief*?"

Isaac stares me down, his tongue rolling inside his cheek. He gets out of his seat and comes around the desk. I stand, too, so we're face-to-face.

"Let's go off the record," he says.

"Let's."

"Nothing leaves this room."

"Agreed."

"What is this fascination with Noah Walker?"

"I don't have a fas—"

"You want to fuck him, don't you?"

I draw back. "*What* did you just say?"

Isaac throws up a hand in disgust. "Always the same with that guy. A juvenile fucking delinquent since the day I met him, but every girl in school fantasized about him. The kid's never been anything but bad. Believe me, I know him a lot better than you, Murphy. Don't be fooled by the movie-star good looks. That guy's nothing but a bad seed."

For a moment, I'm speechless. Isaac's chest is heaving, his cheeks crimson. It's like we're replaying middle school here.

"Did he steal your girlfriend or something, Isaac?"

His eyes flare. He drives a finger into my chest. "Noah Walker killed those people at 7 Ocean Drive and Noah Walker killed your uncle. Noah Walker shot up that school all by himself. You will stop trying to prove otherwise. You will stop right now, or I'm pulling your badge."

I hold my breath, willing myself to calm down. "You're pathetic," I say. "I mean, since we're off the record."

He nods, grins at me, coffee breath and stained teeth. "You think you're untouchable, but you're not. I'm going to run you out of here sooner or later."

"Yeah? Good." I turn and head for the door.

"Oh, and Murphy? Since we're off the record?" He takes a breath and composes himself. "I thought your uncle was a worthless prick."

Chapter 61

THE MAN WHO thinks of himself as Holden is getting restless. No, it's not summer yet, but this March has been one of the warmest on record—is that close enough?

Maybe. For right now, he'll enjoy the sights and sounds at Tasty's. So many people to choose from, men and women both. He'll have to make a list and plan this out. He's good at planning them.

Hell, look at last summer, the summer of 2011. Four victims! In one summer, he doubled what he'd done up until then. Zach and Melanie, that hooker named Bonnie, and the good ol' police chief. The police chief!

And is he in prison?

Nope, he sure isn't. How's that for smart? You kill the chief of police and nobody can lay a glove on you.

His eyes wander beyond the crowded restaurant to the window, where he recognizes someone getting out of a car in the parking lot.

Detective Jenna Murphy, the sexy redhead detective.

Blue jacket over a white blouse, tight-fitting jeans, low heels.

She thinks she's smart. She thinks she's smarter than everyone.

But she's not that smart.

If she's so smart, why doesn't she remember me?

From all those years ago.

It might be fun to remind her one of these days.

Chapter 62

OFFICER RICKETTS AND I are out of luck when we enter Tasty's for lunch—no open tables. We take seats at the counter, with its view of the kitchen, where cooks in aprons and white hats are chopping and broiling and frying, reading orders off slips of paper clipped above them. The smells of garlic and tomato sauce and fried food fill the air.

Aiden Willis is sitting alone at a middle table, always that cap turned backward, the strawlike hair jutting out, those beady, meandering eyes. He's reading something while he eats fried fish out of a paper tray. Time will come, I'll ask him how that "burial" went yesterday, to see if he'll keep lying about it, but I don't want to tip my hand yet.

We both order scallops. Ricketts orders one of those iced-tea drinks served in those giant, colorful cans; ice water for me.

Over my shoulder, I see Chief Isaac Marks, wearing a bib and dipping lobster into butter sauce. Another table for one. He must see me, but after our words yesterday, there isn't much left to say.

"Careful," I tell Ricketts. "Chief's sitting over there. Let's not be too obvious."

She leans into me. "How 'bout I just talk quietly, then? I won't pull out my notes." She taps her head. "It's all up here, anyway."

It's pretty loud in here, so that would probably work.

"Give me the *Reader's Digest,*" I say.

She takes a deep breath. A waiter serves us our drinks, mine in a plastic cup. "The *Reader's Digest,*" she says, "is cree-py."

A ripple of boisterous laughter behind us. I turn back and see a group of guys—construction workers, a testosterone fest—in the corner.

One of them: Noah Walker. T-shirt stretched tight over his chest, dirty jeans, work boots.

I feel my temperature rise and pull my shirt off my suddenly sticky chest.

Something about that guy. I can't deny it. Can't understand it, either.

I have my back to the crowd, but when I'm turned toward Ricketts, I have a good sight line to both Noah and Aiden Willis. Isaac is behind me.

Three men, all about the same age, all at Bridgehampton School.

Ricketts says, "The house at 7 Ocean Drive was built by a Dutch settler named Winston Dahlquist in the late 1700s. He had, like, this massive potato farm on Long Island and was crazy rich. He had a wife, Cecilia, and one son."

Cecilia, O Cecilia / Life was death disguised.

"Cecilia died in 1813. They said she jumped out of her bedroom window. She landed on the spiked fence."

"She . . . *landed* on it?"

"Oh, yeah, they found her impaled on the fence, twenty feet off the ground. Her body was almost cut in half. But the author of the book I read on this—she had someone diagram everything, the angles, the distances. She concluded that if Cecilia had jumped from her bedroom, she would've landed several yards short of the fence."

"So the wife was pushed."

Ricketts nods.

"Tell me about the son," I say.

"His name was Holden. Holden Dahlquist."

Noah's eyes break away from his conversation and catch mine. He does a double take; then he fixes on me, his expression easing, his eyes narrowing.

"Holden was basically insane," she says. "Erratic. Violent. Couldn't be in school. The author of the book thinks Holden's the one who killed Cecilia. He would've been seventeen at the time."

"He killed his mother." I nod along, casually, like she's telling me about a new pair of heels she bought.

"Apparently, after Cecilia died, Winston was never the same. As time went on, Winston started going batty, too. He wrote in a letter—I remember this—he wrote, 'I hesitate to declare what is more alarming, the extent to which my son is beginning to resemble a wild animal, or the extent to which I am beginning to resemble him.'"

Aiden Willis stands up and fishes in his pocket for

money, drops it on the table. Under his arm is a paperback—Steinbeck, *Of Mice and Men.*

A little deeper reading than I might have expected from our Aiden.

"Apparently, after Cecilia's death, a string of murders and disappearances began," Ricketts continues. "Over two dozen people died over the next twenty years."

I turn back to Ricketts. "Tell me about the victims."

"They were hookers or immigrants. They'd go missing in the summer and then they'd be found dead with some kind of hole in their body, usually a through-and-through."

"Impaled," I say, my heartbeat responding.

"Yeah. Always some kind of spear or cutting instrument. And sometimes with all the blood drained out of their bodies."

"Jesus." I draw back. "And they never put this on Winston? Or his kid, Holden?"

My eye catches Aiden Willis, stuffing his hands in his pockets, checking me out with a sidelong glance on his way out, the paperback still tucked under his arm.

Then I look back at Noah, who's watching me while he drinks a bottle of beer, still with his friends at the table.

Then Noah's expression changes, goes cold, hard, and his eyes move away from mine to . . .

. . . Isaac, approaching him, the entire table freezing up. Isaac, with that cop bravado, saying something to Noah that elicits a frown, and I see something in Noah's eyes that makes me think there's going to be violence between them. But then Isaac moves along, heading toward the exit, catching my eye as well, smirking at me.

"They never charged either Winston or Holden," says Ricketts. "Legend has it, Winston had the local constable in his pocket. He was one of the wealthiest people on Long Island."

I watch Isaac leave and think over what Ricketts has told me. "He chose prostitutes and immigrants," I say. "Drifters. People—"

"—who wouldn't be missed. Yeah, there's a saying attributed to Winston. I think I have this right: 'A peasant, any peasant will do, and better still a stranger. Whosoever shall not be missed is welcome in my chamber.'"

Our scallops arrive, with a delicious buttery aroma, but I've lost my appetite.

"Sounds like a fun family," I say.

"Oh, but it gets better," Ricketts says, trying to keep her voice down. "Every generation left a single son, each of them named Holden. Holden Junior, Holden the Third, etc., all the way to Holden the Sixth. All of them suffering some mental illness, most of them suspected of violence. One of them killed his wife. Several committed suicide."

"Where's the most recent Holden?" I ask.

Ricketts spears a scallop with her fork.

"In the ground," she says. "The last Holden died almost twenty years ago, without any children."

Chapter 63

I CHECK MY sidearm for ammunition and holster it.

My head is buzzing after spending hours poring over a copy of the book that Ricketts used for her research, *Winston's Heirs: A Haunted House in the Hamptons*, chronicling the Dahlquists from the time when Winston came to Long Island in the late 1700s until recent years, the many generations of Holdens.

The original Holden, who these days would have been in an institution for the criminally insane, who may have murdered as many as two dozen women.

Holden Junior, who had three kids of whom only one survived, the only boy.

Holden III, who decapitated his wife on their fifth anniversary before jumping out of the same bedroom window from which Cecilia fell.

Holden IV, who went through four wives and a lot of booze before hanging himself at age fifty-two.

Holden V, who married and divorced three times and

overdosed on a combination of amphetamines and alcohol, just days after four vacationers were stabbed to death on the beach not fifty yards from his home at 7 Ocean Drive.

And Holden VI, described by his mother as a "simpleton with violent tendencies and the empathy of a rattlesnake, but other than that a dear boy." Known for his philanthropy publicly, but suspected of multiple rapes and assaults, none of which ever stuck. Holden was found dead in his bedroom in 1994; he slashed his own throat and tossed the knife out the window before dying, thus ending the ignominious reign of the Dahlquist clan.

My sidearm in place, I leave the house, a chill in the midnight air.

I start up my car and put it into gear. The roads are all but empty at this hour, in late March, before the summer vacationers have begun to arrive.

A gray pall hangs over the lonely streets.

I kill the headlights as I approach and let my foot off the gas. I pull my car over on Main Street and kill the engine. I'll walk the rest of the way. One hand on my sidearm. The other clutching my Maglite.

I approach the cemetery from the west. The air is thick, promising rain, but none has yet fallen. As I get closer, the street lighting dims considerably, leaving the cemetery in sleepy black.

This time, I'm more prepared. A sweater instead of short sleeves. Running shoes, not flats. A flashlight.

I pass through the gate quietly and drop down low in the grass among the tombstones. It may take a while, if it happens at all. But just to be sure, I'm not signaling my presence.

The wind kicks up off the ocean, making me wish I'd worn a second layer. Standing still, crouched down, it's not easy to stay warm. My eyes begin to adjust to the darkness, but the effect isn't helpful—it's still too dark to see much of anything, but now the darkness is filled with dancing shadows and fleeting movements.

Keep it together, Murphy.

The sleep deprivation doesn't help. My eyes feel heavy these days, my movements lumbering, my brain fueled by adrenaline but unfocused, sloppy.

A noise. Something soft but persistent. At first, I think it's wind rustling through the trees, but it stays consistent when the breeze ebbs, grows stronger as it draws closer.

Footfalls. Someone walking over the soft earth, heading toward the cemetery.

But no flashlight beam. Nothing illuminating his path.

I steel myself but don't dare move. I can't see anything in the blackness, but the sound is unmistakable now—someone walking into the cemetery.

He's walking in pitch dark without the aid of a flashlight, and without hesitation. He knows exactly where he's going.

Knows it by heart.

And then the footsteps stop.

I look up but can't see anything. Close enough for me to hear, too far away for me to see. Maybe a hood—a sweatshirt with a hood—

A beam of light pops on. Startling me—I almost fall backward in my crouch.

I try to gauge his location from the flashlight beam. But then the light disappears, almost as quickly as it appeared.

Darkness again, and silence. What is—

A new sound. Spray of some kind, a thin stream of liquid slapping against stone.

Sounds like . . .

No, I decide. *Couldn't be.*

Chapter 64

I STAY FIXED in my position until the sound stops; then the footsteps begin again, but now moving away from me. He's leaving the cemetery, same way he came, disappearing into the void of black.

Should I accost him? I'm assuming it's Aiden Willis, as before, but I can't see shit out here. And if I confront him, I might be giving up an advantage.

No. Better I let him leave and try to figure out what he does here at night.

I wait until I can't hear him anymore, then wait another ten minutes for good measure. I keep my eyes focused on where I saw that momentary flashlight beam, trying to use it as a beacon to guide me in the pitch dark.

Once I'm ready to move, I shine my Maglite at that destination point and start walking toward it. It's not perfect, but it should get me where I'm going. Especially if that sound was what I think it was.

Something big up ahead. Something tall. The cemetery has all kinds of tombstones, large and elaborate, small and simple, many variations in between. This one is of the big-and-fancy variety. I run the light over the monument until I hit the name.

Dahlquist

A large stone monument bearing that same family crest with the bird, the shrike. The whole plot surrounded by an iron bar, no more than three feet off the ground, supported by small stone pillars.

My heart skips a beat. I move closer, sweep the beam of light around.

Three tombstones at the monument's base: Winston, Cecilia, Holden. The first Dahlquists. Then, just below them, five more tombstones, presumably for the successive generations of Dahlquists, all males named Holden.

I shine my light over each Holden tombstone, the earliest ones in not nearly as good shape as the more recent ones. Finally, I hit the last generation—Holden VI, buried here since 1994.

There it is.

I bend down to get a closer look at the tombstone. Fresh liquid splattered all over it. I don't dare taste it, but I lower my face close enough to confirm with my nose what I thought I heard with my ears.

Urine.

Whoever crept into this cemetery just took a piss all over Holden VI's grave.

Good thing I looked up Aiden's address.

Maybe it's time to pay him a visit.

Chapter 65

I KILL THE headlights so Aiden won't see my car approaching his house. But he might hear it bouncing over the bumpy, unforgiving roads just north of Main Street.

His house is obscured by trees until I reach his driveway. I pass it and pull the car over on the sloping shoulder of the road.

Only a quarter mile away, last summer, the prostitute, Bonnie Stamos, was found impaled on that tree stump.

The house is dark as I walk up the driveway. It's a dilapidated shingled ranch that almost sags at its sides, a beater Chevy parked in the driveway. I step up onto a cracked concrete porch and can't find a doorbell.

I open the screen door, which is on the verge of falling off, and bang my fist on the door.

"Open up, Aiden. Town police!"

Nothing at first. I bang again. Announce my office once more.

Nothing.

He couldn't have beaten me here by much. Fifteen minutes, tops.

No way he's asleep.

It was Aiden I saw, wasn't it?

"Open up, Aiden!" I pound on the door until my fist hurts.

I check my watch. Half past midnight.

Either he's not home or he's ignoring me.

Either way, I'm out of luck. It's not like I can kick in the door. I don't have probable cause or anything close to it.

But nothing says I can't check the back of the house.

No outdoor lighting on the house, the property surrounded by trees that block any neighboring light, so I use my Maglite to move around the narrow side of the house.

The backyard is equally dark and tree lined. A bicycle lies in the grass. No back porch or patio.

Something moving—

A squirrel or some small animal, sprinting through my beam of light.

I take a breath. Shine the light on the house.

A window well, into the basement. I shine my light inside. Just enough room for me to fit in there.

The window's been unlatched, pulled inward.

I squat down. The window's filthy. I wipe the muck with the sleeve of my sweater, but the light combines with the smears to block any view, like high beams in fog.

I push on the window to open it farther, as far as it will go, to a sixty-degree angle inward.

A noise in the woods behind me, something moving across fallen branches and dead leaves. I shine my light over the woods.

Dry grass moving gently with the breeze. Long, naked trees like skeletons waving at me.

An animal, probably.

The open window gives me, maybe, an inch or two of space. I shine my light directly into the basement and peek inside.

Looking right at me is a woman, sitting in a chair.

Chapter 66

I JUMP AT the sight, fall against the back of the window well. Shine the light through the crack in the window again, make sure I actually saw what I think I saw.

The small circle of light, cutting through the darkness, searching for her—

There.

The woman, seated in a chair, wearing an old-fashioned shawl over her shoulders, her hair pulled back tightly in a bun, her hands resting quietly in her lap. A relaxed expression on her face. Her mouth closed. Her eyes glazed, immobile.

"Town police!" I call out, just to be sure. "Ma'am, can you hear me? Ma'am, are you okay?"

My pulse in overdrive, I draw back, brace my hands against the window well, raise my leg into kicking position.

Wait. Something about that . . .

I lean back in, shine the light once more, find her again.

No movement. Her eyes don't respond to the light. She's dead.

I move the light slowly, probing as best I can the quality of her skin. Hard to do from a distance, with a flashlight.

But little decomposition.

Actually, *no* sign of decomp. None. Her skin looks flawless, even . . .

Inhuman.

I look around her. Next to the rocking chair in which she's seated is a—

"Oh, Jesus—"

My hand jerks, and the beam of light shoots to the ceiling. Hands shaking, I sweep the light through the darkness again, past the woman—

A man. Wearing some kind of coat, tweed. Hair greased back. A thin face, eyes open and vacant. Sitting on a love seat, legs crossed.

Same deal with the glossy skin, the immobile eyes, unresponsive to light.

Not dead people. Not people at all.

Wax figures.

I exhale with the realization. I was two seconds away from kicking in this window to rescue a couple of wax mannequins.

I keep the light moving.

An area rug on the floor. A battered coffee table with a vase and flowers—fresh flowers, not fake.

Against the wall, a faux fireplace—something painted on the wall, complete with logs and a spirited flame.

A television set. I can only see its back, but a soft, flickering glow emanates from it, the only occasional illumination in this basement, other than my flashlight.

A picture over the fake fireplace. A blown-up photograph.

Aiden as a boy, that scarecrow hair and scrawny face, next to a woman.

"What the hell?" I say, repositioning my feet on the bed of rocks.

Which is why I don't hear the footsteps, approaching me from behind on the soft grass.

But I *do* hear the pump action of a shotgun.

Chapter 67

"DON'T MOVE!" A voice calls out.

Startled, I lose my flashlight on the rocks, bathing myself in a little circle of light inside the window well. I turn my head for a look back, but it's no use. I'm below him and lit up; he's above me in the dark.

"I said *don't move!* Put up your hands!"

If I raise my hands right now, squatted down as I am, I'll probably fall over.

"I'm with—"

"Hands up or I shoot!"

"Listen to me, I'm a po—"

"Now!"

"Okay, okay. Easy." I do my best, like a tightrope walker struggling for balance, rising from my crouch and bringing my hands out, leaving my Maglite on the floor of rocks. I'm half turned toward him, so he can see my profile, but I can't see him.

"I'm a cop," I say. "Southampton Town Po—"

"Who sent ya?"

"I'm a *cop*."

"Whatchoo doin' here? What right you got?"

I take a breath. "Aiden—"

"Don't move!"

"I'm not moving. I'm not moving."

Aiden's breath, raspy and heavy.

"Mr. Willis, I just identified myself as a police officer. You don't want to be pointing a shotgun at a cop, do you?"

He doesn't answer.

"The correct answer," I say, "is no, you don't. You know me, Aiden. I'm Detective Jenna Murphy. You saw me the other night at the cemetery."

At which time, I note, the roles were reversed—I had a gun trained on him. Turns out, it's more fun when you're the one holding the weapon.

"Put the gun down, Aiden. I'm not telling you again."

He moves around so he's behind me again, my six o'clock.

"You come ta kill me," he says.

"No, Aiden. I'm a cop. I'm—"

"You comin' ta *kill* me! You been followin' me. You think cuz—"

"No, Aiden."

"Why'd ya have to come back? Ya shouldn'ta come back—"

"Aiden!" I crank up the volume this time, trying to gain the upper hand. "Aiden, I'm a cop. You know me. Now, I'm going to climb out of this window well and you're going to put down that shotgun."

I move slowly, putting my hands on the top of the aluminum well.

"I'll shoot." He shuffles backward as he speaks, feet rustling in the grass.

"No, you won't." I jump and use my arms to push myself onto the grass.

"Don't you move!"

I show my palms, though he probably can't make me out very well.

"Now put down that damn shotgun," I say. I rise to my feet.

I get a little bit of a bead on him, an outline, the hair sticking out, the shotgun in his hand.

"Self-defense," he says, raising the shotgun.

I lose my breath, brace myself, consider my options. If I go for my sidearm, it's a long shot. If I dive, I'm unlikely to miss the wide blast from his gun. Something out of a movie—drop and roll and come up shooting?

"You were at the cemetery tonight," I say.

"No, I wasn't."

I'm calculating how well Aiden can see me now, standing as I am on solid ground in the darkness. Hoping he can't see very well.

"You sure about that?" I put my hands on my hips, as if demanding an answer.

My right hand sliding down to my sidearm.

My fingers fitting into the grooves of the grip.

"Why did you take a piss on the Dahlquist grave, Aiden?"

"I didn't. You're just makin' excuses so you can come here and kill me."

My finger caressing the trigger.

If I draw my weapon, one of us dies.

"Aiden, drop the weapon," I say.

"No." One leg moves back, like he's bracing himself for a shot. "You're gonna kill me," he says.

Maybe both of us die.

"No, Aiden—"

And then we both hear it, footsteps to the west. The beam of a flashlight, coming into the backyard.

"Aiden Willis, put down that goddamn gun."

The chief's voice. Isaac.

Chapter 68

ISAAC SWAGGERS INTO his office and stands behind his desk. He crosses his arms and leans against the wall, next to the American flag and the flag of the Town of Southampton, blue and maize with a pilgrim in the center. He stares at me for a long time in his police jacket, a sweater underneath and blue jeans.

I've been here a good half hour, stewing in my juices, after Isaac ordered me to the substation.

"Is Aiden in lockup?" I ask.

His eyes narrow. "Aiden's probably in bed now, fast asleep."

"You didn't arrest him?"

He stares back at me, his eyes shiny with venom. "Are you carrying?"

Am I carrying? "*Yeah*, I'm carrying."

"Hand over your piece."

"Why?"

Isaac lets out a heavy breath. "Detective, your

commanding officer has ordered you to surrender your weapon."

I blink. Something flutters through my chest.

I reach for my sidearm.

"Slowly," he says.

"Isaac, what the fuck?" I set my Glock, grip first, on his desk.

He picks up the gun, ejects the magazine, catches it in his hand. "You been drinking, Murphy?"

"No. I haven't. What's the chief of police doing out on patrol past midnight?" I ask. "And why are we letting Aiden Willis walk when he was about to shoot me?"

He plays with his goatee, stares at me, almost amused. Having the upper hand is fun for him.

"The better question, Murphy, is what the fuck were *you* doing?"

Not such a good question for me, though. He told me to stay away from the Ocean Drive murders, my uncle's murder, anything other than safety issues at Bridgehampton School. So there's no answer remotely resembling the truth that will exonerate me. I give him most of the cemetery story, only I make it seem like I was simply visiting Uncle Lang's grave, not lying in wait for Aiden.

"You actually saw Aiden take a piss on a tombstone?"

Well, no, I didn't—couldn't make out the actual act; couldn't even make out that it was Aiden. But I'm not going to admit that. "So I went to his house to ask him about it. And yeah, I looked around his place when he didn't answer. There are no lights outside, so I used my Maglite. I just walked the perimeter, Isaac."

He watches me closely. "You were shining a light into his basement?"

"Yeah, and you wanna know what I found?"

"What does Aiden Willis's basement have to do with him taking a piss on a grave? I mean, assuming he even did that, like you claim. You figured, what, you'd find evidence to support a public urination charge by searching his *basement*? No. You're up to something else."

I pause. But he has me. What possible bullshit story could I conjure up?

And besides, I shouldn't have to bullshit. I'm a cop, investigating a series of murders. When did that become a wrong thing? When did following up on a hunch, just to see where it led, become a capital offense?

"It was the Dahlquist grave," I say. "The family that owned the house where Melanie and Zach were—"

"No. No." He shakes his head presumptively, like he's had enough.

"Some strange shit is going on in this town," I say, trying to salvage the conversation. "And there's something about Aiden—"

"Aiden Willis couldn't spell his own name if you gave him all the letters," says Isaac. "And he couldn't hurt a june bug with a sledgehammer. I've known that kid my whole life. That boy is harmless."

"He pulled a gun on me tonight, Isaac."

"Yeah, and you know what? He had every goddamn right to. A prowler on his property, sneaking into his basement? Landowner's got that right."

"I announced my office."

"And maybe he didn't believe you. What's he supposed to think, Murphy? Lucky for us, Aiden's a reasonable man. He's going to let this be water under the bridge."

"Bullshit," I say, getting my Irish up, getting to my feet. "He knows me. Even if he didn't at first. I identified myself. Yeah, okay, maybe at first, I can't blame him. But he knows me, Isaac. I told him who I was and I posed no threat to him at all. And he was *still* going to shoot me. You're gonna let him walk?"

"Hell, yes, I am. A cop of mine, without anything close to probable cause, is looking into a private citizen's basement window? That's a lawsuit right there. The department doesn't need *another* black eye courtesy of you."

I shake my head. "I can't believe this."

"You're behaving in an erratic, irrational manner, Detective Murphy."

My blood goes cold. Magic words, those. The police union's collective bargaining agreement allows the chief to strip a cop whose behavior is "erratic or irrational."

A hint of a smile on Isaac's face. Oh, he's been waiting for this moment.

"Just hear me out first, Isaac, I'm beg—"

"Detective, turn over your badge."

"Isaac, no—"

"You're suspended indefinitely," he says. "I'm stripping you of your police powers. You're no longer a cop. You come back tomorrow, I'll give you thirty minutes to clean out your desk."

He leans over his desk, his eyes boring into mine, a snarl across his mouth.

"Now get the fuck out of my police station."

Chapter 69

THE DIVE BAR'S liquor license cuts off the service of alcohol at two in the morning. That means they have to stop pouring when the little hand hits two, and they can't let in any new customers.

It doesn't mean they can't hand over a bottle to me at 1:55 a.m. and then watch me drink it for an hour, as they close down the place, turn out most of the lights, turn over the chairs and put them on top of the tables, and mop the floors and wipe down the counters.

The good news for me is that I'm a regular, so I get this special treatment from Jerry, the bartender and owner.

The bad news, I suppose, is that I'm a regular.

"I don't like to speak ill of my fellow man," Jerry says to me as he sprays the counter. "But I never much liked Isaac. Worst thing that ever happened to him was getting that badge. Give a guy with an inferiority complex some power and watch out."

I look over at him, my eyes heavy and slow, almost

dreamy. Almost as if, an hour ago, I didn't lose the only thing that mattered to me in this world. Almost like that.

"Fuck Isaac." My tongue thick, numb. All of me feeling numb.

"Okay, three a.m.," Jerry says. "I'm gonna turn into a pumpkin." He lifts the bottle of Jim Beam, three-quarters empty. "I'll hold on to the rest for you, Murph. Your private stash. Let me give you a ride home."

I surrender the bottle but shake my head.

"You can't drive, Murph."

"Not gonna drive. I'll walk. Pick up . . . pick up my car tomorrow." I step off the barstool gingerly, get my balance. "Not like I'll have anything else to do."

"Let me give you a ride, Jenna. C'mon."

"I'm good. I'm good."

The walk will do me good. Or so I think. I'm about a half hour from here, and the cool air helps clear out some of the fog. My hand brushes against my side for my piece, which of course I had to surrender. Because I'm no longer a cop.

I'm no longer a cop. It still hasn't sunk in.

I'm dizzy and unfocused, my emotions careening wildly from utter despair to bitterness to hot rage, grabbing at clues that don't add up, like I'm trying to put together a puzzle that's missing half the pieces.

The start of a massive headache is pressing against my forehead, between my eyes.

By the time I approach my street, the inside of my head is screaming at me. But the blood is flowing again, and much of the alcohol's effect is waning.

All except the emotional part. With the numbness

wearing off, all that's left is my fear of what's to come, a life without a badge.

And sleep, which will end as it always does, with a breathless nightmare.

I rent the bottom floor of a two-flat, all of four rooms inside—living room with tiny kitchenette, bathroom, and bedroom. Always planned to buy a place once I "settled in," but I never really settled in, did I? I never got around to making anything about my apartment feel like a real home, nor did I buy an actual home.

Probably for the best, now.

When I approach the apartment, I see something underneath the porch light. A figure. A man?

I draw closer, feel my hand, by instinct, sweep my side for a gun that isn't there.

A man, sitting up, resting against the outside wall.

"Noah?" I say.

Chapter 70

WHEN I TAKE my first step onto the porch, Noah Walker stirs. He was sleeping.

"Oh, yeah." He pushes himself up, shakes out the cobwebs. Sweatshirt, jeans, sandals.

"Why are you here?"

"Waiting for you," he says.

"Same question," I say, "second time."

"I wanted to tell you something."

"So tell me."

He nods. "I remember now," he says. "Those girls."

"Dede and Annie."

"I saw them. I remember them now. They were at the house, 7 Ocean Drive. I think they were squatting there. I was doing some work. I think . . . patching the lower flat roof. I'm pretty sure it was them. It was five or six years ago, so I'm not positive. They seemed like nice girls. If something happened to them, and I can help . . ."

So that's confirmation. I was pretty sure they'd been

staying there—hard to imagine the initials AC and DP scratched on the windowsill were a coincidence—but it's nice to know for sure.

He looks up at me. He didn't have to tell me any of that. His lawyer, in fact, would have told him to keep his mouth shut.

"It doesn't matter anymore," I say. "Go home."

He steps in front of me. "It *does* matter. You're asking because you think it's connected. Whoever it was who killed those girls might have killed Melanie."

Melanie. Right. He had a relationship with her.

"I loved her. Yeah, she broke up with me and it hurt. And I moved on. But you don't stop caring about someone." He takes a long breath, looks out in the distance. "Y'know, after she died—you guys arrested me right away, and all of a sudden I'm on trial for my life. I never had a chance to . . . I don't know."

To grieve. To mourn her loss.

"And then Paige's suicide . . ."

I didn't even know about that. The woman he was with after Melanie.

"That happened after I went to prison," he says. He slowly nods, gains some steam. "Whoever killed Melanie—in my mind? He's responsible for Paige, too. And a lot of other people, it sounds like. Like those two girls. And your uncle."

This is not the time for me to be thinking about that. The fog may have cleared from my head, but my emotions are on the verge of bursting. It's over for me here in Bridgehampton. Over. I didn't solve the cases, and I'll never be a sworn officer again.

"Let me help you," he says. "Let me help you find him."

"I'm not a cop anymore," I say. "I've lost my badge. I lost everything," I add, for some reason—whiskey-induced self-pity.

"You didn't lose as much as me. And you don't see me running."

I look at him. Still standing tall, after what he's been through. Wrongly accused of a crime—yes, I believe that in my gut—crucified at Sing Sing by white supremacists he refused to join; losing two women he loved; and still being harassed by our police force. And here he is, volunteering for duty. If it were me, I'd have run from this town as soon as I left prison.

No, you wouldn't have. You're too stubborn.

Just like Noah.

That shield that has stood between us, suddenly gone.

I start to say something but don't. Everything swimming through me now, all the regret and anger and yearning, that familiar heat filling my body whenever I see him, but none of the typical restraints, all washed away by the alcohol and emotion, and I don't know if I'm going to burst into tears or—

Or—

"I can help you," Noah says. "I'm not as dumb as I look."

"I'm not a cop anymore."

He shrugs.

"Then what do we have to lose?" he says.

Chapter 71

"THE KEY TO all this," says Noah, "is someone who's been dead for twenty years?"

"Eighteen," I say. "And yes."

We're walking the next morning along Main Street, the sun blistering overhead. I skipped my morning run and pounded aspirin and water to ward off my hangover. The adrenaline helps, too. Funny that I feel almost reborn after the pep talk Noah gave me last night—that losing my badge actually has the effect of motivating me to work harder.

That's the thing: I may have lost my official authority, not to mention my gun, but I have gained some freedom—now Isaac can't prevent me from asking questions and probing where I wish.

I'd just better be careful. Because without said authority, and without said gun, there are limits to how far I can push things.

Noah follows me into the cemetery, all the way up to the Dahlquist plot.

"A family of violent, mentally deranged, suicidal men named Holden," I say. "The first Holden killed, like, twenty or thirty women."

"According to that book." Noah read most of the book after I gave it to him last night. He must not have slept at all. The dark circles under his eyes attest to that fact. "It may not be true."

"Doesn't matter if it's true. All that matters is that he believes it."

"Who?"

"Our suspect," I say. "Our killer."

Noah looks at the plot, the large memorial, then back at me. "He's mimicking what the first Holden did a couple hundred years ago? He has some kind of obsession with the family or something?"

"Very good," I say. "You're smarter than you look."

"Well, dagnabbit, Ms. Murphy—that makes me happier'n a puppy with two peters. I been a-hankerin' for your say-so—"

"All right, enough."

"Yes'm, I'm as pleased as a goat in a briar patch, I am."

I shake my head. "If it's okay with you, can we get back to the point now?"

Noah looks pleased enough with himself, but he turns it off and gets serious again. "Okay, so this guy has a thing for the Dahlquist family. Okay, I get that. But you said this is about the last Holden. The guy who died twenty years ago."

"Eighteen."

"Okay, whatever, eighteen—you're talking about Holden the Sixth."

"Right. Holden the Sixth."

"The guy who died without any heirs," says Noah. "The guy who said—let me find this." He reaches into his satchel and pulls out the book, opens to a page he has dog-eared. "The guy who said, 'The greatest gift I can bequeath mankind is to avoid procreation at all costs.' "

"Yes, that guy."

"The guy who killed himself by downing two fifths of Jack Daniel's, popping some pills, then slitting his own throat and tossing the knife out the window."

"Yes, that guy," I agree.

"The guy who was suspected of raping and assaulting a bunch of women, but the charges never stuck."

"Yes, that guy."

"The guy who, as far as we know, never committed a single murder."

"Yes, that guy."

"Not one murder that we know of."

"Correct," I say. "That guy."

Noah closes the book. "It all starts with *that* guy? He had no children, he committed no murders. I mean, he was a bad guy—he raped women, they think—but the guy running around right now isn't raping anybody. He's killing them in violent ways."

I smirk at him.

"Am I missing something?" Noah asks.

"I think you are," I say. "Our killer is mimicking what the original Holden did. And he's pretty damn good at it. But the question is why."

Noah stares at me, then shrugs. "I have no idea."

"I think he feels a sort of obligation," I say. "He thinks it's his destiny."

Noah opens his hands. "But . . . why would it be his destiny—"

His jaw drops.

I smile at him.

"Oh," says Noah. "You think?"

"I do," I say. "I think, no matter how much he didn't want to, Holden the Sixth left behind a son. A son who wants to restart the family tradition."

Chapter 72

I LEAVE NOAH at the cemetery with a research assignment and continue walking up to the turnpike. It's a little before eleven, so Tasty's is probably not even open for business yet, which is how I prefer it. Because I'm not here for the delicious scallops.

The gravel parking lot is almost empty when I walk up to the door. It's open, so I push through and enter the restaurant. In the back, chefs and servers are busy preparing for the lunch rush, boiling and steaming and chopping, wiping down counters, filling out the chalkboard with today's selections, shouting to one another in English and Spanish. The smells of garlic and butter make me reconsider whether I'm here for business only.

Seated in the dining area, alone, is Justin Rivers, wearing a flannel shirt that he fills out very well, thank you very much, and blue jeans. He's got a pencil poised over a section of newspaper—a crossword puzzle.

Must be nice, being the owner, relaxing while the employees bust a move to get the diner open.

He glances up at me with those boy-next-door looks and smiles widely.

"Detective!"

It's like a punch in the stomach. But I don't correct him. I'm not going to lie if he asks, but if he wants to think I'm still a cop, all the better.

"Hi, Justin. How're you doing?"

"Great, great." He looks down at his watch.

"I'm not here for lunch," I say. "I was hoping to speak with you a moment."

"With me? Okay." He stands up. "You wanna . . ."

"Maybe we could step outside?"

"Sure. I'll be right back," he calls out to his staff, though nobody seems to notice.

He follows me outside and faces me, beaming, clean-cut and handsome.

"Good to see you," he says. The million-dollar smile, the hair swept to one side, the broad shoulders.

"Um—thanks. You too. Listen, I was hoping to ask you a few questions."

"Oh, you mean, official stuff?" His face dropping a bit, like he's disappointed.

I nod. "If that's okay. Did you think there was some . . . other reason?"

"Oh, uh." His face turns red. "Now I'm embarrassed. Oh, I feel stupid."

It sometimes takes me a while, but I get there. He thought I was going to ask him out.

"A guy can hope," he says.

Now we're both embarrassed.

"Oh, Justin, I'm sort of—I mean it's not that I wouldn't—"

He raises his hands. "No explanation required. My fault. My fault totally. God, this is embarrassing." All the blood has reached his face at this point. "Go right ahead and ask, Detective." He nods for emphasis.

"Okay," I say, hoping that if I get down to business, both of us will feel less awkward. "Melanie Phillips. Your waitress."

"Sure." The mention of her name is enough to sober him up. "Great kid. Everyone loved her."

"Well, I'm wondering if anyone seemed to take an interest in her while she worked here."

He looks at the sky, thinks it over. I'm tempted to prompt him with a name, but I want to see if he comes up with it himself.

"Well, I mean, she was very pretty, so lots of guys would stare and stuff. But, like, obsess over her?"

"Yes, obsess."

He runs his hand over his mouth. "Mmm . . . nah, not really. I mean, she and Noah had that breakup, like everybody knows."

Noah. Not the name I was looking for, but since he mentioned it, I might as well see where that goes.

"What did you think about Noah for a suspect?"

"Me? Oh, jeez, I'm no cop. I always liked Noah, tell you the truth."

"I noticed he still eats here, since he's been out."

"Yeah, sure. We get a lot of blue-collar types. Probably because we're cheap."

"But . . . I assume if you thought he did harm to Melanie—"

"Oh, right."

"—you wouldn't let him back in."

"Definitely. I never thought Noah would do something like that. He always seemed like a good guy."

"Okay." I scribble a note in my little pad. "Change of subject. What can you tell me about Aiden Willis?"

"Aiden?" He smiles, shakes his head. "Well, he's a good guy. He's one of a kind, but a good guy."

"Could you be more specific?"

"I mean, he's . . . unusual, I guess. I don't know. Maybe we all are. Good man, though. Good man."

This guy's Mr. Sunshine. *Never speaks ill of his fellow man,* as my favorite bartender would say.

"You said he was unusual."

"Well, I mean—he comes in alone. Sits there and reads some book. Doesn't talk much. Comes in for beers at night sometimes but pretty much keeps to himself. Grew up here. Went to Bridgehampton School. I think Noah did, too."

"What about you?" I ask.

"Me? I grew up in Sag Harbor. Not far."

"You didn't go to school with Aiden and Noah?"

"No, I went to Lanier Academy in East Hampton."

Oh, a private school. A rich kid. I was hoping to talk to someone who went to school with Aiden and Noah.

"You didn't know them growing up?"

"Aiden and Noah? Nope. Hey, Aiden's not some kind of suspect, is he?"

I give a noncommittal shrug. "Just basic questions, at this point."

"I mean, he's kinda odd, but not like that. Odd, but in a funny way, not scary."

That seems to be the prevailing sentiment. I don't remember laughing last night, when he had a shotgun aimed at my head.

"Well, anyway," says Justin, "Aiden didn't kill Melanie."

I snap my focus off my pad to him. "How could you know that?"

"Because he was with me, here," says Justin. "We have a liquor license until two a.m. I was pouring, and Aiden closed down the place with me."

I feel some air deflate from my lungs. "You're sure? You're positive you have those dates lined up? It was a long time ago."

"I'm positive," he says. "The next day, Melanie missed work. We were calling her cell phone, even sent someone over to her condo. Then the cops showed up and told us she was killed the night before at the house on Ocean Drive. They asked me who was here that night. I gave them a list. It wasn't that hard. It was just me and Aiden."

I scribble a note, trying to hide my disappointment.

My biggest lead has just swirled down the drain.

Chapter 73

OFFICER RICKETTS, STILL in patrol uniform, shakes her head as we look out over the Atlantic Ocean. "I still can't believe they did this to you, Murphy."

"You should take my advice and stay away from me."

Ricketts nods and looks over at me, looking younger than her age, her cropped blond hair just long enough to show a hint of curl on the ends. "I'm not so good at taking advice," she says.

"If Isaac ever knew—"

"I'd be fired. I get it."

We are quiet. The sky is darkening and the ocean is reacting in kind. A storm on the way.

"We're supposed to catch the bad guys," Ricketts says. "The day I'm not supposed to do that is the day I look for another job."

I like this girl. She's way more poised and mature than I was as a rookie. And just as stubborn.

I look at her. "Are you sure?"

"Don't ask me that again, Murphy. Just tell me what you need."

"The last Holden was suspected in a number of rapes, right?"

"That's what the book said."

"So let's see if we can find out if anyone filed a criminal charge. Someone must have. Maybe one of his victims got pregnant."

"Okay. What else?"

I shrug. "That's it."

"That's not it," Ricketts says. "We should see what else may have been going on back then, in the early nineties. Missing-persons reports, unsolved murders. The last time you had me do that, I only went back ten years. Now I'll go back to the early nineties."

"To what end?" I ask.

"Who knows? Let's just do it. See what shakes loose."

I let out a long breath. "Ricketts, you're going to make a good detective someday."

"If I don't get fired first."

I take her hand. "That can't happen. I wouldn't be able to live with myself if you got canned for helping me."

She waves me off. "I just want you back on the force. We solve this thing, maybe I'll have my mentor back."

"Let's not get too optimistic."

She looks at me. "You know what you need, Murphy? If I may be so bold."

"Shoot. Be bold."

"You need to get laid."

I let out a laugh. It feels good.

"I was thinking Justin," she says.

I hem and haw. "Yeah, I mean, he's . . ."

"He's really cute. And I saw the way he was looking at you."

I've already told Ricketts about my conversation with Justin today, the substantive part. Now I tell her the personal part.

"He actually said 'A guy can hope'?" She pushes my shoulder. "What do you need, a written invitation?"

"Yeah, I know." I let out a low moan. "Honestly, I mean—he's a really nice guy, but I don't know."

"What, he's too nice?"

I sigh. "Something like that."

"You like the bad boys, don't you? The guys with an edge? The dangerous types?"

"That's my curse."

"Murphy." She puts her hands on my shoulders. "He's a super-nice guy. He runs a diner with incredible food and he could double the prices and still fill the place, but he doesn't. I mean, c'mon. He's hot and he's sweet and he has a crush on you. You're gonna pass on that guy because he's *too nice?*"

I just . . . I just can't see it.

"I don't have time for romance," I say. "I have too much to do."

"I didn't say romance. I said *sex*. Just have dinner one time with the guy and then fuck his lights out. And then, of course, tell me all about it."

"The dinner or the sex?"

"Both."

I shake my head. I just . . .

"You know what you are? You're afraid to be happy," she says.

"Thank you, Doctor."

She hits me on the arm. "I'll get you that research," she says.

"Hey, Ricketts?" I call out to her as she's halfway up the beach. "I don't even know your first name."

She smiles. "It's Lauren."

"Well, thanks, Lauren. Seriously. Thank you."

She nods back at me. "One more piece of advice?" she says. "Get some sleep. You look like crap."

Chapter 74

TWO IN THE morning. The promise of a violent storm no longer just a promise. The windows rattling from the wind and rain, the sky a deep purple.

Pages and pages of notes, all over my desk, pinned up on the wall. I take a sip of wine and arch my back, roll my neck. My head aching, my eyelids heavy.

The answer has to be here. There has to be something. Just keep shaking trees and something will come loose. Keep connecting different dots and you'll find it.

You're getting closer.

Just keep telling myself that.

I'm getting closer . . .

Getting closer . . .

Closer . . .

Let me out

Bam-bam-bam

Let me out

Bam-bam-bam

I can't see can't breathe

Darkness, then penetrating light from above, a shadow blocking it

A face coming into focus, backlit by blinding yellow

A boy, long hair, a hand

Don't touch me, please don't touch

Get away, please don't hurt me

I wanna go home

My head snaps upward, my hands shooting out across the desk, sweeping off papers, knocking the wineglass to the floor with a hollow *clink*. I take a long breath and shake out the cobwebs.

The boy. The long hair. The hand reaching for me into the darkness.

And the face. This time, I saw his face.

A face I've seen before.

The boy in my nightmare is Aiden Willis.

Chapter 75

NOAH WALKER PULLS his Harley up to the curb outside Jenna Murphy's apartment. The streets are still slick from the heavy downpour last night. His sandals squish in the grass on his way up to the door.

He raps on the door and waits, adjusting the satchel over his shoulder.

When the door opens, he sees the face of a ghost.

Jenna's hair is matted and unkempt, her face drawn and pale, her eyes deep-set and dark. A black Yankees T-shirt and men's boxers are all she's wearing.

She squints in the sunlight, doesn't make eye contact with Noah. "You sure about Aiden?" she says as she turns back into her apartment.

"Good morning to you, too." He wishes he'd brought coffee. She looks like she could use some.

The main room of the apartment looks more like an office than residential quarters. Papers everywhere—on the desk perched in the corner, covering the floor, lining the walls. Newspaper clippings, copies of police files scribbled over with notes in Magic Marker, Post-its haphazardly stuck everywhere. Organized in columns for the various victims, Annie Church and Dede Paris, Brittany Halsted, Sally Pfiester, Melanie and Zach, Bonnie Stamos—and Chief Langdon James, her uncle.

"You sure about Aiden?" she asks again, pacing the room, disappearing into her bedroom and coming out again.

"Am I sure Aiden's not a killer? Yes, I'm sure. Why?"

She shakes her head absently, still pacing. "I've been having these . . . nightmares. Ever since I came here."

"What kind of nightmares?"

She throws up her hands. "Like I'm trapped. Enclosed. Pleading to get out. And there's someone above me, a boy, reaching down for me, going to hurt me. And I'm begging, *Please, let me go, don't hurt me,* that kind of thing."

That explains the sleep deprivation he's noticed since he met her. She must have had a doozy of a nightmare last night, because it looks like she didn't sleep much at all.

"Last night, Aiden showed up in the dream."

"Aiden was the boy?" Noah nods. "That's because you have Aiden on the brain, Murphy. You think there's some meaning to your dream? Like, you're assuming the role of one of the victims? Or you're . . . seeing the future or something?"

"How the hell should I know?" She's still pacing; then she stops and puts her hands on the wall. "Sorry. I don't know. I . . . there's probably no meaning to it. I don't know. It's just . . ."

It's just making you crazy, he thinks.

She turns and looks at Noah, sizes him up, narrows her eyes.

"What?" he asks.

"The BB gun shooting at the school," she says. "Back when you were a kid."

"Oh, come *on*, Murphy."

"I'm shaking trees," she says.

"You're what?"

"Tell me." She walks toward him, then stops short, her hands on her hips. She could practically fall over. "Someone did it with you. A second shooter. And then set you up to take the fall. And you let him get away with it. Some kind of . . . code with you. Never rat out your friends or something."

Noah looks down, pinches the bridge of his nose. All these years, all the investigation that took place back when it happened—everyone was sure it was Noah and Noah alone. Nobody ever questioned that. Any evidence to the contrary was swept aside, and the unanimous conclusion was that Noah shot all those kids on the playground, all by his lonesome self.

Not until sixteen, almost seventeen years later, when Detective Jenna Murphy from Manhattan came along and patched together a couple of interviews and some dry reports and reached a different conclusion.

"If you're right," he says, "and I live by the code that you don't rat out your friends, why would I rat them out now?"

She works her jaw, her deep-set eyes burrowing into him.

"What's it matter, Murphy? It doesn't have anything to do with—"

"You were set up," she says. "You were set up for Melanie's and Zach's murders. You were set up for the murder in the woods, the hooker, Bonnie Stamos. You were set up for my uncle's—"

Her voice falters. Her whole body is trembling now.

She clears her throat hard, like an engine struggling to start. "And you were set up to take the fall with the BB gun shooting."

Noah shakes his head. What happened in that school yard doesn't have anything to do with the murders. It was close to seventeen years ago now. She doesn't need to know this.

"This guy is smart," she says. "He's careful. He might be deranged, he might be schizophrenic or a psychopath, but he does *not* make mistakes. He handed you to us as a suspect. Shit, I almost shot you myself, I was so sure you were guilty."

That's true. Something he'll never forget, when she broke into his house after her uncle was attacked.

"Look, I'm grasping at straws, I'm looking for anything I can," she says. "You said you wanted to help. You gave me this bullshit pep talk about—"

"I do want to help." Noah slings his bag off his shoulder. "You didn't even ask me why I'm here. Remember the research assignment you gave me?"

Jenna's eyes move to the satchel.

"You found something," she says.

Chapter 76

"IT'S NOT MUCH," Noah tells me, opening his satchel. "I searched all the public records. Turns out I knew one of the clerks there, someone who grew up down the street from me. She helped."

He removes a manila folder from his bag. "Holden the Sixth was part of three lawsuits in Suffolk County that we know of," he says.

"Anything on paternity?" I ask.

"No, but my friend at the clerk's office said, a lot of times, paternity lawsuits are filed under seal. She said that means the—"

"The names are redacted from the lawsuit," I say. "Kept out of the public domain. So it's possible there was a paternity suit, but we wouldn't know it."

"Yeah. I made copies of the three lawsuits I *did* find. They aren't criminal cases. They're civil. One is a property dispute and one is a defamation suit, whatever that means, and the last one is a lawsuit for assault and battery brought by a neighbor, some guy who said Holden punched him at a party."

He hands me copies of the three civil complaints. He's no lawyer, and neither am I, though a cop knows a thing or two about the legal system.

"Nobody claiming rape, nobody claiming paternity," I say. "So we don't know anything."

"We know one thing." Noah takes the papers and flips through each of them to a particular page.

He hands them to me. Each of these lawsuits has a sheet attached to the front of it, with the names of the attorneys representing the plaintiff and defendant.

"We know the name of Holden's lawyer," Noah says.

Chapter 77

THE WAITER opens the bottle of wine and hands the cork to Justin, who defers to me. The waiter pours an inch of Pinot into my glass and I swirl it, sniff it, taste it, and nod my approval.

"Cheers," says Justin, looking very nice in a white shirt with an open collar, and a blue sport coat. We clink our glasses.

It's a nice place near the intersection of Main Street and the turnpike—not very far, really, from Justin's own restaurant, Tasty's. But this is more than a slight step up from his diner—dark oak and caramel leather, dim lighting, people dressed as formally as it gets in the Hamptons.

"What made you change your mind?" he asks me.

I shrug. "My friend told me I should have dinner with you."

That, and I've gone about seventy-two hours straight obsessing about the case. A little battery recharging may be in order.

"Well, I'm glad." He takes a drink of the wine. "Hey, this is good."

"It *is* good." If I saw the price correctly on the menu, this bottle was over two hundred dollars, a 2011 Pinot from the Russian River Valley. All I know about wine is what I learned from Matty, who would always line up the year it was bottled with the vintage and location to find the "perfect" bottle to pair with our meal.

"I gotta say, I don't know anything about wine," says Justin. "I'm the kind of guy who picks based on the label." He laughs at himself.

"Me too."

An awkward silence follows. He seems a little nervous. Not so adept at small talk, that's for sure. But that part, I like. I've had enough of the smooth talkers.

Still, with two people who aren't good at chatter, there is a palpable sense of relief when the appetizers arrive—chilled zucchini soup for me, burrata with peaches for him.

"So what brought you to the Hamptons?" he asks.

I stop on that one. "I thought everyone knew about that," I say.

"Well, I remember the trial," he says. "Some trouble you had with the NYPD. But I always figure, there's two sides to every story. I mean, if you want."

An initial buzz is kicking in from the wine, maybe loosening me up a little.

"I was working undercover," I say. "Going after meth dealers. High up on the chain. I got close to the top guy."

"How'd you do that? Get close to him." He settles his elbows on the table.

"I slept with him," I say. "I became his girlfriend."

"Wow." He leans back. "Wow."

"Yeah, it was pretty intense. Only way to do it, though. These guys are wired tight. They don't trust anybody. But when it comes to sex, they don't use their brains so much."

"That's—that's pretty—wow."

"So anyway," I say, "I came to find out that some of the people helping the boss were cops. There was a whole ring set up. The cops were running protection for the dealers. So I sent that information back to headquarters. I reported it. I made a big mistake, though."

"What?"

"I didn't report it to IAD. Internal Affairs."

"Who'd you report it to?"

"My boss, my lieutenant."

"Why was that a mistake?"

I gesture with my wineglass, take a sip. "Two days later, totally out of the blue, three cops are suddenly claiming that I skimmed off the top of a drug raid before I went undercover."

"Skimmed off the . . ."

"They said I stole money and drugs from drug dealers. That I arrested them and only turned in some of the money and some of the drugs—kept the rest for myself."

"That kind of thing happens?"

"It happens if you're a dirty cop," I say. "The drug dealers aren't going to complain, right? If you're busted, would you rather be busted with a thousand grams of cocaine and a hundred thousand dollars, or with ten grams and ten thousand bucks? Either way, you're not getting any of it back. But you get a lesser sentence this way. It's a pretty classic shakedown. If you're a dirty cop."

He nods slowly.

"Which I am not," I say. "I touched a nerve in the department, I told the wrong person, and they wanted to silence me. So they trumped up these charges and gave me a choice—resign or go to prison."

We don't speak for a while. I drain my first glass of the Pinot. *Easy, Murphy. Don't let the emotions bubble to the surface.*

"Do you regret it?" he asks.

I let out air. "Do I regret not staying and fighting for my job? Every single day."

"But it was three cops against one," he says.

I nod. "That's what Lang said. He said I couldn't beat those odds. He said, 'Get out while you still have your badge, come work for me.' So I did."

"Well, I'm glad you did. Hope you like it here."

I shrug. "I won't be here much longer," I say. "I'm just staying until I figure out who killed my uncle."

His smile loses a few degrees of wattage. It seems he might have had some ideas about me. I figured I should let him know, up front, that I'm not in his long-term plans.

For the main course, I have scallops with sweet corn and shishito peppers. They are absolutely delicious—but really no better than the ones at Tasty's.

"They get their seafood from the same place we do," Justin says.

"Really? You guys and this restaurant?"

"Yeah," he says, cocking his head, surprised at my surprise.

I put down my fork. "Your food is as good as this place's," I say. "But you can't be operating Tasty's at a profit with the prices you're charging."

"Who said I was operating at a profit?" He smiles and takes the last sip of his wine. He calls over the waiter and orders a second bottle.

"Okay, so what's your angle?" I ask. "This whole man-of-the-people thing about not raising prices for ten years."

"Angle? Why does there have to be an angle?"

I look him over. Good looks, private schools growing up, an expensive dinner tonight, a restaurant that loses money . . .

"I'm no saint," he says. "We come close to breaking even some years. It's . . . fun to have a place where everyone comes and enjoys themselves. It's fun for me, too."

"There's gotta be something wrong with you," I say. "Are you sure you're not a serial killer or something?"

"I never said I wasn't." He smiles and wipes his mouth with his napkin. "You've been a cop too long, Jenna. You only see bad people. There are lots of good people in the world, too."

Maybe he's right. Maybe not everyone in this world has an angle. Maybe I've been so closed off in the cocoon of crime and punishment that I've lost sight of some things. Maybe losing my badge is a good thing.

Maybe there's hope for me yet.

Chapter 78

"I'LL WALK YOU to the door," Justin says, pulling his Jaguar up to the curb. It's a nice ride, this car.

Nice dinner. Nice car. Nice guy.

"This was fun," he says as he steps up onto the porch.

My cell phone vibrates in my purse.

I stand at my door, fishing for my keys.

"So listen." Justin claps his hands together. "I had a great time. I had a . . . great time. It was a . . ."

"Great time?" I rise up on my toes and kiss him softly on the lips. He responds, but awkwardly, his hand touching my arm, unsure whether he should open his mouth.

Shy and clumsy.

"It was fun for me, too," I say as we draw back. His face has lost a bit of color.

Very shy.

"Call me," I say.

He nods, then cocks his head. "Why would I call you?"

I draw back. "Oh, I mean, if you want to . . . have dinner again."

"We already had dinner. Why would we do it again?"

I stare at him, at a loss for words.

"Gotcha." He breaks into laughter. "You should see the look on your face."

Score one for him. He did get me. A little corny . . . but he got me.

"I will call you, Jenna. For sure."

He pauses, like he's thinking about another kiss, but he steps off the porch and heads to his car, whistling. I don't know very many people who whistle. I don't know anybody who whistles.

Snap assessment: nice guy, but not a lot of sparks.

Then again, that's always been my problem. I look for chemistry right away and if I don't feel it, I walk. Maybe that can develop over time. Maybe if I just let someone in . . . someone really nice . . .

Someone without an angle . . .

Justin drives away with a brief toot of his horn.

Yeah, I don't know . . . maybe . . .

I walk inside my tornado of an apartment and fish my cell phone out of my purse.

The call was from Lauren Ricketts. I punch her up and she answers on the second ring.

"Murphy," she says.

"Ricketts. What's up?"

Suddenly my enjoyable Saturday night with Justin is over, and I'm slipping back into the darkness, the quagmire, slogging through evidence and driving myself crazy.

"I finished going through criminal complaints and missing-persons reports," she says. "I went back to the eighties and got through the mid-nineties."

"And?" I say, my heartbeat kicking up. "Did you find any criminal complaints?"

"No. Nobody ever filed a criminal charge against Holden the Sixth."

"Shit." I really thought that was promising. "And what about unsolveds or missing-persons bulletins?"

"No unsolveds that look interesting, not from that time period."

"And no missing-persons reports that looked interesting?"

"Just one from 1994," she says. "I guess it would go under the category of interesting. I wish you'd prepared me for it."

"Prepared you for what?" I ask. "Who was the missing person?"

A pause on the other end of the line.

"You don't know?" she asks.

"Ricketts, just freakin' tell me," I say. "Who went missing?"

Another pause. As if she's debating. As if she's thrown for a loss. And then, finally, she speaks.

She says, "*You* did, Murphy. You were the missing person."

Chapter 79

SUNDAY NIGHT, 7 p.m. The sun almost completely fallen now, a blanket of darkness, the air mild and pleasant.

April Fools' Day, which feels appropriate. I was a fool ever to have returned to this place.

I pull my car into Uncle Langdon's driveway just as Aunt Chloe is locking the house up. Some final boxes to remove, some papers to sign, before the sale of the house goes through this month.

"I was so glad you called," she says. "We could grab a quick bite . . ."

She has a big smile on her face, until she gets a look at mine.

I stop short in front of her, no hug, no nothing.

"What happened to me here in 1994?" I ask. "When I was eight years old."

Her face falls. Her mouth works, but no words come out.

"I asked Lang why my family stopped coming to the

Hamptons when I was a kid," I say. "He never told me. 'A story for another time,' he said. And then I asked you, and you said, 'If you don't know, I don't know.' Whatever that cryptic bullshit is supposed to mean."

"It means just what I said." Chloe looks me over. "I don't know what happened. Nobody knows. Apparently, not even you."

"I saw a missing-persons report, Chloe. From July of 1994. It ended seven hours after it began."

Chloe slowly nods. "That's right. 'Seven hours of hell,' your mother called it. You went missing. You were playing down the street, just right down this street. And then you were gone. Nobody could find you." She places a hand at the base of her throat. "It still gives me a sickening feeling when I remember it. We looked everywhere. Lang had the entire Southampton Town Police Department searching for you. Your mother and I searched for you. Your father and Ryan searched for you. Everyone searched for you."

"And then?"

"And then . . . we found you." Her eyes shine with brimming tears. "Seven hours later. We found you on the beach. You were just . . . sitting there, looking peacefully out at the ocean."

I roll my hand impatiently, like I want her to continue.

"I don't know what else to tell you," she says. "You wouldn't tell us anything. Lang said you were in shock. We took you to the hospital and they checked you out. Nobody had . . . done anything . . . or hurt you—"

"No evidence of any assault," I say, "sexual or otherwise."

"No, nothing like that," she says. "Just this."

She takes my hand, turns it over, palm up, and traces the small scar on my hand, about an inch long.

"You had that cut on your hand."

"That's how I got that cut?" I look at Chloe. "Mom always said I got it chopping a tomato when I was little."

Chloe nods. "Sometimes we tell our children little white lies to protect them," she says. "Anyway, your family left the island that day and never came back to the Hamptons. They asked you about it for a while afterward. Days, weeks. But you wouldn't talk about it. Or couldn't. And then . . . life went on. Finally, they just dropped it. The nightmare with a happy ending."

I don't remember any of this. Or at least, I thought I didn't remember.

"I was at the beach the whole time?"

Chloe looks at me like she's unsure of the answer.

"For God's sake, Chloe, speak."

She breathes out. "No. That's the thing. The spot where they found you—I had personally looked there with your mother. It was one of the first places we checked. I'm sure of it. You weren't there at first."

"So I wasn't at the beach, and then seven hours later, I was."

She nods.

"But you don't know where I was for those seven hours."

She shakes her head, her expression grim. "Seven hours of hell."

I look over her shoulder at Lang's house, now empty, soon to be sold to a young couple with a baby. A new life in a new town. New memories, new dreams.

"Get in the car," I say.

"Jenna—"

"Get in the car, Chloe."

"Why?"

"You're going to show me."

The drive doesn't take long. She directs me, but I'm beyond being surprised at this point. There are any number of roads that lead to the sweeping beach, but I know which one before she says it.

I drive down Ocean Drive and park in the parking lot and make her get out and walk onto the beach until she shows me the exact spot where I was found.

"Right here," she says. "I'll never forget the sound your mother made when she saw you sitting here."

Those nightmares—they aren't random spooky dreams. They aren't some glimpse into the future. They aren't telepathic visions of other victims' experiences.

They're my memories. Repressed memories.

I look out over the ocean, then turn my back to it, looking north.

Looking at the second house from the end, looming over the coastline. The house at 7 Ocean Drive. The Gothic facade, the spears aimed at the sky.

The memories, the flashbacks are at their most intense when I'm inside that house. Paralyzing panic attacks, every time I set foot inside that mansion.

That's where I was for seven hours, when I was a little girl.

I was inside the Murder House.

Chapter 80

MY CAR BUMPS violently over the rough road, sending my head banging against the roof. I stop on the shoulder, not wanting to pull into his driveway—not wanting to announce myself in advance.

I remember you now, he said to me when I accosted him at the cemetery.

I find his driveway, walk up to the front porch, and reach the door.

"Open up, Aiden!" Pounding the door so hard that my knuckles start to bleed.

Nothing.

You shouldn't have come back, he said to me when he caught me looking into his basement.

My chest heaving, my emotions skittering about, I move to the window closest to the front door and look inside.

The window is open, a screen letting in fresh air. I lean in, kick the screen off, push it into the house, and get one leg and my body through the window.

Just as Aiden is rushing past me, panic on his face.

He cries out in surprise and tries to avoid me, but I grab hold of his arm, getting a poor grip, enough to spin him slightly before he wrests his arm free. I'm off balance, my back leg just coming through the open window, and I fall to the floor as he continues to run.

"What did you do to me?" I shout as I get to my feet and race after him.

He reaches a door—looks like a bedroom door—and opens it and closes it quickly. I reach it a moment later, just as I hear the *click* of the dead bolt.

I pound on the door.

"What did you do to me? What did you do to me when I was a little girl?"

Punching the door like it's his face, the blood from my knuckles smeared across the white wood.

I rear back and give the door a kick. An interior door, not as substantial as an outside door. And it's been a while, but once upon a time when I was training, I had a pretty good kick.

I kick at the doorknob and the adjacent wood. After three furious blows, it splinters, and then my foot breaks through. I reach inside and unlock the dead bolt and the button on the knob.

He could have anything inside there. He could have the shotgun. He could have a knife. Nothing I've done so far is smart, fueled as I am by insatiable rage—but I charge through, anyway.

A dark room, but fresh air sweeping in.

The window, open.

He escaped out the back window.

I climb through the window and run into the backyard, into a vacuum of blackness.

He's gone. This is his home turf. He probably knows every nook and cranny of those woods behind his house. He's long gone.

The darkness, suddenly interrupted by colored, flashing lights.

A car engine, tires crunching over gravel.

A patrol car, pulling into Aiden's driveway.

I move to the side of the house and peek around to the front. I hear a car door open and close. I hear footsteps, but not coming my way. Moving into the house.

I place myself flat against the house, not moving an inch. The only sound the gentle swaying of the trees in the wind.

Then a light comes on in the bedroom, where I just came from. I hear the footsteps inside.

A head pops out of the window, looking outside. I hold my breath.

It's our beloved chief of police, Isaac Marks, illuminated by the light of the room. He's only twenty feet or so away from me, but I'm bathed in darkness and far to his right—I don't think he can make me.

"Shit," he says into the darkness.

A noise; then I hear beeps. He's dialing a cell phone.

"You okay?" Isaac says. "Where are you? No, she's gone. I don't know, do you? She said what? Okay. Don't worry about her. I'll take care of her. I said I'll take care of this. You gotta relax. Listen to me . . ."

His voice fading as he leaves the room, as he moves into the interior of the house.

Chapter 81

AFTER WAITING OVER an hour in Aiden's backyard, I head back to my car. Aiden's not coming back, and Isaac left long ago.

My car is tucked away on the shoulder of the road down the street. Did Isaac spot it? I don't see an ambush awaiting me. No doubt there's an APB out, possibly a warrant for my arrest.

I don't know what Isaac has planned. I don't know what he meant when he told Aiden he would "take care" of me.

And I'm not anxious to find out.

I have to get my car out of sight. I have to get *myself* out of sight.

I pull my car into his driveway and ring the doorbell. Nobody likes unannounced visitors at midnight.

"Who's there?" he calls through the door.

"It's Murphy."

When he opens the door, Noah Walker is wearing an undershirt and sweat pants. He's clutching a hand towel, his face still dripping with water.

As always—that heat across my chest.

There. That's the difference. That's the spark. That's what's missing with Justin.

No time for that now, Murphy.

"You okay?" Noah asks.

"No," I say. "I can't go home. The police are looking for me."

"The pol— Well, come in." He moves out of the way to let me in. "So what happened?" he asks.

"I broke into Aiden's house," I say. "I know it was him."

"What, that dream again?" Noah closes the door and locks it.

"He did something to me," I say. "A long time ago. Back in ninety-four. The dream is a flashback, Noah. It's a memory. I saw the police report myself."

"Then why wasn't Aiden arrested or—"

"Aiden's not in the report. I didn't tell anybody anything. I couldn't. But now I know."

"Look, Aiden's a strange bird," he says, "but he's a sweet kid."

"That's what everyone says. That's what *everyone* says." I grip my hair as if I'm going to yank it out at the roots, feeling a buzz of nervous energy. "What happened to me was in 1994," I say. "And in 1995, there was the school shooting. I know Aiden was involved in the first of those. Was he involved in the second?"

Noah's head drops. "Murphy—"

"Tell me, Noah. Tell me what happened in that school yard."

"Let me make you some coffee or—"

"Fuck coffee," I spit. "I don't give a shit about some stupid code or promise you made seventeen years ago. People we care about have died. More will die. Was Aiden a part of that school shooting or wasn't he?"

Flustered, Noah puts his hands on his head. Looking off in the distance. Probably pondering the importance of a promise made, or maybe just reliving what happened back then.

Finally, he drops his arms, clears his throat.

"I always met Aiden by that bench before school," he says. "Back then, people used to pick on him. I tried to help him out. So we'd meet at that bench and walk into school together."

I suck in a breath. *Aiden*. I knew it.

"So that day, I sat on the bench, listening to music on my headphones. Then all of a sudden, a gym teacher, Coach Cooper, is running up to me and telling me I have to come with him, I'm in big trouble."

I stare at him, waiting for more.

"You didn't participate?" I ask. "You had nothing do with the school shooting?"

He shrugs. "I didn't even know it was happening. I was on the other side of the school, down the road, blasting music in my ears."

I step closer to him. "What about the rifle they found in the bushes behind you?"

"Don't know anything about it. Never saw it."

"And—what did Aiden say to you afterward?"

"Nothing." Noah raises his hands. "I was suspended for the rest of the year. I didn't see Aiden for months.

When I did—I mean, what was there to say? I don't rat people out. And it's not like I knew Aiden had something to do with it. I *still* don't know that. I just know I didn't."

I start pacing. "Reports said the shooter—the one they saw, over by the woods—was wearing a Spider-Man costume. Just like you were."

"Yeah."

"Did Aiden know you were going to wear a Spider-Man costume to school?"

Noah thinks about that. "Probably. Yeah, he probably did."

"And it never occurred to you that Aiden set you up?"

"It crossed my mind. But I didn't know. And I'm not a rat."

I bring a hand to my forehead, push my hair off my face.

"The second shooter," I mumble.

"Yeah, you keep going on about that," says Noah. "You're sure two people did this?"

I nod. "That's the only way it could've happened. So if you didn't do it . . ."

"Then someone else helped Aiden," says Noah.

And after tonight, I think I know who. I think I know who was working with Aiden, who's been working with him all along.

The man who was in Noah's house with my uncle when Lang planted the incriminating evidence to frame Noah.

The man who always seems to show up conveniently to rush to Aiden's rescue.

The man who demanded that I stop investigating the school shooting, my uncle's murder, all of it.

The man who told Aiden tonight, *I'll take care of this.*

"I have to go," I say.

"No, don't." Noah puts a hand on my shoulder. "You said yourself, you can't go home."

"I can't stay here."

"You could, actually," he says, his voice quieter.

I look at him, his eyes peering directly into mine.

He puts his hand on my face and moves in for a kiss.

Like a surge of electricity through my body. Realizing that I've always wanted this. His hands in my hair, my hand cupped around his neck, letting myself surrender—

"No," I say, breaking away. "I have to go. They'll look for me here. It might not be the first place Isaac looks, but he'll get here eventually."

"So let him."

"Why?" I gather myself, fix my hair. "So we both get in trouble?"

He concedes that. "Where will you go?"

I don't know. Hotel, not an option—no cash to my name, and using a credit card would be the same as handing the address to Isaac. Ricketts's house, negative. Uncle Lang's house, nope, I already gave back my keys.

Someone I can trust, but close by, so I don't have to drive the streets very long.

"Justin," I say.

"Justin . . . Rivers? The guy who owns Tasty's?"

I nod, suddenly feeling awkward admitting that to someone I just kissed.

"I . . . didn't know," says Noah, taking a step back.

"No, it's not like that," I say. "I mean, we went on one date."

Noah's eyes trail away. "Okay. I understand. He's a nice guy."

"Hey," I say, and when he looks back at me, I grab his shirt and draw him in and kiss him hard.

Then I pull away and leave his house.

Chapter 82

I PULL MY car into the lot at Tasty's Diner and park around the back, out of sight. There's only one other car in the lot, Justin's Jaguar. I walk in and find him behind the bar, reading something on his laptop.

I admit—one of the reasons I came here tonight was the small chance that I might run into Aiden Willis, who apparently spends a lot of nights at Tasty's drinking. But no luck. Justin is here alone.

"Hey there," he says when he looks up, not unhappy to see me.

"Slow night?" I ask.

"It picks up in the summer," he says. He looks me over. "You doing okay?"

I take a long breath.

"You must not be," he says, coming around the counter, walking up to me, unsure of how close to get, whether to touch me—the whole awkward thing again.

I give him the short version of my lovely evening,

that in the course of investigating my uncle's murder, I may have bent the law tonight and found myself on the wrong end of an arrest warrant.

"I don't know for a fact that I'm wanted for questioning," I say. "Or that an arrest warrant was issued. But my guess is they're looking for me."

"You need a place to stay," he says. "You can't go home."

"Well . . ."

"That's no problem. You can stay at my place. I have plenty of room."

"If you're sure it's not a bother," I say. "Technically, you wouldn't be harboring a fugitive. But you might want to give this some thought."

He thinks about it for a moment. "I've always wanted to harbor a fugitive."

I laugh, in spite of the circumstances.

He looks at the clock on the wall. It's half past one in the morning. "Let's go," he says. "Nobody's coming at this point."

We take our own cars. I follow him into East Hampton, checking my mirrors at all times, feeling very conspicuous out here on Main Street at this hour.

But I don't see any patrol cars.

Justin has a house by the ocean, a beautiful two-story cedar A-frame. I park my car next to his in the garage and he lowers the door, shielding my car from any inquisitive law enforcement.

Inside, he leads me to a family room. What a place. Clean and spacious and updated. He directs me to a couch that's more comfortable than my bed, perched next to a floor-to-ceiling window overlooking a large backyard.

I sink into the couch, exhausted. Next to me, on a side table, are two framed photographs of Justin as a child. The first with his mother and father, at a Yankees game. Justin must have been, what, four or five? All of them wearing Yankees caps, smiling for the camera. Justin looking like a miniature version of his father.

The second, just the boy and his mother, when Justin is older, probably ten or so, on the beach, the Atlantic Ocean as a backdrop.

"Nice family," I say.

"Yeah." Justin nods at the photographs. "That's the last photo I have of my father. He died two days later. Crazy, right?"

"Gosh, I'm sorry," I say. "How did he die? Not to pry."

"No, that's okay." He waves me off. "He had a brain aneurysm. Healthy as a horse, worked out regularly. Then all of a sudden, he dropped dead. He just dropped."

"I'm . . . so sorry."

"Yeah." Justin puts his hands on his hips. "The truth? I don't even remember him. I was only four. That's why I keep the photograph around." He waves his hand around the room. "And that's how I have money. A healthy life insurance policy."

"Sure."

He works his jaw. "I'd give it all back to have a father." He claps his hands, shakes himself free of the memory. "Now, Miss Murphy, have you eaten?"

"Have I—oh, listen, that's not—"

"Did you eat, ma'am? It's a simple yes-or-no question."

I chuckle again. "No."

He nods in the direction of his kitchen. "I have cold cuts and some cheese and crackers. Maybe even some fruit. I'd like some myself."

"That sounds great," I concede.

He starts to leave but turns and spins. "And what are we drinking? I can't tell if you need coffee or wine."

I look at him.

"Wine," we say together.

He returns first with two glasses of Chardonnay. "Cheers," he says. "Our second date."

I realize my hands are shaking as I clink glasses with him. "You're trembling," he says. He puts his hand on my free one.

"You're safe here, Jenna. Just relax."

I nod and take a sip. It's on the sweeter side, but alcohol feels good right now, a little numbing of the anxiety.

"I'll get the snacks." He pops off the couch and heads into the kitchen.

Justin's right. Isaac would never look for me here. I'm safe for tonight.

But so much to do. I have to reach out to Ricketts to see what my status is. I need to find out more about Holden VI. I have his lawyer's name, but—

No. Justin's right about that, too. I have to slow down. If I don't get some sleep, I'm going to fall apart.

I look over the room. Picture windows on two sides. Expensive leather furniture. A big-screen TV mounted on one wall. An oak bookcase lining another wall.

A nice, handsome, rich guy. Yeah, run away from this one, Murphy. You wouldn't want to be happy and comfortable, would you?

"You look more relaxed now," he says. He's carrying a tray of cheese and salami, some sliced tomatoes and grapes, a small fancy knife, the Chardonnay bottle tucked under one arm.

He sets it all down and sits next to me on the couch.

"Now eat," he says. "And drink. And be merry."

I pick a couple of grapes off the bunch and pop them in my mouth.

"You're spoiling me," I say. "I show up unannounced, with the cops on my tail, and you spoil me."

When he doesn't respond right away, I turn to him. He's watching me.

"Maybe I like spoiling you," he says, touching my hair.

Is this guy for real? Are there actually guys like this out there? In that other world, I mean, the one Justin mentioned, where people are truly decent and honest?

And handsome, too.

He leans into me slowly, giving me the chance to decide, and I lean into him as well. This kiss is better than last time, less inhibited, more natural, each of us more at ease.

He pulls back. "You can stay here as long as you need to," he says. "You're safe here."

And then we both hear it, footsteps from a distance.

From behind us, outside.

And then a piercing smash, as something—or someone—comes crashing through the picture window.

Chapter 83

SHARDS OF GLASS everywhere, something hard striking my head, and Justin and I are thrown from the couch as another body sails into us.

All three of us hit the hardwood floor.

Darkness.

Chaos and shouting and thumping and grunting and smashing.

Darkness.

I open my eyes, my head reeling, my vision blurred.

Justin and . . .

Aiden.

Struggling on the floor. Aiden on top, with the knife raised. Justin grabbing his arm to hold him off.

Telling myself to move, begging my arms and legs to work, the room angled sideways, spinning—

Move.

I lunge forward, both hands aiming for the knife. The knife, the most important thing, disarm the suspect, disable the weapon.

All my body weight, plowing into Aiden, both hands gripping his wrist, sending Aiden and me over Justin to the floor. I hit the floor again, hard, colorful bursts dancing around my eyes.

But I have the knife.

Behind me, the shuffling of feet. With everything I can muster, I manage to crane my neck around.

Just as Aiden Willis is climbing up on the couch and jumping out through the window, the same way he came.

Justin moans. Blood coming from his forehead, his breathing shallow.

Around us, chaos. A piece of lawn furniture, the one that helped Aiden break through the window, the one that smacked me in the temple, lying by the bookcase. The glass table overturned. Food everywhere. Broken glass littering the couch and floor.

And blood. Justin's blood. And mine, some of which is spilling into my eyes right now from the head wound.

"Are you . . . okay?" I ask.

"Yeah," he says, short of breath. He props himself up on his elbows. Several cuts across his cheeks and forehead from the glass. Nothing too serious, nothing life-threatening. "How about you?"

"Were you cut?" I crawl toward him. "By the knife, I mean."

He shakes his head. He looks about as stunned as I am. "What the hell just happened?"

The wind gusting through the open, shattered window.

"We have to call the police," I say, just now catching my breath.

"But . . ." Justin forces himself to sit up, grimacing. "If there's a warrant for your arrest, you can't be—"

"It doesn't matter. We have to report this."

He reaches over and grabs my hand. I squeeze back. After a moment, we help each other to our feet. He brings me close, hugging me, our chests heaving, our hearts pounding in tandem.

"I'm . . . so sorry, Justin," I say into his chest. "I brought this to you. I never should have come here."

"No, no." He cradles my head with his hand. "I want you here."

"I think . . . you just saved my life," I say.

"I'm just glad you're okay. And here I told you . . . you were safe."

I close my eyes and nestle in the comfort of his arms.

I *was* safe. Or at least, I should have been safe. How did Aiden even know I was here? I wasn't followed in my car. I checked the rearview mirror the whole time for patrol cars. The streets were deserted. Nobody followed me by car.

So how did Aiden know?

Nobody knew I was coming here.

Then my eyes pop open.

A chill courses through me.

One person knew.

Chapter 84

THE EAST HAMPTON Town Police respond to Justin's call. I know some members of that force from working on the multijurisdictional drug task force, but I don't know any of the ones who arrive at the scene. It's clear the officers know who I am when I give them my name, thanks to the Noah Walker trial. They are respectful and courteous as they scribble their notes and take photographs and scan the living room and backyard for evidence.

I sit quietly for hours, letting them do their work, waiting for one of them to inform me that there's a warrant outstanding for my arrest, or an APB, from the STPD. But it doesn't happen. No handcuffs come out. No perp walk. They just promise to keep us updated on their investigation and leave.

An armed invasion in East Hampton is something the cops take seriously, so I know they're going to be looking hard for Aiden now.

Which also means that, if Aiden has a single

functioning brain cell in his head, he's in the wind now. Gone. Skedaddled.

"I'm sorry about this," I say to Justin. "He was after me, not you. I brought him to your house."

"He brought himself." Justin touches my arm. "You're the good guy, remember?"

Not sure about that. I'd say *Justin's* the good guy. And dammit, I really wish my feelings for him went deeper than that. I wish I could manufacture some chemistry, a spark between us.

The wind whips up, straining the large pieces of cardboard that we used to cover the shattered window.

"I have to go," I say.

"Stay. It's after four in the morning. And you can't go home."

I probably *can* go home, actually. Apparently, Isaac's plan to "take care of" me doesn't include issuing a warrant for my arrest for breaking into Aiden's house.

So yeah, I can probably go home. But I won't. Not yet.

Aiden's surely not home, after all. What better time to visit his house again?

Chapter 85

I PARK MY car on the shoulder of the road, just as I did last night, and I approach his house with caution, just as before.

First blush, I see nothing different about Aiden's house. The front window through which I climbed, almost grabbing Aiden as he raced past me to his bedroom, is still open. If Aiden had come back, surely he would have closed it.

Same deal in the backyard. His bedroom window still open.

Isaac didn't close up the house? Not his job, I suppose. And he was probably distracted.

Or maybe not. Maybe he knew I'd come back. Maybe I'm walking into a trap.

The front window would be an easier entry point, but the backyard is more private, nothing but a sloping yard and swaying trees, and total darkness.

I climb into the bedroom and stand for a moment, silent. Hard to hear much of anything inside the house.

Wind coming in from windows in the front and back, simultaneously, like the entire house is whistling to me.

Daylight will come in an hour. I want to be home by then.

Start with the bedroom. A battered dresser with a framed photograph on top, one of those side-by-side frames. On the left, a beautiful young woman, probably in her late teens, with strawberry-blond hair and elegant features. On the right, the same woman, propped up against pillows in a hospital bed, her face pale, her hair unkempt, no makeup, but a radiant, beaming smile as she holds a newborn. Pretty much a standard postbirth hospital photo.

I remove the hospital photo and flip it over. On the back, handwritten in cheap blue ink:

Aiden and Mommy, 6-8-81

Aiden as a baby. And this very attractive woman, his mother. He doesn't look a thing like her.

Then again, I haven't seen the father yet.

I replace the photos and open some drawers, having no interest in his clothes or underwear but hoping for anything else that might be tucked away in here.

When I get to the final drawer, I don't find clothes at all. I find a small photo album, a cheap one you'd get at a convenience store with plastic sleeves to hold the photos.

Most of them are of his mother, going back as far as the hospital photo. Little Aiden, with those raccoon eyes even as an infant, appears once or twice. And I get the first shot of the father, his cheek pressed against Aiden's, smiling for the camera. A strong resemblance to Aiden, deep-set eyes and straw-colored hair, not by any means a handsome man.

But the mother dominates these photos. About twenty photos in all. Starting with the hospital and moving forward, chronologically I assume, but—

But she looks different as time moves on in these photos. Not older, but different. Hard to tell how much she has aged—not too much, a year or two, at most—but a definite change. Her eyes darker, deeper. Looking more gaunt, more tired.

Sick? Can't tell, but—darker, for sure. More troubled, more weary, as the photos progress, like I'm watching the story of her decline in time-lapse photography.

And then the last photo, her head turned from the camera, her hand raised in a *stop* gesture, as if she didn't want to be photographed.

And a baby bump, unmistakable, protruding from her belly, beneath her black T-shirt.

My heartbeat kicks up. A second child?

The last page doesn't contain photos. It contains two news clippings, one of them a vertical column, the other merely a headline and photo. Old articles, each of them, faded, with the crispy texture of aged newspaper.

The vertical column, stapled to the album page, has this headline:

Hit-and-Run Kills BH Woman

They're talking about Aiden's mother. Gloria Willis,

age thirty, of Bridgehampton, pronounced dead at Southampton Hospital after being hit by a car on Sugar Hill Road the previous night. The article claims she had several priors for prostitution and drug possession. Her blood analysis revealed the presence of narcotics and alcohol in her system at the time of her death.

The article is cut out of the bottom quarter of a newspaper page, so there's no date. But it can't be that hard to find out when Aiden's mother died.

Gloria Willis was a drug addict and a prostitute?

Holden VI liked prostitutes. It seemed to be a family trait, in fact.

The other news clipping isn't even an article. It's a photo, likewise ripped from the center of the newspaper and thus undated.

The photo shows Uncle Lang, in his chief's uniform, holding a child swaddled in blankets.

Beneath it, this caption:

Newborn Abandoned at Police Station

Southampton Town Police Chief Langdon James holds a newborn child, left abandoned at the entrance to the Bridgehampton substation last night. The infant will be turned over to the Suffolk County Division of Child Protective Services.

What does this all mean? Is this abandoned child Aiden? No. No, of course not. There are photographs of Gloria and Aiden in the hospital at birth.

The baby bump. The second child.

I close the photo album and leave the bedroom. In the kitchen, there is a door that could possibly be a door to a pantry, but my money says it's a door to the basement.

The basement with those wax figures, arranged perfectly, like a family portrait.

It's time I got a better look at them.

Chapter 86

I OPEN THE basement door, flip on the switch, and head downstairs.

The basement is unfinished, with an aging washer and dryer, an unused sink.

I walk toward the back of the basement, the part I saw through the open window last time. But this time, the lights are on.

The creepy wax figures, the Norman Rockwell setting around a coffee table, the faux fireplace.

On the love seat, the wax figure of the man, in a tweed coat, hair greased back, beady eyes, looking a lot like the man in the photo album.

In the rocking chair, the woman, seated and wearing a shawl over her shoulders—a dead ringer for Aiden's mother.

A third chair, empty. For Aiden?

For Aiden to sit down here and play "let's pretend" with his family?

Weird. Creepy.

Sad, actually.

I get a closer look at the woman and see, for the first time, something I didn't notice when I was shining a flashlight in here from the backyard.

On the floor, next to the woman's chair.

A tiny toy crib, for an infant.

Not a wax figure this time, just a doll—a naked doll, a tiny, bald newborn, swaddled in blankets.

A newborn.

Trying to connect it now.

Aiden at the cemetery, urinating on the tombstone of Holden VI.

Holden VI, the man notorious for frequenting prostitutes.

Gloria Willis, a prostitute—in that photo, pregnant with a second child.

The caption from that photograph in the paper: NEWBORN ABANDONED AT POLICE STATION.

"Shit," I mumble. "That's it."

Gloria Willis had two children. Aiden first, then a child she gave up at birth, abandoned anonymously at the police station.

And why would she abandon her son at the police station anonymously?

Because she didn't want him? Because she didn't want a child whose father was a monster? Because she didn't want the father to ruin the son?

I don't know. There are still some questions.

But at last, finally, I might have a few answers.

Aiden Willis had a brother. Or more accurately, a half brother.

Whose biological father was Holden Dahlquist VI.

And somehow, in some way, that abandoned boy found his way back into dear old Dad's life.

Book VI

BRIDGEHAMPTON, 1993–94

Chapter 87

TONIGHT IT WILL be the beach. Sometimes it's a park, sometimes one of the taverns as it's closing and drunk patrons are stumbling out. The beach is always the best. Because there's always someone there, and they're asleep, unaware—easy prey.

His trombone case feels heavy. The boy alternates hands as he carries it along Ocean Drive toward the Atlantic, the beach, just past two in the morning.

The wind coming sharply off the ocean. Darkness, and roiling, chaotic waves.

And light.

Three small beacons of light. Lanterns, or some form of them, for the beach bums, the ones not comfortable sleeping in pitch darkness. He knows how they feel—he slept with the closet light on for years, his mother yanking on the shoestring to turn it on, then sliding closed the closet door, leaving it open just a crack. He'd beg for another inch, for additional light, and they'd negotiate it every night. She usually let him win.

Kind of funny, though, that they'd sleep out here on the beach, in a natural setting, and still require the comfort of artificial light.

What are they afraid of, scary monsters?

What scares you? Dr. Conway always asks him. *Scary monsters, things like that? Or does something else scare you?*

The boy climbs to the small perch where the parking lot meets the sand. He opens the trombone case and removes the BB rifle, fully loaded.

Safely enveloped in darkness, further shielded by the wild grass on his perch, he closes his left eye and nestles his right eye against the rifle's scope, slowly moving the barrel of the air gun through the deep blackness, through the dark, until he finds the small glow of light.

You wanna know how I feel, Doctor?

When the rifle's sight is perfectly aligned with the lantern, when the circular scope is filled with nothing but the yellow-orange glow, he pulls the trigger.

A quick, hollow *clink* as the glass breaks, and the light disappears.

Over the wind, over the rush of the crashing waves, he hears it, ever so faintly. Movement. Rustling. Someone jarred awake.

He imagines that person's reaction: disoriented. Confused. Alarmed. And worse—not knowing. Not knowing whether he should be scared. Not knowing whether he's safe. Not knowing whether something really bad is about to happen.

That's how I feel, Doc. That's how I feel, all the time.

The boy places the rifle back in the trombone

case and slides down from the sandy perch. He steps back onto the pavement of the parking lot and heads north.

The house, the Murder House, on his right, just two houses from the beach.

He knows the house. His mother comes here once a week for her job.

He stops at the iron gate. Looks up at the sad monster of a mansion, at the gargoyles and the spears on the roof, aimed at the sky, as if angrily threatening the gods—

A loud, sudden noise, the slap of doors flying open, wood hitting wood.

The boy crouches down, fear swirling inside.

A man's mumbling, angry voice carrying in the wind.

The house, still dark. But the boy finds it. The second floor, south end.

His eyes adjust. He makes out a bedroom. A balcony that wraps around the west and south sides. Double doors, flung wide open.

A man—*the* man, it must be him. *Six*, they call him, or *Number Six*, or just *The Sixth*. But it's him. Holden Dahlquist VI.

Shirtless, hair blowing in the wind, leaning over the balcony, looking down.

Trying to get his leg up on the top of the railing that borders the balcony. Trying to stand on top of it?

The boy gently places his trombone case on the ground.

Unlocks the latches.

Removes the air gun.

Looks through his scope, moving through darkness

until he finds the man, illuminated by the bedroom light behind him.

With a final thrust, the man pushes himself onto the top of the railing. He rises, wobbly, standing on a narrow perch, a tightrope walker getting his balance.

He's only on the second story, but this is no ordinary house. The man must be thirty, forty feet up. No way he'd survive a fall, especially when his landing would most likely be on the spiked fence below him.

The man arches his back, raises his arms as if beseeching the heavens. As if preparing to jump, as if preparing to fly off the balcony to another world.

The boy watches all of this through the rifle's scope.

He pulls the trigger.

The man takes the blow, staggers, flutters on his perch, his arms doing tiny circles, his legs buckling, before he falls backward onto the balcony.

Aim-fire-click. The boy can do it well. He fires two, three pellets at the man. The man, injured from his fall, confused, reacts to each shot, jumping with surprise before scurrying back into the bedroom, out of sight.

The boy smiles. Then he packs up his rifle and runs back to his house.

Chapter 88

THE BOY RETURNS the next day. An itch he has to scratch. He hasn't stopped thinking about the man. Can't get the images from last night out of his head.

No trombone case this time. And this time, during the day. No school today, and Mom says dinner isn't until two.

Ocean Drive is empty. The beach is empty. Even the beach bums, the drifters, have found someplace else to be today. It seems like everybody has someplace else to be on Thanksgiving.

The boy slips through the iron gates. It takes some effort, but he's small enough.

He walks into the front yard, which slopes upward to the house. Colorful leaves dancing all around him, the air brittle with cold, the wind coming off the ocean downright treacherous.

He's staring at the monument by the fountain—*Cecilia, O Cecilia / Life was death disguised*—when he hears the noise in the back.

He rushes to the back of the house, his feet crunching the blanket of leaves.

The first thing he sees: a rope, dangling from a tree branch, knotted in such a way that an oval circle hangs down, bobbing in the wind.

A noose. He knows the word for it. That's a noose.

A ladder. A man—the man, it's him—standing on the top rung, reaching for the noose, struggling to fit it over his head. Crying, sobbing, cursing.

And then suddenly noticing him, a trespasser, a boy, having just come around the corner.

"Get . . . get outta . . . get outta here . . . kid." His words thick and slurred. The noose in his hands, not yet around his neck.

He is so terrified, he can't respond to Mr. Dahlquist.

"I said . . . get out . . . get—" The man swaying, the ladder rocking, the man losing his grip on the noose as the ladder topples over, the man falling with the ladder to the blanket of leaves below with a muted *thump*.

The man cursing, then sobbing, his shoulders heaving. Punching the ground, swatting leaves, gripping his hair, grunting and screaming, like something inside him is trying to get out.

Then he stops. He's worn himself out. He looks around and he finds the bottle, half-filled with some brown liquid, obscured by the leaves. He unscrews the top and takes a long guzzle, empties most of the bottle, wipes his mouth with his sleeve.

Then he turns and looks at the boy.

"It was . . . you . . . last . . . last night," says Holden

Dahlquist VI. The words struggling to escape his mouth, heavy and blurry.

The boy doesn't answer. Doesn't confirm, doesn't deny.

But he walks toward the man.

"You my . . . guardian angel . . . or some . . . something?"

The boy stops short in front of him.

Mr. Dahlquist, dressed in a flannel shirt and pajama bottoms, yanks open the right side of his shirt, ripping off a button, revealing a small, deep-red wound.

"You . . . shot . . . shot me . . . last night." His eyes red and heavy and unfocused, his face unshaven but handsome. Thick auburn hair. Tall and lean.

And then the boy sees the handgun, nestled in the leaves, three feet from him, and three feet from Mr. Dahlquist.

The boy reaches down and picks it up.

It is tiny, and light. Gold and silver. A short barrel. A big looping circle in the middle of the brass grip. Nothing like the guns that cops have, or that you see on TV.

"My great . . . grandfather's revolver," says Mr. Dahlquist. "Over a . . . a hundred . . . years old. A knuckle . . . knuckle duster."

The boy wraps his fingers in the circle. Can't even fire the trigger.

"I'm a good shot," the boy says.

The man's eyes grow wide for a moment, his lips parting. His eyes shift from the gun to the boy. "That gun's . . . loaded," he says. "It has . . . bullets—"

"I know what *loaded* means."

Mr. Dahlquist stares at the gun, as if lost in a deep dream, his body swaying slightly, his chest heaving. "Give it . . . to me, kid."

The boy doesn't move. He cocks the gun, which produces the trigger, protruding against his index finger.

"What . . . are you . . . doing?" Mr. Dahlquist reaches out with his hand, palm open. "Gimme it." He lets out a noise, air whooshing out of him, and pushes himself to his feet, unsteady.

The boy doesn't move. Holding the gun, aiming it at the man. The sensation it brings, the feeling of power, control, over another person.

The boy isn't scared anymore. For the first time he can remember, he isn't scared or confused. He feels . . . in control. For the first time in his life, he's composed, in command.

He relishes that feeling. He doesn't ever want to lose that feeling. He wants to remember that feeling forever.

He doesn't ever want to go back to those other feelings he has.

He puts the barrel of the gun against his temple.

Mr. Dahlquist raises his hands, palms out. "No . . ."

The boy pulls the trigger.

Nothing but a loud *click* against his temple.

He cocks the gun again, pulls the trigger again.

Nothing again. The boy hurls the gun like a tomahawk across the yard. Adrenaline swirling inside him, his heartbeat rattling against his chest.

Mr. Dahlquist, chest heaving, eyes bugged out, looks at the boy, then at the gun in the grass, then back at the boy.

"You . . . think about . . . about doing that . . . a lot? Kill . . . killing yourself?"

The boy doesn't answer.

Every day, he thinks. *I think about it every day, every hour, every minute.*

"Me too," says Mr. Dahlquist.

Like the man can read his thoughts. Like he's the first person who understands him.

"Good thing . . . that gun's a . . . hundred years old." And then Mr. Dahlquist starts laughing. He laughs for a long time, wiping at his eyes.

The boy doesn't know what's so funny.

"We're quite a . . . pair. Can't even . . . kill ourselves . . . right."

Holden Dahlquist VI brushes himself off. "I'm cold. Are you . . . cold, kid?"

He picks up his bottle, drinks the remaining liquid, and staggers toward the house.

The boy follows him inside.

Chapter 89

A SECRET. THAT'S part of what has made these last six months so fun. It's a secret, the two of them. Nobody knows he comes over every day after school. Not his mother, not his friends—nobody knows about his new and special friend, Holden.

Well, six days a week, not seven. His mom comes here once a week. The boy doesn't come on that day.

But all the other days, the boy slips through the gate and comes around the back.

"Did you kill yourself today?" he asks Mr. Dahlquist.

"Nope. Did you?"

"Nope."

Their running joke.

"I won't . . . if you won't," Holden always says at the end. "Prom . . . promise?"

Sometimes Holden looks happy to see him. Most days, he doesn't look happy about anything else. Always unsteady on his feet, always reeking of alcohol—"my medicine," he calls it—always slurring his words, forcing them out in small spurts.

Every day there is a chore, and the reward of ten dollars. Usually the task is really small, like raking a meager pile of leaves or shoveling snow off the front walk or washing a few dishes. The boy can tell that most of this work has already been done by someone else, and only a small portion of the project has been reserved for him.

Most days they talk. The boy, mostly. He tells Holden stories about his life, or his day at school, or the things that bother him. Holden doesn't like to talk about himself, or even his family, for some reason. He likes to listen more than talk.

The boy watches Holden sometimes, even when he doesn't come in for a visit, standing outside the gate and just watching. Holden doesn't leave the house very much. He lives alone, save for the servant who comes in every other day to clean and cook and run errands.

He doesn't have any other visitors, except the pretty women who come by once in a while and stay for a few hours, looking disheveled and sometimes bruised, sometimes limping, when they leave. Holden doesn't like to talk about them, either.

Sometimes Holden paints. Sometimes he reads. Always, he drinks.

Canvases fill his upstairs, nearly all of the artwork dark, macabre. Storms ravaging houses, angry oceans, portraits of people dying, sometimes in bloody, grisly fashion, spears protruding through their midsections, gaping wounds in their chests. Anguished, tortured faces, death and destruction.

"You don't . . . have to come here . . . every day," Holden tells him one day.

"I want to."

"You have . . . friends . . . friends your . . . age? Kids in . . . school?"

"Not really," he says, when the true answer is a hard *no*. "I'm not really—" The boy isn't sure how to finish the sentence. "They're not . . . like me."

Holden turns away from his artwork and looks at him, appraises him.

"I'm not like them," the boy says.

Holden nods.

I'm like you, the boy does not say.

His other secret—the one he hasn't even told Holden: the journal.

Or diary, whatever you call it. The thick book, bound in red leather, more than two hundred years old, which the boy found around Christmastime in Holden's parlor. Wrapped in plastic for preservation.

He doesn't understand every word of what's written in that journal. Some of the words he has to look up in a dictionary. But he gets the gist of it. Some passages he reads and rereads. He doesn't dare dog-ear the pages, but he slips makeshift bookmarks into those pages.

From Winston, the patriarch:

> I've come to surrender my inhibitions and any pretense of civility. I may be able to fool the

authorities, but I'm far too advanced in age to fool myself. There is a monster inside me. It can sleep for days, for months. But it will never go away. It will feast on me, prey on me, until the day I die.

From Holden III, Winston's great-grandson:

The lust has taken up permanent residence within me. I can no longer resist it, any more than I can resist my very existence. Blessing or curse, it is now my identity. I will use an axe, and I will watch Anna bleed, and then I will pray for death.

Holden VI:

Like Winston before me, I have surrendered. I can say that I'm filled with remorse over the four dead tourists, but in fact what swims inside me is neither dread nor sadness, but relief.

They can't help it. That's what they're saying. It's not their fault. They can't stop it. It's a part of them. It's outside their control.

They don't want to do it. They *have* to do it.

He reads it every day. It makes him feel different. It makes him feel better. As if something inside him is blossoming, something changing, like a drug releasing its contents into his bloodstream.

He's not the only one.

He's not the only one who feels like there's a monster inside him.

And he knows that Holden's just like him, too. No matter how hard he tries to resist it, Holden's no different from him, no different from his ancestors.

So he will wait. It may take months. It may take years.

He will wait for the moment when Holden is ready to show everyone what lies inside him.

Book VII

BRIDGEHAMPTON, 2012

Chapter 90

IT'S LATE, SO late that now it's technically called early. Predawn, nearly five in the morning.

The man who sometimes thinks of himself as Holden positions the note card carefully on the desk, his fingers covered in rubber gloves. He considers cutting the words out of a magazine or newspaper, like an old-fashioned ransom note, but there is no time for that. So he will write with his nondominant hand, to avoid detection by any handwriting expert.

Again, this is him being smart.

The words come out wobbly—especially the words *bodies* and *Aiden,* for some reason—but they're legible, which is all that matters.

He closes up the envelope but, of course, does not lick the adhesive. That would be something, wouldn't it? After all this time, to make a mistake like that, leaving his DNA on the envelope?

On his way, he makes a detour and turns down Ocean Drive. It's still dark, and nobody will see him. He likes to visit this time of the day.

When he reaches 7 Ocean Drive, he steps out of his car and crosses the street to the magnificent wrought-iron gates, leans against them, pokes his nose between the bars.

He can't fit between the bars anymore.

"Bet you never expected this, did you, Holden?" he whispers.

Who could have expected this turn of events? But it's happening.

He pushes himself off the gate and returns to his car. It's not far from dawn, and he wants to deliver the note under the cover of darkness. He throws the car into drive and heads back toward town.

It isn't difficult to find the car, parked on the street, and nobody is out at this hour. He tucks the note on the windshield, safely and securely beneath the wiper blade, like a flyer advertising a liquidation sale at a sporting goods store or a buy-one, get-one-free at some fast-food restaurant.

This note, of course, has a bit more gravity to it than a coupon.

This note's going to turn everything on its head.

Chapter 91

I LEAVE AIDEN'S house and get home before dawn. My apartment is a slum, papers strewn about, the bed unmade, unwashed glasses in the kitchen sink, a musty smell.

I'm exhausted but propped up by the hum of adrenaline. I look again at the newspaper photo I pilfered from Aiden's scrapbook, with the caption NEWBORN ABANDONED AT POLICE STATION.

I must be right. It makes everything fit. Aiden's mother, a prostitute, had a second child, one fathered by Holden VI. She gave the boy up for some reason—because she didn't want a child fathered by Holden, or because she didn't want Holden to have any influence over him. But in some way I can't possibly know, father and son were reunited.

But then—why is Aiden a part of this? How does he figure in?

And more importantly—who is that second child, Aiden's half brother?

Is it Isaac Marks? He seems to be working with Aiden against me.

Is it Noah? He's the one who must have tipped off Aiden that I'd be with Justin last night, when Aiden came through the window and tried to kill me.

Isaac and Noah. Each of them a grade younger than Aiden.

Three kids who grew up together, who went to school together. Did they learn more than reading, writing, and 'rithmetic while they were in school together?

I'm buzzed but exhausted at first light. Everyone else is just beginning to waken, to start a new day, and I'm about to collapse. My brain is fuzzy from sleep deprivation. I have a lot to do, but I can't function without sleep. . . .

Bam bam bam

Let me out

Buzz buzz buzz

Please let me out

Buzz buzz buzz

My eyes pop open, mid-dream, adrenaline swirling. My cell phone vibrating. I pat the bed until I find it, pick it up, stare at it through foggy eyes.

The caller ID says NOAH WALKER.

A flutter through my chest. I'm not ready to answer it. I wait until the buzzing ends. A NEW VOICE MAIL message pops up.

I look at the clock. It's one in the afternoon. Wow. I slept for almost six hours. It felt like six minutes.

Then I play the voice mail.

Murphy, it's Noah. Just want to make sure you're okay. I have an idea I wanna run by you. Give me a call.

I punch out the phone and drop it on the bed. He has an idea he wants to run by me? *Yeah, I have something to run by you, too, Noah—why don't you explain to me who told Aiden Willis that I'd be at Justin's house last night?*

And by chance, were you adopted? Were you left abandoned at the police station as a child? Did you later discover that your biological father was part of a family line of deranged killers going back centuries?

Did you decide to pick up the mantle where they left off?

And was I, Detective Jenna Murphy, the dumb shit who sprang you from prison?

I move slowly, as if I'd been drugged last night, as if I'm recovering from a hangover. I eat some toast and drink some coffee and sit under a cascade of scalding shower water until the hot water runs out—which, in my apartment, doesn't take very long.

My cell phone rings again. I find it in the bathroom through the steam. Noah, again. I ignore it, again.

Somehow, it's four in the afternoon now.

I have to find Holden Dahlquist's son. If that baby was abandoned at the police station, he would have been turned over to Child Protective Services, like the news clipping said. He would have entered the system—he would have been adopted, or placed in a foster home. Something that would have generated a paper trail.

Did the child trace that paper trail back to Holden? Or did Holden trace that paper trail back to the boy?

I don't know. And I don't care.

Because however it happened—a paternity suit, an

adoption, whatever—Holden would have involved his attorney. And I have his lawyer's name, thanks to Noah.

So how do I get this information from Holden's lawyer, who will assert his attorney-client privilege?

No clue. All I know is that I'm getting closer, shaking some trees, and people are getting nervous.

Maybe all I can do is wait for their next move.

My phone rings again. It's Lauren Ricketts.

"Hey there," I say.

"Murphy!" Her voice excited, breathless.

"What's going on?"

"You're not going to believe this."

I push my laptop computer aside. "Try me."

"Annie Church and Dede Paris," she says. "We just found their bodies."

I close my eyes. Somebody—Aiden, Isaac, Noah — just made their next move.

Chapter 92

MY THIRD TIME in two days driving in this neighborhood. But this time, it's not directly to Aiden Willis's house. And this time, traffic is at a standstill, logjammed as far as the eye can see, traffic down to a single, narrow lane on the turnpike.

I inch forward until I reach the barricades blocking access to the very road on which Aiden Willis lives. TV crews have lined up their vans and satellite feeds, well-coiffed reporters taking their turns before the cameras with their microphones. Once past the barricade, the turnpike opens up again, so I head north another quarter mile to Tasty's, where I park in the lot and head back to the scene on foot.

Two bodies discovered in the woods, almost directly behind Aiden Willis's property line in the backyard, buried ten feet belowground.

That was all I got from Lauren Ricketts, one of the officers on the scene. She didn't have much time to talk to me; I was lucky to get as much as she gave me.

I walk down to the barricaded street. A reporter from one of the local stations, a guy with hair so brittle from hair spray that he could weaponize it, recognizes me. He probably doesn't know I've lost my badge. Either way, he allows me inside the van and shows me the feed his station's helicopter is getting, an overhead shot.

The overhead view: A lot of the work has already been completed. A bulldozer has already excavated the dirt, and a crane has somehow lifted the bodies out of the crater. The team is on the ground, officers and forensic investigators and medical examiners.

Two gurneys are loaded into a hearse and driven off the property. I step out of the news van. Five minutes later, I see the hearse approaching the turnpike barricade, officers removing the barriers to allow it to leave.

Annie and Dede. Why now? And how did it happen?

I send a text message to Ricketts: I'm here on the scene when you have a minute. It will be a while, I expect, before her work is done.

But thirty seconds later, I get a reply: Where?

I text back, then wait. Ricketts, looking the worse for wear—dusty and dirty, like a soldier emerging from battle—but excited, too, approaches the barricade.

"It's Annie and Dede?" I ask.

She nods. "I think so. One of the fingers was missing."

Right. He cut off one of Dede's fingers and left it for the cops to find, a few years ago.

"The knife was there, too," she says. "The murder weapon."

Wow. He left the murder weapon with the girls? Our

killer was probably too careful to leave fingerprints on the knife, but you never know.

"I found the bodies," Ricketts says. "It was me."

I put my hand on her shoulder. "How the heck did *that* happen?"

"Well, that's the thing—someone put a note on my windshield this morning."

I draw back. "What?"

Ricketts looks around at the bedlam, the reporters and onlookers, practically shutting down the turnpike. "A note said I could find their bodies back here. By the large elm tree with the *X* in red spray paint." She shrugs. "Why would someone do that? Why would someone write *me* a note?"

I think about that. But she knows the answer, same as I do. The note was written to her because she was working on this case with me.

"Whoever did this—he wants you to know," she says. "Since I'm the responding officer, it's my case. I have access to all the data. He wants you to have the information, Murphy. He knows I'll tell you."

She's right. It makes sense.

"Aiden didn't work alone," I say. "There are at least two people doing this. Aiden and someone else, maybe two somebody elses. Someone who knows we're working on this case together."

She thinks about it, nods. "So what do we do now?"

"Do your job," I say. "Find out all you can. And then, when it's safe, you and I should work through this."

"Okay. Right. Okay."

Ricketts takes a deep breath. This is a big moment

for her. It's not every day a rookie patrol officer breaks a major unsolved case.

"Watch your back, Officer," I say. "They may be trying to communicate with me, but they're using you to do it."

I walk back to my car as a light mist begins to fall, my mind racing with questions. He's messing with me now, telling me something, sending me in a certain direction. But which direction? And why? How does showing me Dede's and Annie's bodies help him?

My head starts to ache. Another new piece of evidence, yielding nothing but more questions.

When I reach my car, Noah Walker is leaning against it, his arms crossed.

"Hello, stranger," he says to me.

Chapter 93

"I'VE BEEN CALLING you," Noah says. He pushes himself off my car. He's in his construction gear, jeans and T-shirt, boots, protective vest. Off work now, catching dinner at Tasty's.

I feel something between us, always that radiating heat, but this time more penetrating, turning my stomach sour.

"I guess you heard about Annie and Dede," I say.

"Yeah. You have any information?"

"None," I say. "I'm not on the inside anymore."

"But you have that friend, that young cop. What's her name again?"

Playing dumb. I'm not going to play back. "What do you want, Noah?"

He opens his hands. "Same thing you want," he says, like it's obvious. "I thought we were a team."

So did I. Before you tried to help Aiden kill me.

"What's wrong?" he says.

Ask him. Just ask him and see what he says.

"Were you adopted, Noah?"

He gives me a funny look. "Adopted? No."

"You sure?"

"Am I sure I wasn't adopted? I think I'd be sure about that."

I look him over, try to read him. I'm not getting a solid hit either way.

"It's public information," I say. "I can find out."

"I don't think so," he answers. "I don't think adoptions are public information."

"For a guy who wasn't adopted, you seem to know a lot about them."

"Murphy, what the hell?" He steps toward me. "What's with this bizarre interrogation? I've been leaving you messages—"

"By the way," I say, getting my Irish up now, "I went to Justin's last night, like I told you I would. And guess who paid me a visit?"

He shakes his head. Playing dumb again.

"Aiden," I say. "He came through a window at me. With a knife."

"He *what?* Are you okay?"

"I wonder how he knew I'd be there, Noah. Got any ideas?"

He waves his hand, like he's erasing something. "Wait a second, wait a second. You don't think it was *me*—"

"Oh, no, of course not. It was probably the long list of *other* people who knew I was going to be at Justin's last night. Oh, wait—*nobody* else knew."

"Murphy, just hold on a second."

He reaches for me, but I pull back.

"Don't you touch me," I say. "Don't come near me ever again. Just know something, Noah—I *will* figure this out. You tell your buddies, whoever's a part of this: I'm close. I'm going to nail all of you. Or die trying."

Noah steps between me and my car.

"Okay, you got to talk," he says. "Now I get to talk."

Get out of my way, or you'll be sorry."

"Hey!"

Noah and I both turn. Justin is jogging toward us, from the restaurant.

"Is there a problem?" he asks.

Noah glares at him. Something primitive in his eyes. These two are casual acquaintances—each has said a kind word about the other—but something passed between Noah and me last night, until I mentioned Justin. I remember the look on his face, the blow he suffered, even though I insisted Justin and I are just friends.

"Nothing that concerns you," Noah says to Justin.

Justin stops short of us, looks at me. "Jenna?"

"It's none of your business," Noah says.

"You're on my property, Noah. And you're bothering my friend. So I think it *is* my business."

"Stay out of this, Justin." Noah squares off on Justin. "This is a private conversation."

Two men, the macho thing, battling over the damsel's honor. Only this damsel ain't interested.

"Uh, guys? Over here?" I wave my hand. "I'm leaving. I'll call you later, Justin. And Noah? Stay away from me."

I climb into my car and slam the door. I start up the engine and throw it into reverse, gravel flying in my wake, then head north on the turnpike, unsure of my destination, only certain that wherever I'm going, I'm going alone.

Chapter 94

I DRIVE HOME as darkness sweeps over Bridgehampton.

Aiden's still out there, and while I seriously doubt he'd be dumb enough to hang around the Hamptons to take another shot at me, I take simple precautions. I lock the dead bolt and prop a chair against the door, and I move the dresser against the small window. It's not much of a deterrent, but at least it will keep Aiden from doing another nose dive through a plate of glass.

I have almost nothing in my cupboard but some noodles, so I boil some water and drop them in.

Eat and sleep, Murphy. Or you'll crumble like a stale cookie.

But I have no appetite. My stomach is a pool of nerves and chaos.

You're getting closer, Murphy.

I push the plate of noodles aside.

But you're not there yet.

Then two things happen at once, causing me to jump from my seat.

My cell phone buzzes, and my doorbell rings.

The phone is Ricketts. I punch it on while I move to the door.

I look through the peephole at the man standing at my door.

It's Isaac Marks, our beloved chief of police.

"Ricketts, let me call you back," I say into the phone. "Your boss is at the door."

"No, Jenna, wait—"

I punch the phone off, release the dead bolt, and open the door.

And stare at the man who just might be responsible for the murder of eight people. Including the man he replaced as chief.

"Murphy," Isaac says, nodding. Wearing his uniform. Probably did some press today on Annie and Dede.

"Need you to come down to the substation," he says.

"You can talk to me right here."

He takes a deep breath, grimaces. "Don't make this difficult. Come down with me voluntarily. Make a good decision for once in your life."

"You don't have anything better to do?" I ask. "After finding two dead bodies today?"

He gives me a funny look.

"The two dead bodies," he says, "are the reason I'm here."

Chapter 95

I SIT IN the same interview room where I've sat many times, only on the other side of the table. I used to be good at this, questioning witnesses, sizing them up, reading them, making them sweat, gaining their trust, taking them on a roller-coaster ride from fright to horror to despondence to remorse to confession.

The door opens, and in walks Isaac Marks. He stands against the wall, arms crossed.

What is he capable of? Did he kill all those people, with Aiden as his accomplice? And maybe Noah, too?

Did he do something to me, along with Aiden, at 7 Ocean Drive when I was a little girl?

I've never had a bead on the guy. I was his partner for less than a year, and he was a phone-it-in cop, a guy who liked to strut around with the badge, enjoyed the power more than the responsibility. Never one to put in the extra hours necessary. Never one to go the extra mile.

But a killer? If it's true, I missed it. Never saw it.

Then again, I wasn't looking for it.

"I want some answers, Murphy," he says. "Some straight answers."

"So do I."

He shakes his head. "Doesn't work that way. Maybe you forgot."

"It does now. Or I take Five."

Most people are afraid to invoke their Fifth Amendment rights. They think it makes them look guilty. They're right, but they're wrong. Yeah, you look bad if you won't talk. But how you appear at that moment to a cop pales in comparison to the damage you do by answering detailed questions, locking yourself in.

Maybe I should be heeding that advice right now.

"The bodies were Annie and Dede?" I ask.

Isaac closes his eyes, nods. "We have a rush on DNA. We won't have it for another day or so. But there was a missing finger, and some personal articles on the bodies that the families confirmed. It's not official, but unofficially? There's no doubt."

"How did you make the discovery?" I ask.

Still planted against the wall, still stoic, but now with a gleam in his eye. He knows Ricketts and I are friends. He knows I know.

"Anonymous tip," he says.

"How convenient."

He cocks his head. "Convenient? How so?"

I shrug. "Maybe someone was getting too close to solving this whole thing. Maybe Aiden's being given up as a sacrificial lamb. A scapegoat."

"A scapegoat." Isaac's eyes narrow. "Meaning he's innocent."

"Meaning," I say, "that he wasn't the only one. He has a partner."

Isaac doesn't move. Expression doesn't break. Tough to read, because interrogators are playing a role, acting out a scene, so it could be just him doing his job. Or it could be he's sweating bullets underneath that uniform.

"A partner," he says. "Two people?"

"At least two," I say, "and the partner just fucked Aiden."

Isaac pushes himself off the wall and pulls out the chair across from me. He takes his time getting seated, settling in, training his stare on me.

"How did the partner fuck Aiden?" he asks.

My heartbeat ratcheting up. He has me in an enclosed room, in his custody. But it's a police station. There are witnesses, other cops watching through the one-way. It's not like he can silence me.

Do I want to do this? Right here, right now?

Hell yes, I do. With other cops as witnesses.

"Let's say Aiden was getting nervous," I say. "He talks to his partner. He says, 'They're getting close.' So his partner tells Aiden to leave town. Get out of Dodge for a while. Let things settle down."

Isaac nods, listening intently.

"Maybe the partner tells Aiden, 'Don't worry, I'll take care of this.' "

Isaac does a double blink with his eyes. I've just quoted what he said to Aiden on the phone last night—when he didn't see me hiding outside.

"Go on," he says, his voice flat and cold.

"But once Aiden scrams, his partner makes an

anonymous tip to the cops. Bodies are discovered a stone's throw from Aiden's property line. And ten gets you twenty there's incriminating evidence found at that burial scene, evidence that implicates Aiden and Aiden alone. My guess? Aiden's fingerprints on the murder weapon."

Isaac is silent, his eyes deadened.

"So now Aiden's an obvious suspect," I say. "Gift-wrapped, practically. And his partner walks away scot-free."

Isaac takes a breath, leans back in his chair.

"Cat got your tongue, Chief?"

His fingers tap the table. "You think Aiden's a part of this."

"Yes. I've suspected him for a while now. In fact, I tried to confront him last night at his house. He ran from me before I could question him. But . . . you already know that, don't you, Isaac?"

The dam has burst. I've all but accused him now. I don't know if this is the smart move here, but I'm running out of options. Smart or not, it's time to move.

Isaac tries to smile. It doesn't work very well.

"Tell me more about this second killer," he says.

I shrug. "He's lasted this long, eight murders over five years, so he's smart, and he's able to function in society as a normal person. A classic psychopath. He could be anyone. He could be a construction worker. He could be a ditch-digger."

I look Isaac squarely in the eye.

"He could be a cop," I say.

"A cop? Interesting." Isaac purses his lips. "Well,

Murphy, it turns out we *did* find Aiden's fingerprints on the murder weapon."

"You have Aiden's prints on file?"

"He was arrested once, long time ago, for retail theft. Shoplifting. His prints are in the database."

"Did you run *all* the databases, Chief? Even the government employees' database? Every cop in our department has their prints in that database. Did you remember to check that database, too? Or did it . . . slip your mind?"

My blood is boiling now. But the cops who are watching this interview need to hear this, all of it.

"You figure," says Isaac, "that if we found another set of prints, we'd have the second person—Aiden's partner."

"Worth a shot."

"Someone who can act perfectly normal in society. Like a construction worker."

"Or a cop," I say again.

"Yeah, you said that before," he says. "A cop?"

"Why not? It's the perfect cover. He could manipulate the evidence. He could influence the investigation."

"True," says Isaac. "That's true."

I open my hands. "What are you afraid of, Isaac? Check the government database. Or . . . are you worried that maybe your hand slipped, and your prints accidentally got on that knife?"

Now his smile comes on, full glow. He shakes his head.

"We did run the prints on the murder weapon through the government database," he says. "And we got a match."

He rises out of his chair and leans over the table, so he can whisper his next words.

"Aiden's prints weren't the only ones on that murder weapon," he says. "We found yours, too, Jenna Murphy."

Chapter 96

I SPRING OUT of my chair. A slow burn through my chest.

"No," I say. "No way."

Chief Isaac Marks is suddenly enjoying himself very much. He sits back in his chair, crosses a leg. "I suppose now you're going to claim that I manipulated the process somehow. Planted your fingerprints. Right?"

My mind racing, my throat full, everything moving too fast.

"Well, let me put you at ease, Murphy. I had no part in the gathering of the evidence or in running the prints. If you don't believe me, you can ask your bestest buddy, Officer Ricketts."

The walls closing in. The heat turned way up. This isn't right.

It can't be right.

"You can't possibly think . . ." My throat closes before I can finish the sentence.

"I can't possibly think what?" he says whimsically.

"That you had something to do with Annie's and Dede's murders? Well, let's think about that. Have a seat, if you would."

I put my hand against the wall to brace myself. My prints are on the murder weapon? That can't possibly be right. Somebody, somehow, must have—

"I said sit the fuck down, Murphy."

My legs unsteady, I find the seat and plant myself.

"So let's think this through," he says. "You have very persuasively argued that there were two killers—Aiden Willis and another person. You have also persuaded me that the second killer could be a police officer, that it would be the perfect cover for a psychopath."

"I didn't mean me—"

"So we have two girls who were murdered in the summer of 2007. Since we don't know the exact day, or even the exact month of their death, it's impossible to know your whereabouts at the time. You were a cop in Manhattan, but how easy would it have been to drive out here and do the deed, then drive back without anyone knowing? *Very* easy, I'd say."

"No. No." I push myself out of the chair, knocking it over with a clatter. "You can't actually believe that. No."

My pulse soaring. Sweat covering my brow. This is like a bad dream. This can't be happening.

"You did this, Isaac. You think I don't know what's going on?"

"Oh, Murphy, I think you know *exactly* what's going on."

Two officers, uniforms whose names I've forgotten,

step into the room. Isaac nods to them. Cool and collected, he is having the time of his life.

"Jenna Murphy," he says, "you're under arrest for the murders of Annie Church and Dede Paris."

Chapter 97

NOAH WATCHES. And waits. Two hours pass, while the midnight air moves from brisk to cold. He's underdressed in his black sweatshirt and black baseball cap and black jeans. They may not keep him warm, but they serve another purpose.

Nobody can see him in the dark.

He hears a noise—probably just the wind—and scrapes his cheek against one of the shrubs. He's been crouched low for a long time, so he stretches out, kicking out one leg at a time, like a sprinter preparing for a race, so he'll be loose when the time comes.

No police, no security.

Probably a burglar alarm on the outside door. But on the window?

Well, let's find out.

He steps out into the clearing, a small expanse of grass behind the building, but still outside the reach of the overhanging lights. Still in the dark. Still invisible.

The window has iron bars over it. He'll deal with the bars if necessary, but first he wants to see if the window has an alarm.

He raises his tire iron to eye level, angles it through the bars, and jams it against the glass. The glass shatters, an unmistakable sound, but not a very loud one, especially with a light wind. And really, nobody should be around right now, past midnight in an empty industrial park.

After shattering the glass, Noah steps back, ready to retreat into the darkness.

He hears no glass-shatter alarm. No police sirens.

But there could be an alarm on the window itself, triggered when it's opened.

So he tries that next, slipping his hand between the iron bars, carefully through the half-shattered window, until he finds the interior latch. He unlocks the window. Then, with both hands, he pushes it up from the bottom frame.

A few more shards of glass fall onto the floor inside.

But no alarm sounds. The window is not armed.

They must have figured the iron bars were enough.

They figured wrong.

Noah shines his flashlight on the screws. They are deeply embedded, some of them rusted. They won't be easy to unscrew. But his cordless drill will get the job done, sooner or later.

It will make some noise, but nothing too loud, and he's out here alone.

He just needs to hurry.

Noah puts on his rubber gloves. Then he fits the drill bit into the first screw and gets to work.

Chapter 98

"HEY THERE."

I'm sitting upright, against the wall in a holding cell beneath the substation, on a mattress about as thick and comfortable as a piece of paper, my thoughts scattering about.

My head turns toward the cell bars, toward the voice.

Lauren Ricketts, in uniform, giving me a sympathetic smile.

"Had to wait until the chief went home," she says. "He didn't want anyone visiting you. Least of all me."

I push myself off the wall, pain running down my neck and back.

"What the hell's going on, Murphy?" she asks. "How can this be right?"

That's all I've been thinking about.

"No clue," I say. "No freakin' clue. These girls were murdered in 2007. I wasn't even *here* in 2007. I didn't come here until last year—four years later."

"But you can't prove that," she says.

"How can I prove I never came here?" I throw up my hands. "Like Isaac said, nobody knows when, specifically, those two girls were murdered. June? July? August? There's no specific day or even month that the murders happened. So how can I produce an alibi? Am I supposed to have an alibi for every single day of the entire summer of 2007? It's impossible."

"Oh, Murphy. What a clusterfuck."

"And this hunting knife they found, the murder weapon? I haven't so much as touched a hunting knife since I came back here. I'm not sure I've ever held one in my life. I mean, it's not physically possible."

Ricketts doesn't have an answer for that. Neither of us does.

"What about Aiden?" I ask. "They're looking for him?"

"Oh, yeah. His prints on the weapon, the bodies behind his property—and we heard from East Hampton PD about what happened at Justin's house last night, the attack. There's a manhunt."

"We have to find him, Lauren," I say. "We have to find Aiden."

"Believe me, we're trying—"

"No, I mean, *we* have to find him. *Isaac* doesn't want Aiden found. He's the one who told Aiden to leave. And if he *does* find Aiden, he'll kill him. Y'know, make it look like a shootout with a suspect or something. He wants Aiden gone or dead. So Aiden will take the fall all by himself."

Ricketts looks at me, doubt creeping into her eyes. "Jenna . . ."

"You think I'm wrong?"

She lifts her shoulders. "I'm not sure. Are you? Are you so sure it's Isaac? That Isaac's a killer? That he framed you for this?"

I'm not sure of anything anymore. Aiden, Isaac, Noah—or some combination thereof. My fingerprints magically appearing on murder weapons without my knowledge. I feel like I'm in the Twilight Zone.

"The fingerprint match was clean," Ricketts says. "I found the murder weapon, that hunting knife, myself. And I delivered it directly to our forensics team. I watched the guy run the analysis, Murph. Isaac didn't tamper with that. So how could Isaac get your fingerprints on the knife?"

"How could anybody? But somebody did. Probably easier for him than anybody else."

Ricketts steps back from the cell bars, her focus dropping to the floor.

"You don't believe me," I say.

She shakes her head slowly. "I'm not ready to believe our chief of police is a serial killer. No."

I stare at her. She looks suddenly uncomfortable, shifting her weight from one foot to the other.

"He got to you," I say. "He told you what a great job you're doing. How a big promotion could be in the works. A bright future. 'But just watch out for Jenna Murphy! Don't believe anything she says. She's bad news. She'll take you down.' Is that about it, Officer Ricketts?"

"No, that's *not* it." Some steam in her voice, color to her face. "I'm following the facts wherever they lead."

“Including my prints being found on that hunting knife.”

“Yeah, including that.” Her eyes rise to meet mine.

A gulf between us, suddenly, the cop on the one side, the suspect on the other.

“So we’re done?” I say. “You and me?”

“I told you, Murphy. I’ll follow the facts wherever they lead.”

Another one bites the dust. First Noah, now Ricketts. My “team” has been reduced to a team of me, myself, and I.

“Then I have some facts for you to follow,” I say. “Aiden’s mother. Gloria Willis.”

“Yeah?”

“She was killed in a hit-and-run,” I say. “Find out when.”

She thinks about that, nods. “I can do that.”

“And while you’re at it,” I say, “find out whether Isaac or Noah Walker was adopted.”

Chapter 99

JOSHUA BRODY, ONCE Noah Walker's attorney and now mine, walks into my holding cell as Lauren Ricketts leaves. He looks around and then looks at me.

"Thanks for coming in the middle of the night," I say.

"Part of the job." He scratches the back of his neck, his eyelids heavy. He looks around again. "So is this the cell where Noah supposedly confessed to Chief James?"

I shake my head. I'm not in the mood. Joshua beat me up pretty good over that during the cross-examination.

"Talk to me," I say.

"The arrest is solid," he says. "Your prints on the murder weapon are sufficient for probable cause."

"We don't know it's the murder weapon," I counter. "They don't have DNA back yet. We don't know that it's Annie's and Dede's blood on the knife."

Brody looks at me like he would look at a child who

just doesn't get it. "The hunting knife was covered in blood and was found with the bodies," he says. "You're right. They haven't conclusively tied the knife to the dead girls, but c'mon. Dead women with stab wounds, a bloody knife found inside . . ."

"Did they die of stab wounds? I thought their skulls were crushed."

"I don't know," he says. "Autopsy's tomorrow. But whatever the cause of death, they have sufficient evidence for an arrest. Remember, they don't have to show guilt beyond a reasonable doubt until trial."

The trial. I can't believe it. I'm going to be tried for murder?

"You have to get me out of here," I say.

"Best I can do is try to get a reasonable bond," Brody says. "The hearing's tomorrow. But on two counts of murder? It will be hard. If you get bond at all, it will be a million dollars. Maybe two million. Which means you'll need to come up with ten percent. A hundred thousand, two hundred thousand, whatever."

"Noah Walker bonded out. He was charged with a double murder."

"Noah Walker had a girlfriend for whom a million dollars was pocket change. I don't suppose you have a trust fund or anything like that?"

I let out a bitter laugh. I have a little bit of money saved up, but nowhere near that kind of scratch.

"I'll come back tomorrow," Brody says. "Unless there's anything else I can do."

I drop my head against the wall. But then it comes to me. There is one thing.

"You're a lawyer," I say.

"Last I checked, yeah."

"Maybe you can help me with something," I say.

Chapter 100

JOSHUA BRODY RUBS his unshaven face, mulling over everything I've just told him.

"So you think the sixth and last Holden Dahlquist had a son. A son who's running around killing people."

"That's my theory, yes. A pretty good one, I think."

"And you think this boy is the younger half brother of Aiden Willis, the other person whose prints were found on the knife."

"Yes. The half brother was abandoned at birth. But somehow, in some way, he was able to discover his biological father, or vice versa."

"So you figure there might be some records of this? Maybe the biological mother filed a paternity suit. Or there'd be adoption records. Or both."

"Something," I say. "But whatever it may be, I'm pretty sure—"

"It would involve his attorney," Brody says. "Yes, I agree with that much. If a guy like Holden Dahlquist had a problem like that, his first call would be to his lawyer. Sure."

"So that's why I'm asking about his attorney," I say.

"Okay. Well, to answer your question: These days, most files are stored electronically. But Holden the Sixth, as you call him, he died . . . when, again?"

"He died sometime in 1994," I say.

"Okay." Brody nods. "So any records would be no later than ninety-four. And back then, nobody was creating the kind of electronic files we have today. There would be hard copies."

Hard copies. That's what I thought. That's what I was hoping.

"Where would those hard copies be?"

"Something that old, they would be in off-site storage," he says. "But it's not like you have access to them. These are attorney-client documents. You'd need a court order."

"Then let's get one."

"On what grounds? Your hunch?"

"Yes, my hunch."

He shakes his head. "It would be hard. Nearly impossible."

"How long would it take?"

"Very long. Months. There'd be a vicious court battle."

"I don't have months, Mr. Brody. I have to know this *now*."

"Murphy," he says, "you haven't even been indicted yet. When you are, there will be a court case, and maybe we can explore that. But now? Right now? No chance. Zero."

I deflate. He's making sense, I know it. It would take months to get court-approved access to those files, if they even exist at all.

Unless . . .

"Just out of curiosity," I say, "where would the law firm keep its old hard copies of files?"

"Oh." Brody shrugs. "Most law firms around here use a place out in Riverhead called Dunbar Professional Storage."

Dunbar Professional Storage in Riverhead.

"I know the name of Holden the Sixth's lawyer," I say. "A guy named Finneus Rucker. Do you know him?"

"I *knew* him," says Brody. "He died a few years ago. Cancer, I think."

I deflate. "But I looked up his law firm online. Rucker, Rice and Spong."

"Yeah, his firm still exists. But he doesn't."

"But—his firm would still have the records."

Brody nods. "I'm sure they do."

"Well, do you have any idea if his firm uses that storage facility?"

Brody's eyes narrow. "No, I have no idea. But like I said, wherever they keep those records, you'd have to go through a judge."

"Absolutely," I say.

"Don't get any dumb ideas. You're in enough trouble already."

"Of course."

Dunbar Professional Storage in Riverhead.
Remember that.
That's my next stop. If I ever get out of this jail cell.

Chapter 101

NOAH REMOVES THE third iron bar from the window and decides it's enough.

He tosses his cable cutters in through the open window.

He stuffs the flashlight into his front pocket.

Using the remaining iron bar as a brace, he hauls himself up and onto the window ledge.

His head through the open window, his body dangling outside, he looks around. It's dark, but he can see enough to get the drift.

An office. A desk covered in paper, a chair, file cabinets.

He has no choice but to fall in headfirst. He can't see the floor, but he knows it's littered with broken glass now.

He lunges forward and catches the chair to break his fall, but fall, and fall hard, he does. An awkward landing, his jeans doing enough to protect him from the glass. Could have been a lot worse.

He brushes himself off and turns on his flashlight just for a second. Then he opens the locked office door, looks beyond it.

Darkness, until he finds the light switch.

And then: a warehouse, a wide and long and high expanse of space, filled with nothing but rows and rows of shelving, a rolling ladder in each row to reach the higher shelves. He looks around long enough to get his bearings. Then he kills the lights. Those overhead lights are no good. Someone could detect an intruder from a mile away.

With his flashlight, he roots around the office and finds the index. He leafs through it until he finds what he's looking for.

Then he walks into the warehouse, his footsteps echoing, the space pitch-dark except for the beam from his flashlight.

He finds the right row, and then the right shelf. He's ready to break a lock with the cable cutters, but there aren't any locks on the doors.

Even better.

He riffles through the files, the flashlight in his mouth. It takes him longer than expected, the risk of detection growing with each moment that passes.

When he finds it, he flips through the pages briefly—time does not permit a thorough review—shining his flashlight over each page, before he closes it up, the story from the newspaper on top:

Newborn Abandoned at Police Station

He takes the news clipping and the other documents, stuffs them back in the file folder, and places the folder under his arm. Then he closes the doors and climbs down the ladder.

He retraces his steps, closing the office door, climbing back out the window, falling into the grass.

He scrambles back to his hiding spot in the shrubs and looks over his handiwork. If he had all the time in the world, he could replace the iron bars. But he doesn't. And there's no replacing a shattered window.

But that's okay. He didn't leave any prints. He didn't even have to break any locks. The file doors he opened are now closed up, like before, with no evidence that Noah looked inside that door versus any of the other hundreds of doors in the facility.

So tomorrow, when the employees of Dunbar Professional Storage arrive at work, they'll know someone broke one of their windows and got inside, but that's all they'll know.

They won't know who broke in. They won't know where he looked.

And they'll have no idea which files he took.

Chapter 102

THE COURTROOM, FILLED with media and spectators. The discovery of the Yale students, plus the ex-cop who starred prominently in the Noah Walker case—too much for the reporters to stay away. I've become tabloid fodder.

Justin, sitting in the front row, trying to give me an upbeat expression when I walk into court. I can't bear to make eye contact with him.

The lawyers make their arguments. Joshua Brody argues that the evidence against me is weak—the fingerprints on the knife, but that's all. No motive. No evidence that I even set foot on Long Island during the summer of 2007.

Sebastian Akers rises for the prosecution. Oh, how he must savor the opportunity to prosecute me. He's never forgiven me for blowing his conviction against Noah Walker.

"Of course she's a flight risk," he says. "These women were stabbed, and her prints are on the knife. It's hard to imagine more direct evidence of guilt, short of capturing the whole thing on video."

The judge, an old guy I've never met named Corrigan, raises his hand.

"Bond will be set at two million dollars," he says. "In the event bond is made, the defendant will surrender her passport and will submit to electronic monitoring. She will be restricted to home confinement with waivers for work, attorney or medical visits, religious observation, and household errands under the supervision of the sheriff's office."

The judge bangs his gavel.

We won, but we lost.

Two million dollars? That means I have to come up with two hundred thousand to get out of here. I don't think I have *ten* thousand to my name, and what little I have is going to Joshua Brody as a retainer to defend me.

"I'll pay it," Justin calls out to me as the courtroom grows noisy. "It'll take me a day or two, but I have it."

"I—can't ask you to do that," I say.

He looks at me, almost wounded. "You didn't ask," he says.

I don't know how to respond. I absolutely hate being dependent on someone else for anything. But I don't have any other options.

Before the deputies escort me from the courtroom, my lawyer asks for a moment.

"We're lucky to get bond at all," he says. "Whoever that guy is in the front row, if he's offering to pay it, you should say yes."

"But I have to wear an electronic ankle monitor? And home confinement?"

"It's pretty standard these days," he says.

I know—but then I can't do what I need to do. I'll be trapped.

"And Jenna," he says. "I called that facility, that off-site storage place I use. Dunbar Professional Storage?"

"Yes?" I perk up.

"I know someone there. I'm a longtime client. Anyway—Holden's lawyer, Finn Rucker? His firm *does* use that facility."

I nod. "Okay, good."

"But you should know something. Someone broke into their facility last night."

"What?" I draw back from him.

"Yeah. Broke through a window. Removed the iron bars. Had the run of the place. So just in case you were getting a dumb idea like breaking into that warehouse—which we both know you were thinking—you should know that they've doubled down on security. They're posting guards around the clock now."

"What—what was taken?" I ask.

"They don't know. Practically impossible to tell. I think they're doing an inventory, but it's so hard to know. There are literally millions of files there." He looks at me, cocks his head. "Why? You think this is related to your—"

"Of *course* it's related," I whisper harshly. "Whoever broke in there—he did it so I wouldn't find those files."

"Jenna." He squeezes my arm. "You're watching too many conspiracy shows."

"He took it so I wouldn't find it," I say. Realizing that I probably sound paranoid to him, just another irrational client.

The guards intervene, place me in handcuffs, and escort me out.

I glance back at Brody, who looks like he's never felt sorrier for anyone.

Then I glance at Justin, who looks like he's just lost his best friend.

Chapter 103

BOND WAS SET at two million dollars this morning for Jenna Murphy, the former Southampton police detective arrested for the murders of Dede Paris and Annie Church, the Yale sophomores whose disappearance in the Hamptons five years ago sparked a massive manhunt. . . .

Noah Walker paces back and forth in his living room as the newscast—*News at Noon*—talks about Murphy and the murders of the Yale sophomores.

Noah is exhausted, not having slept last night, after breaking into the storage facility and removing those files. He needs to sleep, he needs to shower—but he can't do anything but think about his next move.

He passes the couch, the pile of documents he took from the warehouse.

The news clipping with the catchy headline, NEWBORN ABANDONED AT POLICE STATION, which tells most of the story right there.

And the letter, aged and dusty, having sat in a file inside that storage facility for the better part of twenty years now. The nice stationery, the fancy letterhead bearing the name of the private investigator hired by Holden VI, with tabs behind the letter, supporting documentation:

Mr. Dahlquist:

This private investigation was undertaken on your behalf, at the direction of Mr. Finneus Rucker, Esq., your attorney. This investigation is thus covered by the attorney-client privilege and will remain confidential.

You asked us to determine whether a woman named Gloria Willis, of Bridgehampton, mother of Aiden Willis, gave birth to a second child approximately eight years ago.

Noah looks away from the documents, thinks of the things Jenna Murphy has said to him over the last few weeks.

At the cemetery, when she told him her theory for the first time: *Holden the Sixth left behind a son,* she said. *A son who wants to restart the family tradition.*

And yesterday, in the parking lot at Tasty's: *Were you adopted, Noah?*

Holden left behind a son. Were you adopted, Noah?

He looks back down at the letter:

The answer to your question is yes. Eight years ago, Ms. Willis did give birth to a second child at Southampton Hospital but left the hospital with her child only hours later, without filling out any paperwork. We believe that she abandoned this child later that evening at the Bridgehampton Police Substation (see attached news headline).

He reads through the packet of information behind the letter—the hospital records, the county adoption records, the photographs.

Noah goes upstairs to his bedroom loft, finds the handgun he hasn't held in years. Checks it for ammunition. Stuffs it in his pants. Puts on a clean shirt, pulls it down over the gun.

He grabs his leather jacket on the way out and hops on his Harley.

Her apartment isn't far. And she's definitely not home. She's in jail, stuck on a two-million-dollar bond.

He parks his Harley outside her apartment and approaches it. It's broad daylight, and cars occasionally whisk by on Main Street. But no pedestrians approach.

His heartbeat speeds up. Should he do it?

Yes.

He slams against the door, four times, five times, violent thrusts, wood splintering, sharp pain in his shoulder, until enough of the door frame has been compromised that he can reach inside and unlock the dead bolt and open the knob from the inside.

He pushes open the battered door and he's inside Jenna Murphy's apartment.

A mess. A train wreck.

A timeline, on her wall, covering all of the murders. Right. He's seen that before.

But there's something he hasn't seen before. On her desk, beneath the timeline. A newspaper clipping, jagged edges, still with tape attached to all four corners, as if she removed it from something:

Newborn Abandoned at Police Station

Noah's heart skips a beat.

She knows, he thinks. *She already knows.*

Knowing what he has to do now. Wishing it hadn't come to this.

He was really starting to like Jenna Murphy.

Chapter 104

ANOTHER DAY IN this cramped, drafty jail cell. A special kind of torture for me, listening to the hustle and bustle one floor above me, hearing the police department at work, reminding me of how far I've fallen in such a short time.

Isaac wanted it that way. He normally would transfer me to the Suffolk County Jail after my bond hearing, where I'd be placed in administrative segregation because I'm a former cop, who can't be put in with ordinary inmates. But the jail is overcrowded, which gave Isaac the excuse to keep me here, so close and yet so far from the job I once had, the job I loved.

Footsteps. Somebody approaching my cell. It's not lunch. I ate a half hour ago. Tea and crumpets, maybe? A complimentary massage?

No, and no.

It's Isaac, staring at me, looking . . . not so happy. I mean, he's not Mr. Sunshine on a good day, but . . . why shouldn't he be happy? He should be dancing a jig, the way things are going.

He produces a key from behind his back and opens the door. He walks in and sizes me up. I try to put on a brave front, to look like I'm holding up much better than I really am. But I can't hide the dark circles under my eyes, and I haven't showered in two days; my hair is flat and oily. My clothes look exactly as they should—like I've slept in them for two nights.

He doesn't just look unhappy. He looks like he just swallowed a bug.

Why the long face, Isaac?

"You have the right to remain silent," he says to me. And then he runs through the rest of the Miranda warnings. I could say them backward by now.

"Why are you Mirandizing me?" I ask.

"I want you to acknowledge I've made you aware of your rights," he says.

"Fine. Done."

But fresh Miranda warnings? Only one reason for that.

He wants to question me on a new topic.

"What happened in 1994?" he asks.

I draw back. Why is he asking me about 1994? When I was just a kid. The year that thing happened, when I disappeared, only to be found on the beach by 7 Ocean Drive. The day my parents whisked me away from the Hamptons, never to return during my childhood.

Seven hours of hell, Aunt Chloe called it.

"There was a missing-persons report that summer," he says. "It lasted less than a day. I saw it myself. July—"

"I have nothing to say to you, Isaac. Zilch."

Isaac steps back. He can't be surprised that I'd clam up. His face turns tomato red.

"I just want you to know," he says, "that I know you're behind this. I don't know what kind of crap you're pulling here, but I'm going to figure it out. You may have won this battle, but you won't win the war."

What the hell is he talking about? What battle did *I* win? As far as I can tell, right now I'm getting the royal crap beaten out of me.

He opens his hand. "You're free to leave," he says.

Oh. Justin came through with the money that quickly? Quicker than he thought he could.

But this doesn't seem right. Isaac doesn't have any handcuffs.

There's a protocol when you bond out. You're transported to the sheriff, who makes arrangements for your home confinement, gets a list of addresses for doctors and lawyers and grocery stores so they can input the coordinates into the GPS. Then someone fits the ankle bracelet on you.

But until then, you're still locked up. You're handcuffed and transported.

"I said you're free to leave," he says. "You're being released."

"I don't understand."

Isaac shoots me a look. He thinks I *do* understand. He thinks I've pulled some kind of fast one, that I'm just playing dumb.

"You're no longer under arrest for the murders of Dede Paris and Annie Church," he says.

My head spins, some strange version of hope floating through me.

"The DNA came back on the murder weapon," he says. "None of the blood on the knife matches those girls. Their stab wounds don't match up with the knife blade, either. That knife wasn't used to kill Dede and Annie."

I stand up for the first time, unsteady, certain I'm not hearing this correctly. A bloody knife, with both Aiden's and my fingerprints on it, but . . .

"We did get matches on the blood, though," says Isaac. "Not Dede or Annie, but two matches. One of the matches was you, Murphy."

Like the floor has dropped out from beneath me, like I'm spinning, falling . . .

"My . . . blood?"

My blood on the knife? My prints and my blood?

"And . . . who else's blood?" I manage. "You said . . . two matches."

"You know," says Isaac, fuming. "You damn well know. Tell me, Murphy. Tell me everything."

But I can't. I *don't* know. I don't know what the hell is going on.

"That knife wasn't used to kill Annie and Dede," says Isaac. "It was the knife used to kill Holden Dahlquist the Sixth, on July 13, 1994. The same day that you went missing for seven hours."

Chapter 105

I STUMBLE OUT of the police station with a bag holding my cell phone, wallet, keys.

I don't know what to do.

I don't know where to go.

I look at my hand, at the inch-long scar across my palm. The only injury they found on me, Aunt Chloe said, after I went missing for seven hours and then was found on the beach, otherwise unharmed.

That scar must have come from the knife. The knife that had my fingerprints on it. It cut my hand. I must have touched it, too.

My prints, my blood.

On the knife that Holden VI used to kill himself.

On July 13, 1994.

I was there. I was there when it happened.

What the hell happened that day?

Aiden, I think. I need to find Aiden.

But how? And whom can I trust at this point? Not Noah. Not Ricketts, not anymore.

Only one person I can think of.

I make the call, and not fifteen minutes later, Justin's Jaguar pulls up in front of the substation.

He pops out. "What happened? How did you get out?"

I shake my head. It's a long story. A story I don't even understand.

"Justin," I say, "I need someone I can trust. That's a rapidly dwindling population, I'm afraid."

Justin nods, a look of concern on his face.

"Can I trust you?" I ask.

"Only one way to find out." He smiles, then realizes the comment fell flat. He touches my arm. "Hey, listen. You know how I feel about you. I haven't made a secret of that. And I know . . . I know you don't feel quite the same way about me. I know I'm not your type."

"No, it's not—"

"I'm not dumb, Jenna. And I'm not blind, either. But I'm here for you if you need me. Maybe—maybe I'll grow on you. Maybe not. But either way, if you need something, you know all you have to do is ask."

I hate this. I hate having to rely on someone else. Especially for this.

"Aiden already tried to kill me once," I say. "He'd do it again. And someone's working with him. There are people in this town who don't want me to figure this out, and they'll kill to stop me."

Justin takes a deep breath, then nods.

"I'm in," he says. "Let's do it."

Chapter 106

JUSTIN DRIVES HIS Jaguar toward his house, having just gotten an earful from me.

"Okay," he says, glancing at me. "So something happened to you here in July of 1994, and you think Aiden had something to do with it."

"Yes. And someone else did, too."

"Okay," he says. "And you think this 'someone else' is Aiden's younger half brother."

"Yes. And his father is Holden Dahlquist the Sixth."

Justin takes a deep breath. "You think Holden the Sixth, and his newfound son, and Aiden, tried to kill you when you were a little girl."

"Something like that," I say. "I don't have it all figured out. Maybe—maybe I was their first. Maybe I was a dry run, a test, to see if they could pull it off. Whatever it was, something must have gone wrong, because *Holden* ended up dead, not me."

"Wow. And now the son is carrying on the legacy."

"I think so," I say. "So the key is, who is Holden's

son? Who is the baby abandoned at the police station? Isaac? Noah?"

Justin shrugs. "Can you ask them?"

"They wouldn't admit it. I asked Noah if he was adopted and he said no. But that doesn't mean he's telling the truth."

"Or maybe he doesn't know," says Justin. "Maybe his parents never told him."

"Oh, come on."

"No, seriously, Jenna—how do any of us know that our parents are our biological parents? We take our parents' word for it, right?"

"There are birth certificates," I say.

"Those are just records. They can be doctored."

"Or there's a strong physical resemblance."

Justin makes a face. "Maybe. But not always. I'm not adopted, but I don't look a whole lot like either of my parents. I'm kind of a blend of them. Do you look like your parents?"

I think about that. "Actually, I got my looks and red hair from my Irish great-grandmother." I turn to Justin. "Okay, point taken. So you think there might be someone running around with Holden the Sixth's genes, and he doesn't even *know* it?"

"Possibly. Do you think there's some kind of serial-killer gene that can be passed down from generation to generation? Even without your knowledge?"

That one is definitely above my pay grade.

"We have to find Aiden," I say. "Aiden's the key to all of this."

"Okay, so how do we do that?"

"I have no idea."

Justin touches my arm. "Don't say that. Think."

Think. He's right, think.

"If I'm Aiden," I say, "I don't have much money. I don't have a car. I can't go to airports or train or bus stations. I can't use a credit card for a rental car or a hotel. How do I run? I could hitchhike."

"Have you gotten a good look at Aiden?" Justin asks. "Would you pick him up?"

"Stranger things have happened. But okay. What else? He could boost a car, I suppose. But I don't have access to that kind of information right now, recent auto thefts or anything else. I don't have any resources at all."

"I'll try not to take that as an insult," says Justin.

"You know what I mean."

If I'm Aiden, what do I do? If I'm Aiden . . .

If I'm Aiden . . .

Wait.

"Maybe he didn't run at all," I say. I turn to Justin. "Maybe he's right here in town. He's lived here his whole life, right? If he could find a place to hide for a while, it would beat the hell out of traveling somewhere with no money, no resources."

Justin shakes his head.

I slap my hand on the dashboard. Could it be that simple?

"I can't believe this," I say, "but I think I might know where he is."

Chapter 107

NOAH JUMPS ONTO his motorcycle, his heartbeat racing faster than the bike's engine as he heads across town.

He parks his Harley and removes the gun from his pants, placing it inside the saddlebag on his bike. Cops don't like it when you walk into a police station with a handgun.

Noah enters the police substation. Someone at the front desk, behind a plate of bulletproof glass.

"I'm here to see one of the people in the holding cell," he says.

"Are you a lawyer?" the man asks, though he doesn't seem to think Noah fits that bill.

"No, but this is important," he says. "Jenna Murphy is—"

"Jenna Murphy isn't here," the man says.

"Oh—where are you holding her?"

"We're not. She was released half an hour ago."

"She was *released?* On bond?"

The officer on duty looks over his glasses at Noah. "Sir, whoever you are, I can't give that information to you."

He looks outside. She was released half an hour ago? But . . . he saw her car at her house just now. How did she leave? She wouldn't have walked—

Justin, he thinks. *She must be with Justin.*

"I need to speak with Isaac," he says. "I need to speak with the chief."

"Sir," says the duty officer, "you can't just waltz in here and demand to speak with the chief."

"It's important."

"Sir, the chief isn't—"

"Listen!" Noah slaps his hand against the plate of glass. "I need to speak with him and I need to speak with him now!"

"Hey."

Noah turns at the sound of the voice. A uniformed officer approaching him, a young woman—Murphy's friend, the rookie cop, Lauren Ricketts.

"What's going on, Noah?" she says.

"I have to talk to Isaac," he says. "Right now."

"Why? Tell me what's going on."

Noah thinks it over. He doesn't know Ricketts. He has no idea what she knows and what she doesn't know.

"No," he says. "I'll only talk to Isaac."

Chapter 108

JUSTIN PULLS HIS car into his garage in East Hampton. The garage door grinds to a close behind us.

"So tell me," he says. "Tell me where you think Aiden is."

"Later," I say.

"Later? Why later?"

My cell phone buzzes. Caller ID says it's Lauren Ricketts. I don't dare answer. I let the call go to voice mail and then play the message on my speakerphone:

Murphy, it's Ricketts. I'm not sure what's going on, and I probably shouldn't be calling you, but—but whatever, I'm calling you. Listen, about twenty minutes ago, Noah Walker had a private conversation with the chief, and the next thing I know, Isaac has issued an APB for you. They think you're with Justin.

I look over at Justin, whose face has gone pale.

He mobilized the SWAT teams, Murphy. We're coming after you with everything we have. You should surrender at the station before something bad happens. I can coordinate it with you. Please, call me before this gets out of hand.

Justin turns and looks at me, the gravity of what we've just heard sinking in. "He just released you, and now he's after you again?"

After talking to Noah, apparently. And here I thought Noah didn't get along so well with the chief.

I get out of the car, and Justin follows suit. We go into his house, his beautiful, spacious kitchen.

"You said you have a gun," I say.

"Um—yeah, I do," he says, still distracted. "Hang on."

"And a flashlight," I call out to him as he leaves the kitchen.

I take a breath. Isaac and Noah got together, had a nice little chat, and now the STPD is after me with full force.

Isaac and Noah. They've made a very public show of not getting along so well. An act? An act I fell for hook, line, and sinker?

"Okay." Justin returns to the kitchen with not one gun but two, holding each of them with two fingers, the barrels dangling down.

"A regular arsenal," I say.

But not really. One is a shiny, polished revolver, new and, from the looks of it, unused. The other is a beat-up revolver with a pearl handle, a vintage piece, a .38 special with a very short, maybe two-inch barrel that is probably thirty or forty years old.

"Take your pick," he says, placing them gently on the kitchen table.

I laugh. "Take my pick? How old is that thirty-eight special?"

Justin shrugs. "My dad bought it years ago—probably the seventies. This new one, I bought. I assume it works."

"You assume?"

He shakes his head. "Never used it. Bought it for home protection. Some silly notion that I'm safer with it. I have a feeling if I ever had to use it, I'd end up shooting myself in the foot or something."

"You're probably right." I choose the shiny new revolver, hold the gun toward the floor, pop open the cylinder, and confirm the presence of rounds in all six chambers.

Justin looks at all of this like he's scared to death of guns.

He probably is. This isn't his thing. He isn't cut out for this. He's a nice guy, a wonderful guy, but he lives in a world where people are decent and gracious. He doesn't live in a world full of bad guys. That's where we differ. That's where we'll always differ.

"And the flashlight," I say.

"Oh—right," he says. He removes one from a kitchen drawer and hands it to me.

Then he claps his hands, as if ready for action, but the paleness of his face suggests otherwise. "Where to?" he asks. "Where do you think Aiden is hiding out?"

I stuff the revolver in the back of my pants. "I have to go now," I say.

He looks at me. "Don't you mean *we* have to go?"

"No, I mean I have to go. This is my problem, not yours."

"Jenna—"

"You've done enough. You've given me your gun and a flashlight, and a ride. But I can't ask for anything else."

"For the last time, you *didn't ask,*" he says. He puts his hands on my shoulders. "You can't do this by yourself. I may not be a veteran police officer or some Navy SEAL—shit, I wasn't even an athlete—but you can trust me. I'd do anything for you, Detective Murphy. Haven't you figured that out by now?"

I look into his eyes. Yes, there's something there, something more than gratitude for all his attempts to help me. Maybe what I feel for him is enough. Maybe. But now is not the time to be gauging my emotions.

I have to do this, and I have to do it alone.

"I'll just follow you," he says.

"Not if I shoot you in the leg."

He laughs, in spite of the circumstances.

Then the doorbell rings. We both turn our heads toward the front door. Justin takes a couple of cautious steps backward and peeks beyond the kitchen, presumably through a window.

"Police car," he says.

"East Hampton PD?"

"Southampton," he says. "That's Isaac Marks at my front door."

Chapter 109

"SHIT," I SAY, panic swirling inside me. "*Shit.*"

Justin puts out a hand for caution. "I'll take care of it. Stay here."

"I should hide."

"No place to hide. He'd see you running through the kitchen. Sit tight."

Justin walks out of the kitchen. A moment later, I hear him opening the front door. I steel myself, close my eyes, listen carefully.

"Isaac," he says.

My blood goes cold.

"Hello, Justin. I'm looking for Jenna Murphy. Is she here?"

"Here? No. No, she's not here. Why?"

"Do you know where she is?"

"No idea," says Justin. "Is everything okay?"

"It's a police matter. When did you last see her?"

"I dropped her off at her house earlier today. After she was released from custody."

"And?"

"And nothing. That's it. I dropped her off and I drove here."

"You drove here? Why not to the restaurant?"

A pause. "I'm the boss, Isaac. I come and go as I please. I didn't think I had to get the police department's permission."

"You come and go as you please." A pause, this time from Isaac. "You wouldn't be lying to me, would you, Justin? Because you know it's a crime to lie to a law enforcement officer, don't you?"

"I think I've heard that somewhere," Justin says. "Oh, I know—it was on TV."

I smile but don't dare laugh.

"You think this is funny? Listen to me, and listen to me very closely. We are actively seeking to bring Jenna Murphy into custody. She's not who you think she is."

"I think she's an honorable and decent person."

"Well, she isn't. I'm gonna take her down. The easy way or the hard way, I'm gonna do it. I prefer the easy way. The safe way. But if you're helping her evade us, you become an accessory. You ever heard *that* term from TV? It means you're just as guilty as she is."

Justin doesn't respond.

"I've known you a long time, Justin. Never had a beef with you. You've always been a good egg. And you make the best damn barbecue shrimp on Long Island. So I'm going to give you one more chance. And think about what I said. You can help us find a dangerous person who's committed some very serious crimes. Or you could lie to me and spend a very long time in prison. And I will personally see to it that you do."

My heart is sinking as Justin himself sinks deeper and deeper into my problems.

"I understand." Justin's tone is cold and flat.

"Do you know where Jenna Murphy is?"

I hold my breath. I'd come out right now and show myself, and spare Justin any further trouble. But if I do, it's game over. I'll never know the truth.

"I have no idea where she is," Justin tells Isaac.

Justin returns to the kitchen, his face ashen, after Isaac drives away.

"Well, that was fun," he says, trying to maintain a brave front, but he can't even bring himself to smile.

"I'm so sorry," I say. "I'm going to leave now."

"I'm going with you."

"No. I leave now, you have plausible deniability. I'll scrape the serial number off your gun so it can't be traced back to you. No one will ever know you helped me. But if you go with me, you spend the next decade in prison. Assuming you don't get killed."

"I don't care." He touches my arm. "I understand the risks. But you need help, and the risk of losing you is worse than . . ." He swallows hard. His eyes fill. "I don't usually—I've never responded to anyone like I do to you."

I step away from him. "Justin, you know I can't reciprocate those feelings. I just don't know—"

"Yeah, I know. But I don't care. You just haven't figured out what a wonderful guy I am yet. You will, someday."

I drop my eyes and smile. Still trying to make this

easier for me. Maybe he's right. Maybe someday I'll feel about him the same way he does about me. If there is a *someday* in my future.

"At least tell me where you're going," he says.

"No, Justin."

"Then take my car."

"No. They find your car and that's the same thing as you coming with me. You're aiding and abetting. I'll walk. Better I stay off the roads, anyway. And I'm in no hurry. I need the sun to go down before I make my move. I'll wait until midnight, probably."

"Call me on your cell, then. At least tell me you're okay."

"Turning my cell phone off right now," I say. "So they can't track me."

Justin lets out air, shaking his head. "Oh, Jenna. Don't say good-bye to me. Just—tell me this isn't good-bye."

I walk up to him and plant a soft kiss on his cheek. "This isn't good-bye," I say, before I head out his back door.

Chapter 110

MY THOUGHTS ZIGZAGGING in every direction, trying to make sense of it all—Noah, Isaac, Aiden—not to mention the entire Southampton Town Police Department after me, heavily armed and prepared for combat. But something is telling me that the key to this is Aiden Willis. If I can get hold of him tonight, if I can surprise him and subdue him, I can finally put an end to this.

The walk from East Hampton isn't bad. It's about seven miles, which under different circumstances would be a typical day's jog for me, and it's safer than driving. When you're on foot, you're nimble. You can escape into crowds, cut corners, hide among foliage—you can obscure yourself in any number of ways.

The sky overhead is threatening rain, which will royally suck if it happens, but the good news is that in the meantime, it darkens the sky and brings the rough equivalent of nightfall prematurely.

I make it to the beach and kick off my shoes and

tromp along the sand, the restless Atlantic Ocean to the south, the carefree breeze playing with my hair. I don't look like a fugitive, and unless the police are conducting beach patrol, I'm practically invisible to them.

So I sit in the sand, less than a mile from my destination, watching the foamy tide crash ashore and recede, waiting for the moment to arrive. If my guess about Aiden is right, he's settling in right now, nestled in his hiding spot, his guard slowly lowering.

Somewhere in the house at 7 Ocean Drive.

At midnight, I make the decision—it's time. Hopefully, he's asleep, or at least close to it. Not expecting company, in any event.

I step out of the sand onto the parking lot and look up at the mansion. No lights are on. No visible sign of life. Not that I expected Aiden to be hosting a party.

I walk along Ocean Drive until I reach the front of the house, my nervous system catching up now, sending warning signals to me, filling my chest. Justin's revolver in my right hand, the flashlight in my left.

I try the driveway entrance, expecting resistance, planning to push it open and squeeze myself between the twin gates. But it's not locked. I push one side open and enter, then close it back up, without allowing my imagination to wonder why the gate would be open.

My breathing erratic, my legs heavy, I walk up the driveway to the fork—to the right, the walk heading up the hill to the house; to the left, the driveway continuing on to the carriage house or whatever it is.

For some reason, I don't take the familiar path, the

one I've traveled several times during my investigation, up the sidewalk toward the house.

This time, I stay left, remaining on the driveway, walking toward that oversize carriage house.

Not knowing why. Unable to place it in my brain, but feeling something inside me growing, spreading like poison.

And then a flash through my brain like lightning.

Walking, shoved from behind, forced forward, wondering what it is, a stable, a garage, a separate house, where is it he's taking me?

Walk. Move! Walk faster, you stupid girl!

I suck in a breath. I should turn around now. I know that. If I had any sense, I'd turn and run. Instead, I shine my light forward, just briefly, to see if there's anything in front of me, up the driveway toward the structure.

I move slowly—

Faster! Walk faster!

—as I approach it. Tall double doors for an entrance. On the ground, at my feet, a long chain with a broken lock.

Somebody unlocked this door recently.

He's here. Aiden is here.

I put my flashlight in my mouth and raise my gun. With my free hand, I pull on the door handle and yank it open.

In one motion, I drop to a knee, remove the flashlight from my mouth, and click it on, sweeping it over the space inside.

Open air. Two stories tall. Big, yes, but empty.

Empty.

Stains on the concrete floor from automobiles, once upon a time. A rack on the wall for tools, though none are present right now. A carpenter's desk, too, a wooden top with steel legs, with an old saw and a vise on top.

Empty. But a different kind of empty.

I shine my light along the floor by the desk. There are circles on the floor, dust markings, from where the legs of the tool desk rested not long ago.

"Someone moved that desk," I mumble to myself. Recently. Very recently.

Why move it?

I shine the light along the floor.

In the area where the desk once stood, before being moved, there is a break in the concrete. An outline. A square. Lying on top of it, a short length of rope.

I squat down for a closer look. Same color paint, but the surface of the square looks different.

I try to pick up the rope, but it's stuck to the floor, attached somehow.

And the surface is . . . wood, not concrete.

A wooden square with a rope attached to it.

I grab the rope and, this time, pull on it hard.

The wooden square jars loose.

"What the hell . . ."

I pull harder, and the piece of wood pops upward.

A burst of cool air escaping from beneath it.

"A hidden door," I whisper.

There's something underneath this floor.

Chapter 111

MY GUN POISED, I pull the trapdoor fully open. I turn on the flashlight, dust particles floating in the beam, aiming it down into the darkness below.

A ladder, a wooden ladder, leading down several steps to a floor.

My lungs thirsting for air, my head spinning. A small tremor spreads through my limbs, immediately turning into a full-scale tremble, my hand shaking so hard I can hardly hold my gun. I don't dare cock the revolver's hammer, putting the gun in ready position, for fear I'll start shooting, maybe even hitting myself.

The ladder so wobbly

I don't know how far down it will go

The boy yelling at me, "Move! Move!"

I drop to my knees and suck in air, desperately seeking breath while my lungs seize up.

I was here. I was in this carriage house. I went down this ladder.

Sweat stinging my eyes, my shirt stuck to my back,

my vision spotty, my heart pounding so fiercely I can hardly move.

"Move, Murphy," I whisper. "Move."

I tuck the gun into the back of my pants. I fish around the open space with one leg until my foot finds a rung on the ladder.

I move slowly, hoping to minimize the noise, praying I don't lose my grip, the ladder itself quaking along with my hands, my arms and legs.

Darker, the lower I climb.

Colder.

White noise filling my ears, bits and pieces of memories, the sounds of the boy's voice taunting me—

Move! Keep moving, stupid girl

—my body shivering so violently, my feet hitting the floor, something hard like marble. I remove my gun and aim it in all directions, spinning, somehow keeping my balance, as I shine the flashlight all around.

A tunnel. I'm at one end. The other end, I can't see. High ceilings, width sufficient for two, maybe three people to stand side-by-side.

The lightning bolts between my eyes, the fragments coming back.

Wearing sandals and the bathing suit Mommy just bought me, a Lion King *T-shirt over it. So hard to walk in these sandals, especially when the boy pushes me, afraid that if I fall he'll get mad, afraid of what he might do to me—*

Stepping forward gingerly, every forward advance an effort, half blind from the sweat burning my eyes, electricity filling my body—

I don't understand what is happening, why this boy is

making me go down here, where are we going, where are we going—

The beam of my flashlight dancing along the floor, the walls, the ceiling, and then I see it.

A wall. The end of the tunnel.

A doorknob.

I tuck the flashlight under my left arm, my left hand holding a wobbly gun. With my right, I reach for the knob.

I steel myself. "You can do this," I tell myself.

I turn the knob slowly, then whip the door open.

Chapter 112

I POINT THE gun inside the room, my pulse pounding against my temples.

The smell of bleach and burning oil. A square, windowless room, a single kerosene lamp on one side casting flickering orange light about. Next to the lamp, a sleeping bag, unfolded, but nobody inside it. Nobody in this room, period. No chairs or furniture or anything except—except something near the back—

A spear. Protruding from the floor, a long narrow missile with a sharp top—

"No," I say. "No." Hot tears blurring my vision, running down my cheeks into my mouth.

I step into the room, my words echoing between my ears, the walls moving, the room spinning, the cries, the horrific, ghoulish screams from all directions filling my head, my legs unsteady as I move forward—

—as I move toward the other end of this square room—

—because somehow I know, some internal compass

is directing me, some force is moving me toward a door at the other end of the room, a door I can't see but that I know, somehow I know is there.

Everything slowing down, like I'm moving through quicksand, but *I must reach the door,* I have to reach it for some reason, but my legs are suddenly numb, up is down, down is up, the floor is suddenly rising up to meet my face with a violent smack, sending shock waves through my skull, jarring the roots of my teeth.

The revolver bounces out of my hand on impact with the floor.

Everything fuzz and fog, but I can't let go now, can't let go now.

The flashlight underneath me—I fell on it—but the gun . . .

I need the gun.

My head lifting off the floor, searing pain over my right eye, nausea rising to the surface; I'm woozy and disoriented. Patting the floor around me. Forcing myself to my knees, light flickering in and out from the glow of the kerosene lamp, the gash over my eye making me pay a severe price every time I whip my head from one side to the other, but I need the gun—

Words screaming at me, but I can't make them out, so loud that I can't hear them, echoing through my head with such force that I can't understand them, what is he saying, what is he—

Come with me

Footsteps, coming from the other side of the room, near the door I can't see, footsteps, someone's coming—

Come with me

Come with me
The gun, I need the gun—
Where is that gun?
The click of a doorknob, the groan of a door opening.
And Aiden Willis walks in.

Chapter 113

AIDEN, THE SCARECROW hair sticking out from his baseball cap turned backward, his features lit up with the flickering orange light, holding something in his hand, a thermos, closing the door behind him.

I hold my breath, hold my body still, searching for the gun only with my eyes.

There. I spot it. Justin's revolver, over by the wall.

"Oh—" Aiden jumps upon seeing me on the floor to his left. The thermos falls from his hand, clanging and bouncing on the ground. He falls against the wall and struggles to keep his balance.

I slide my body toward the far wall and grab the revolver, cock the hammer.

"What—how—what do you—"

I grip the gun with both hands, trembling so fiercely that I couldn't possibly aim properly.

My insides on fire, my head ringing, nausea and bile at my throat, oxygen coming in tiny, thirsty gulps—

The door opens

Bright light streaming in, and a boy, a boy with scarecrow hair

With some reserve energy I didn't know existed, as if I'm watching someone else perform the task, I rise to my knees and aim the gun toward Aiden.

Aiden's eyes go wide; he looks ghoulish in the intermittent orange light, pinned against the wall, watching me.

Lightning, thunder between my ears.

Come with me

Come with me

The gun so unsteady in my hand, rising and falling, swaying back and forth.

Aiden watching me, watching the gun bob up and down, back and forth.

Tears filling my eyes again, my chest heaving, my throat so full I can't speak—

Come with me

Sobbing and shaking, the gun moving all over the place—

Aiden watching me, watching the gun.

Come with me

The gun dropping to my side. I can't do it. I know it and Aiden knows it.

Aiden pushes himself off the wall, straightens himself.

Looks at me, just for a single moment, those darting eyes making contact with mine.

Come with me

Then he walks toward me. No sudden movement, just slowly approaching me.

Come with me

The boy with the scarecrow hair

Aiden places a hand over my gun hand, then carefully removes the revolver from it.

I look up at him, on my knees, helpless.

He uncocks the revolver, points it upward, pops open the cylinder, and empties all six rounds from the chamber into his cupped hand. He locks the cylinder back in place and hands the unloaded gun back to me.

"Aiden, wait," I manage, my throat full, my words garbled.

Then Aiden Willis disappears through the door from which he entered.

"Please, wait," I say as I get to my feet, the synapses not firing properly, but I manage to stumble and stagger toward the door.

Chapter 114

NOAH WALKER SITS on his idling Harley, down the street from Justin's house in East Hampton. He's logged a lot of miles tonight looking for Jenna Murphy, driving loops around Bridgehampton, hitting some familiar spots like Murphy's apartment, Tasty's, the Dive Bar, even Aiden's house, but always doubling back here to Justin's place.

Because Justin's the best bet for finding her. Jenna was last seen, according to Isaac, being picked up outside the police station by someone driving a Jaguar, which almost assuredly means Justin. And it would make sense she'd call him.

They aren't together right now, apparently, because all Justin has done for the last couple of hours is pace back and forth in his living room.

There he is right now, standing close enough to the window on the west side of his property that Noah can see him. Checking his watch. Pacing. Running his hands through his hair. Nervous. Anxious.

Maybe it's time to drive around some more, do another loop.

He jumps at the sight of Justin's garage door lifting. A moment later, the Jaguar pulls out of the driveway, backing up not far from where Noah rests on his Harley.

This is it. He's sure of it.

He waits until Justin has turned off his street before he starts up his bike and drives. He turns in the same direction as Justin and follows him from a distance, only a small amount of traffic on the roads but sufficient to hide his presence.

Justin travels west on Main Street toward Bridgehampton. Noah keeps his distance, considers even killing his lights, but he sees no indication that Justin knows he's being followed.

If only he knew where Justin was going. If he knew that, he could—

Justin's car slows near the cemetery. He puts on his signal for a right turn.

Wait.

Wait a second.

He's heading for Ocean Drive. Sure. Of course. He's going to that house.

And I know a shortcut. I can beat him there.

Noah veers off Main Street and drives his bike across the open field of the cemetery, taking a straight line instead of the right angle Justin is forced to take by driving on the streets.

Noah crosses through the south end of the cemetery and hits Ocean Drive before Justin has even turned off Main Street. With a good two blocks' lead on Justin, he kills the lights on his bike and guns it forward, making sure he'll arrive at the mansion at least a full minute before Justin.

He stops at a group of trees just off the street, very close to the mansion. He looks back, seeing the headlights of a car in the distance, heading his way.

He removes his gun and flashlight from his saddlebag. Then he ducks into the shrubbery across the street from the mansion and waits. Only moments later, the Jaguar pulls up in front of the mansion.

Justin gets out of his car without any sense that Noah is nearby, or that he's been followed, jogging up to the mammoth gate blocking the driveway. He grabs it, then pushes it open and heads onto the driveway.

Noah creeps closer, obscured by darkness, in soft grass, watching Justin.

Justin jogs slowly up toward the dark house, looking at it. Looking, as well, at the old carriage house at the end of the driveway.

Noah crosses the street and hides behind the Jaguar.

Justin, at a crossroads, decides to head up the driveway, toward the carriage house. Noah slinks up to the gate by the curb and pushes it open as softly as he can.

A flashlight comes on, Justin illuminating the space in front of him.

Noah sees what Justin saw, the reason he chose to head up the driveway.

The door of the carriage house is wide open.

Justin starts jogging toward it, while Noah follows, moving at a slightly faster clip, closing the distance but taking care not to announce himself.

"Jenna!" Justin calls out in a harsh whisper. "Jenna?" He approaches the carriage house with caution, slowing his pace.

Then Justin disappears inside.

Noah reaches the doors and readies himself.

Chapter 115

NOAH PEEKS INSIDE the carriage house.

Justin is shining his flashlight around. "Shit," he says.

You don't know what shit is, Justin.

But you're about to find out.

Noah springs forward into the room. Before Justin can do anything more than turn around, Noah plows into him, sending him sprawling, crashing into the wall. Noah grabs Justin and throws him facedown on the cement floor, gripping his hair, shoving the gun into the back of Justin's neck.

"Where is she?" Noah growls.

"Noah?" Justin manages, catching his breath. "Is that . . . you?"

"Tell me where she is, Justin, or I'll kill you right now."

His fingers tightly gripping Justin's hair, Noah jerks Justin's head upward and then down, hard, onto the cement floor.

"That's me being nice, Justin. You wanna see me when I'm mean? This is your last chance," says Noah. "Where is Jenna Murphy?"

"I don't—I'm looking for her, too. I thought she might've . . . come here."

Cool air to Noah's right. He looks over, shines his flashlight over the trapdoor, wide open.

"Did she go down there?"

"I'm telling you, I don't know."

"Don't bullshit me."

"I'm not bullshitting you." Justin's voice weaker from the blow to his head. "What . . . what are you going to do to her?"

Noah presses the gun into the soft space beneath Justin's skull. "You should be worried about what I'm going to do to *you*."

"Don't hurt her," Justin says. "Please, Noah, just . . . don't hurt her."

Noah leans down, close to Justin's face. "Justin, I can't tell if you're a liar or a fool."

He cracks Justin's head against the floor again. Justin goes limp with an abrupt groan.

Noah stands and shines his flashlight along the walls, over the carpenter's desk. Some things hanging on the walls that could be helpful.

Then he shines the light back down on Justin, unconscious but still breathing.

He pats Justin down and feels something in the front pocket of his trousers. He removes a tiny gun, one of those old Saturday-night specials, a beat-up vintage .38 with a pearl handle.

“I think I’ll take this, Justin,” he says. He stuffs the little gun into his pants pocket, a nice complement to his own gun.

“I haven’t decided what I’m gonna do to you yet,” he says. “Let’s see how I feel after my nice, friendly chat with Jenna Murphy.”

Chapter 116

I STUMBLE THROUGH the door, the door through which Aiden Willis just escaped, away from the smooth marble onto something different, the floor broken and dirty. Once I'm clear of the doorway, I slam the door behind me.

And take a deep, delicious breath of oxygen.

The air is dry and stale, but I don't care. I'm breathing again, on two feet again. I'm out of that awful room.

Come with me

I put one foot in front of the other, my legs unsteady but better, feeling better now.

"Aiden," I try to call out, my throat and mouth so dry I can hardly speak.

A small room, it feels like, not open air. I'm reaching out for the walls when something slithers across my face—

I jump back and wave my hand around, connect with it again.

A string, dangling in the air.

I reach out, making my hand still, and the string falls

back against my hand. I grip it and pull down.

A light, a single naked overhead light, comes on.

Hanging from the walls, medieval weapons. Lances, stars, battle-axes, cat-o'-nine-tails, maces. A full menu of torture devices.

I shudder but shake it off. I need to figure out a way out of here.

Three of the four walls are covered with this weaponry, but one wall is naked. Nothing hanging on it. Nothing but smooth wood.

Immediately next to it on the adjoining wall, a small button.

A buzzer?

With a trembling hand, I press the button.

I know, somehow, what will happen next: The wall slides open.

I drop to a knee, my weapon useless now without any bullets, and click on the flashlight.

A corridor. Naked walls, concrete floor.

The basement of 7 Ocean Drive.

Follow me

C'mon

"Aiden!" I call out, but I get no response. The hallway turns a sharp left into a giant room, just as dark as everywhere else in the basement. I shine my flashlight over the room, though the beam is weakening and I need to preserve the battery.

"Aiden!"

Boxes, old furniture, photographs and artwork—the kind of stuff in any basement.

And a staircase, leading up.

C'mon

Follow me

Be quiet

I approach the staircase slowly, not trusting my rubbery legs, my head throbbing like I have a hangover from being inside that room.

I take the stairs just as carefully, lightly touching each step before transferring my weight, unsure of the stability of this staircase.

When I reach the top of the stairs, the door is ajar.

Aiden must have blown through here a few minutes ago.

I take a breath and push the door open.

I turn the corner and shine the flashlight, the dwindling beam, over the open foyer of the house. The front door is straight ahead of me, across the foyer and the two ornate anterooms.

The words coming at me so fleetingly, like smoke, whispers—

Run go get out of here

Run!

"Aiden!" I call out again, my voice shakier this time, echoing upward, nothing in response but a groan from this haunted mansion.

I hear something upstairs, an elongated sigh. A house sound or a human sound?

I take a step up the stairs.

You don't wanna go up there

Squeezing my eyes shut, as if it will lock out the whispers between my ears.

Don't come up here

Go, leave, don't come up here

"Aiden, please talk to me!" I cry.

The pressure mounting inside my chest again, the momentary reprieve I felt after leaving that room vanishing in the snap of a finger, everything returning like an avalanche, my heart pounding again, sweat on my face once more.

Every step an effort, every instinct telling me to turn back, run out the front door, there's danger upstairs, but I move forward regardless, because I have to know, I have to finally know.

Even if it kills me.

I reach the landing on the second floor, the double doors open onto the second-floor hallway. I walk through like I'm in slow motion, like I'm wading upstream, but I'm not stopping now, so I turn left and head toward the master bedroom, the bedroom where Melanie Phillips and Zach Stern were brutally tortured, where various Holdens over the years committed brutal acts on others and on themselves.

"Aiden Willis!" I call, forcing the words out. "Aiden, I was wrong about you! I know that now! You—you saved my life that day. I remember now. You got me out of this house. Just—just please, *please* talk to me!"

One foot in front of the other down the ornate red-and-gold hallway, shining my dwindling flashlight beam in front of me, until I reach the threshold of the master bedroom.

"Aiden, are you in here?"

I shine my light over the room. Empty. Nobody here.

But near the bed, a lamp—another kerosene lamp,

the liquid full in the hourglass-shaped clear bowl, a short wick protruding from atop the metal dome. Next to it, a book of matches. I tuck my gun in the back of my pants and pin the flashlight between my arm and body. I strike the match and light the wick, producing a healthy orange glow about the room.

Light, precious light, as my flashlight is on the verge of dying.

I head to the corner of the room, to the French doors and the wraparound corner balcony outside. I push open the French doors, cool air hitting my face, the wind swirling, and look out over Ocean Drive to the west.

I see a glimpse of him, the signature straw hair, the slight hunch to his posture—Aiden Willis running north on Ocean Drive, away from the Atlantic, from this house, from me and my questions, and disappearing into the woods.

I lean against the railing, the wind playing with my hair, my eyes fixed on that point where Aiden ducked into the woods. I'll never catch up with him. He's too far ahead, and much more familiar with every nook and cranny of this town.

Come here, he said to me as a boy. *Follow me.*

I'm trying to pull more from that memory, but the more I reach for it, the farther away it gets. I shake my head. It's no use trying to force it. It's like turning on high beams to see through fog; it only muddies it up more.

I remember his face, remember his words, remember the relief sweeping through me when he guided me out of that basement and up those stairs.

"But then what?" I whisper.

And why—why did Aiden come through Justin's window the other night and try to attack me with that knife?

Deflated, defeated, I push myself off the railing. I curve around the corner to enter the bedroom from the south.

Where Noah Walker stands, training a gun on me.

Chapter 117

"DON'T MOVE, MURPHY. Don't move or I'll shoot."

I show him my empty hands. The flashlight left behind, on the bed. Justin's revolver stuffed in the back of my pants, which he can't see.

Focus, Murphy.

Assess—assess the situation.

I'm on the balcony by the railing. Noah is maybe eight, ten feet away, inside the room but just at the entrance to the balcony. The lamp, behind him, is sufficient to give me a decent look at his features—his eyes narrowed from the wind licking his face, stinging his eyes, his face crumpled up in anger, the gun trembling in front of him.

Anger—at me? For screwing up his plans? I guess he was having a pretty easy time killing people before I came along.

"I should kill you right now," he hisses.

"What's stopping you?" I say. My eyes cast about for options, but it's pitch-black out here on the balcony.

About my only option is jumping from the balcony and hoping I avoid the spiked fence, hoping I survive with just some broken bones.

Or charging him. He doesn't look that comfortable holding that gun. Most of the people he killed were cut or stabbed or impaled. Maybe firearms aren't his thing.

Still, he's so close to me. He couldn't miss me if he tried.

"I have a few questions," he says.

"And you think I'm going to answer them?"

"Yeah, I do," he says, "because I still haven't decided whether I'm going to kill your boyfriend Justin."

Justin. Roped into this because of me.

"Justin has nothing to do with this, Noah. Leave him out of it."

Noah pauses. "He doesn't know anything?"

"Nothing."

"Nothing?" he asks.

"Nothing."

"Don't fuck with me, Murphy. I'm done with you screwing with my head. You know I actually started to *care* about you? What a freakin' joke."

Emotion in his voice with these last words, choking on them. Shifting his weight from one foot to the other. He's upset, coming unraveled.

Something I can use, maybe.

"I started to care about you, too," I say.

"*Shut up!* I don't wanna hear that!"

He takes another step closer to me. I can almost feel the bitterness radiating off him. His chest heaving now.

Shaking his head. "Why?" he asks. "Why did you do all this?"

"Do all what?" I ask as calmly as I can. "Try to catch a killer? Because it's—"

"Stop it! Is that how you wanna play this? Even now, when there's nobody else here to hear your lies? Do you *want* me to put a bullet through your head? Because I'll do it. I swear I will."

The gun bobbing slightly. Do I have a move here?

Dive to the ground and make him shoot wildly in the dark? Then I see it, over Noah's shoulder, at the far end of the bedroom, where the hallway meets the doorway.

The beam of a flashlight, searching along the floor.

Justin, limping forward down the hallway.

The swirling wind drowning out any noise he's making, at least for me, and probably for Noah, too—at least I hope so.

Stall. Stall for time, Murphy.

"You're the one who broke into the warehouse and stole those attorney files, aren't you?" I ask.

"Damn straight I am," he says. "Guess I beat you to them."

Justin drawing closer. I'm willing myself not to look too closely at him, not to signal Noah.

Keep that flashlight beam down, Justin, or Noah will see it.

The flashlight turns off—Justin is at the threshold of the bedroom now, and the glow from the kerosene lamp is sufficient.

But the closer he gets, the more likely it is Noah will

hear him, no matter how violently the wind swirls through this balcony and into the bedroom.

No matter how quietly Justin approaches, with long tiptoe strides.

Keep Noah talking.

"That was a nice move," I say. "Getting those lawyer files before I could."

Something in Justin's hand, something long and thin—a golf club?

A golf club.

"Are those the last remaining copies?" I ask.

"You tell me, Murphy."

Justin raising the golf club, holding it with two hands.

"How the hell should I know?" I ask.

"Shut up," Noah spits. "Just stop with all your bullshit."

Justin is only a few steps away now. It's all I can do to pretend I don't see him, not to tense up, not to give away his presence.

"What bullshit?" I ask.

"I said *shut up!* I'm done with this, Murphy. You know what's in those lawyer files. You've known all along."

Justin stops, the club poised like a baseball bat, ready for the most important swing of his life.

"I have no idea what's in those files," I say.

Noah does a double take, his head cocked, a hint of doubt crossing his face.

Then his eyes suddenly become alert, and he spins to his right just as Justin swings the golf club.

Chapter 118

ALL AT ONCE—

Noah spins to his right and instinctively ducks—

The violent swing of the golf club, grazing the top of Noah's head before continuing its momentum and splintering the wood on the balcony doorway—

Noah's gun, hitting the other side of the doorway during his spin, falling from his hand onto the balcony floor.

I lunge for the gun as Noah, stunned, falls against the opposite side of the doorway.

I scoop up the gun in my hands and fall forward into the bedroom.

"Don't move, Noah," I say, jumping to my feet.

Noah, dazed, has managed to remain upright. His woozy eyes drift over to me and his gun, his Glock, now in my hands, now pointed at him.

"Shit," he says. He touches the top of his head and finds blood on his fingers.

"Hands where I can see them," I say. "Show me your palms."

"Or what? You'll shoot me?"

"He has my gun," Justin says, still clutching the golf club with two hands, like a weapon.

He doesn't mean the revolver he lent me—that's stuffed in the back of my pants.

"That old thirty-eight I showed you at my house," Justin says. "Noah has it. He jumped me and took it off me."

I look Noah over. In one jeans pocket, something—some papers rolled up and shoved inside, the edges protruding. The other front pocket, unclear, but a slight bulge, which could be the .38 special.

"What are those papers in your pocket?" I ask him.

"The lawyer papers," he snarls. "In case you didn't believe I had them."

"And the other pocket?"

He shakes his head. "Nothing. I threw Justin's gun in the front yard."

"Show me your palms," I say. "The first second you don't, I shoot."

Noah, his brows curled in a frown, shakes his head, a bemused laugh escaping from him as his eyes bore into me. "You're good, Murphy. You're very good. I gotta give you that. But guess what?"

He takes a step toward me.

"Don't, Noah."

"Isaac's preparing warrants for your arrest as we speak," he goes on. "For all of the murders. All of them.

Did you know that, Justin?" Noah nods in Justin's direction. "Does he know everything?"

"Shut up, Noah. It's not going to work. And you take one more step, I start shooting."

He takes another step toward me, but slowly, still showing his palms.

Pushing me, but not pushing me too far. Testing me.

"Why didn't you kill me when you had the chance?" he asks. "That night you broke into my house? You buzzed a bullet right past my ear, but you couldn't finish me off."

"That's enough, Noah."

"Why'd you get me out of prison?" he says.

"Because your trial was unfair," I say, my voice shaking. My hands are shaking, too.

"My *trial* was unfair?" He lets out a bitter laugh. "You kill, what, eight people but suddenly you care about the justice system?"

He takes another step.

I fire a round into the floor near his feet. Noah jumps back, startled for a moment. But he quickly recovers.

"That's the second time you deliberately missed me," he says. "Why, Murphy? Why not kill me?" Heat coming to his face now, the snarl returning. "Why? So you could kill everyone I ever cared about and watch me suffer?"

His eyes are filling with tears now, his shoulders trembling.

"I don't know who you think you're fooling," I say. "I didn't kill anybody."

My mind racing. Signals flying in all directions. *He's screwing with you, Murphy. He always does this. Anyone who could be this good, for this long, made a living out of mind-fucking people.*

He takes another step toward me.

This time, I take a step back.

"Jenna, what are you doing?" Justin says.

"Yeah, Murphy, what are you doing?" Noah says, tears falling down his cheeks, his hands clenched in fists. "Aren't you going to kill me?"

"I'm taking you in."

"Jenna, you heard what he said," says Justin. "Isaac's gonna arrest *you*. We know that's true. You heard Isaac say it himself at my house. Noah's gonna walk away from this!"

Noah takes another step toward me, his eyes searching mine, pure bitterness in his expression.

I take another step back, an earthquake inside my head.

"You can't let him get away with this!" Justin cries. "He killed Melanie! He killed your uncle! He sent Aiden to my house to kill *you!*"

Aiden.

Aiden at Justin's house with a knife, coming through the window.

Noah shakes his head slowly, his eyes still on mine.

Aiden.

And then it happens. It comes to me, all at once, just with the mention of Aiden's name.

I can't be sure. I couldn't prove it in a court of law.

But I think I finally figured it out.

I fire another round into the floor. Noah jumps back again.

His momentum temporarily stopped, I reach into the back of my pants and remove the revolver Justin lent me.

"Justin, catch," I say.

Justin drops the golf club. I toss him his revolver, which he catches in both hands.

Noah steadies himself, looks to his right; Justin is now pointing his revolver at Noah.

Then Noah turns again and looks into my eyes, the odds against him mounting now, me holding Noah's Glock, Justin holding his own revolver. Two people, two guns, two different angles.

I search his eyes for an answer. Every time I've looked into those eyes, I've received mixed messages, a series of crisscrossing signals, heat and passion and rage and lust and pure hatred.

My gun wavers as I replay everything in my head, sorting through it all, trying to make the puzzle pieces fit, everything flying at me at once like a tornado.

"Justin," I say.

"Yeah?"

"Aiden didn't come through your window to kill me."

"What—what do you mean?" he asks.

"He came through that window to *protect* me," I say. "To protect me from you."

Chapter 119

STILL FACING NOAH, the Glock in my hand still trained on him, I see, in my peripheral vision, Justin move the gun away from Noah, toward me.

"I'm so tired," I say. "I'm so tired of all of this."

"You're not thinking clearly," Justin says. "But all the same—keep that gun aimed at Noah. If it moves one inch toward me, it's a bad outcome for you."

"It was you," I say. "You're the one who brought me to this house when I was a little girl. You and Holden the Sixth were going to kill me. Your first murder together, your initiation into the family or something, I don't know. But I *do* know that Aiden rescued me. For some reason, Aiden never told anyone about you. Maybe you held something over him. That bloody knife, I'd guess—the one with Aiden's and my fingerprints on it. The one that killed Holden the Sixth?"

Justin doesn't say anything. I keep my eyes on Noah, who returns an intense stare.

"If I'm guessing," I continue, "Aiden came here that

day out of revenge, after Holden the Sixth killed his mother. He got his revenge. He killed Holden with that knife. And somehow you got hold of the knife, the murder weapon, and you held it over his head all these years. You threatened him, blackmailed him, whatever. Aiden would be easy to intimidate. He's practically a kid even now."

"Jenna—"

"And then you grew up. The boy who tried to kill me that day became the man who's killed eight people. Then, when I started getting close, when it became convenient to pin all these murders on Aiden, you tipped off Officer Ricketts about the whereabouts of the knife. How'm I doing so far?"

"You're doing quite well, Detective. *Quite* well." Justin moves a few steps closer. "Now lower the gun and drop it, Jenna. Slowly, or I'll get nervous."

Noah remains motionless, save for the drop of his jaw, as I do what Justin says. I lower the Glock to my side and let it fall from my hand.

"You must have *just* figured this out," he says. "Or you wouldn't have tossed me the gun."

"You mentioned Aiden," I say. "He wouldn't hurt me. I know that now. And you just confirmed it."

"I guess I did. Quite true about Aiden. He's your hero, after all, the young lad who rescued the damsel in distress all those many years ago. Too bad you realized it after you tossed me this gun. Life's a game of inches, isn't it? If it had come to you just a few seconds earlier, I wouldn't be holding this gun. That's gotta sting."

Justin moves behind me, keeping both Noah and me

in his sight and positioning himself beyond our reach. The right move, strategically. He didn't get this far, for this long, without being smart.

"For what it's worth," Justin says, "I'd hoped that tonight would end differently."

"You wanted me to kill Aiden when I came here looking for him. You knew this was where I'd come to look for him. You wanted me to kill him, to keep you clean. But you followed behind me, with your other gun, just in case it didn't work out that way."

"But I sure didn't expect Noah," he says. "The best-laid plans and all."

Noah's jaw clenches. I look at his left front pocket—was Justin right? Does Noah have Justin's other gun, the .38 special?

"By the way, Noah," Justin says. "In the future, if you think you've knocked someone unconscious, be sure they're not faking. Stick 'em with a pin or something. And if you're going to tie someone up with a rope, don't just bind their hands behind their back. Bind their feet, too, and then bind the feet and hands together. It makes it a lot harder to get out."

Footsteps behind me as Justin presses the revolver into the base of my skull.

"Not that it matters now," he says, "but for the record, Jenna, I didn't want anything to happen to you. You may find this hard to believe, but I really did want us to be together."

I let out a bitter laugh.

"I did. Think of how good we'd have been together. Think of our children! Holden's grandchildren."

I stifle the urge to vomit, the bile at my throat. "You're sick," I say.

"Everyone's *sick*," he spits, pushing the muzzle of his gun into the base of my skull, forcing my head forward. "Everyone has it inside them. Some of us are a little more liberal about releasing it, that's all."

Noah is trembling, his eyes smoldering with pure hatred. "You killed Melanie," he growls. "Right here in this room."

"But that's not even the best part," says Justin. "The best part is *you* took the fall for it! Just like old times, with the school yard shooting. You've always been a reliable fall guy, Noah. I've never properly thanked you for that. How have those hands healed up, by the way, from your fun at Sing Sing?"

A furious, tortured smile plays on Noah's face. "You're gonna find out," he says, "when I put them on your throat."

"No, I think your hands are going on top of your head. And you're going to move back toward the balcony. I know you have my thirty-eight special on you. If you make me nervous, this gun goes off. You'll be wearing Jenna's face on your shirt."

Noah blinks, snaps out of his fury, looks at me, the gun shoved against my skull.

He backpedals from us, puts his hands on his head.

"You'll never get away with this," I say.

"Sure I will. *Sure* I will. The happy-go-lucky millionaire philanthropist who serves low-cost food to the middle class? Everyone loves me. Oh, and Jenna?" he says.

"Yes, Justin," I say evenly.

He says it in a whisper. "After I kill you and Noah, I'm going to find your aunt Chloe and kill her, too. She's going to *love* our little fun room downstairs. I'm thinking *shish kebab*."

And then I feel the vibration against the back of my skull as Justin pulls the trigger.

Chapter 120

CLICK.

Justin pulls the trigger again.

Another hollow *click*.

I dive for the Glock I just dropped, sliding to the floor, then spinning back, faster than Justin can say *Damn, this revolver must not be loaded.*

Thank you, Aiden, for emptying the bullets.

Justin looks at the gun, then me. A bitter smile on his face, then he shakes his head and throws the gun to the floor.

"No one will believe it," he says. "Like Noah said, Chief Marks already has arrest warrants out with your name on it. So the only way you'll get that *justice* you so richly seek is to shoot me."

I get to my feet, the gun steady now, aimed at Justin's chest.

He raises his arms in surrender. "How about it, Detective? Are you gonna shoot an unarmed man? Please, please," he says in a mocking plea, dropping to his knees, "don't shoot me, Ms. Murphy! Don't shoot me!"

Sirens, in the distance, but not that distant. A 911 call, no doubt, after the gunshots I fired. Once Isaac heard that the shots came from the house on 7 Ocean Drive, he'd send the whole force.

I lower the gun slightly—not so low as to give Justin any ideas, but not pointing it directly at him.

"You're not gonna do it," says Justin, as if disappointed. "You're really not." His chest rises and falls, his face locked in a grimace.

It hits me then—he wants to die. He doesn't want to spend his life in prison. Not one member of the Dahlquist clan ever spent a day in prison. He doesn't want to break the streak.

"My favorite was your uncle," he says. "Heating up that poker in the fireplace and driving it through his kidney."

I shake my head. I'm not going to let him bait me.

"Do you wanna know what he said before I did it?"

The sirens getting closer. Multiple squad cars approaching.

"He said, 'Help me, Jenna.' He was begging."

I close the distance between us, the gun aimed at his head.

"He was in so much pain," Justin says.

I rear back, then drive my foot into his ribs, kicking him as hard as I can.

He doubles over on the floor.

"Pain like that?" I say.

He lets out a noise—pain, yes, but also amusement. "That's the spirit," he manages. "I knew you had it in you."

"You're gonna rot in prison, Justin," I say. "You don't get to go out in a blaze of glory, some dramatic suicide, like all your ancestors."

Justin focuses on me with a hint of amusement. He gets himself to his hands and knees. "*My* ancestors?" he says.

"Shut up, Justin," Noah says, suddenly stepping forward.

"*My* ancestors?"

Noah pulls the .38 special from his pocket and aims it at Justin. "I'm warning you, Justin, *shut up*."

Justin lets out a wicked laugh. "Oh, Jenna, you think Holden is *my* father?"

I look at Noah. "What's he talking about?"

"Nothing," Noah says. "We'll talk about it later, when everything's calmed down."

I step back, instinctively, separating myself from both of them. "We'll talk about it now, Noah. And put down that gun!"

"Murphy—"

"Drop the gun, Noah! Now! Slide it over to me."

The sound of tires squealing outside as the squad cars pull up to the mansion.

"Tell her, Noah," says Justin, regaining an upright position, still on his knees. "Or better yet, show her those papers in your—"

Noah throws an uppercut, a violent left fist, connecting just under Justin's chin, sending Justin off his knees and sprawling backward. Justin's head smacks the floor, and this time he's truly unconscious, no faking about it.

Noah with his back to me. The gun in his right hand.

"Don't move, Noah. Don't make a move."

The sounds outside: officers rushing through the gate, up the walk, the front door of the mansion slamming open, footfalls downstairs, their voices, announcing their office, clearing each room on the lower level.

My mind races, thoughts bouncing every which way, trying to make it fit. Noah—Noah—it was Noah all along? Noah is Holden's son? Everything spun upside down, everything unraveled, like a fist coming down on a jigsaw puzzle, scattering the pieces in all directions.

"Tell me, Noah," I say, my voice shaking.

Noah slowly bends down and places the gun on the floor. Though Justin is no longer a threat, he kicks the gun across the room for good measure.

"I want to see those papers," I say.

His back still to me, Noah removes the papers from his pocket, rolled up like an ancient scroll, and turns to face me.

"Put the gun down first," he says.

"No chance. Toss them over."

Noah drops his head, then starts walking over to me.

"Stop, now," I say. "Keep your distance and toss them to me."

He looks up at me, not breaking stride. "Jenna," he says.

"Stop, Noah, or I'll shoot!" My gun is aimed at his face, my feet spread.

"No," he says.

He draws closer to me. Five steps. Three steps.

Footfalls on the stairs as officers race up to the second floor.

"I'll shoot," I say through my teeth.

"You're not gonna shoot me, Jenna."

My finger is on the trigger as Noah's eyes lock on mine, as I feel the familiar heat of his approach.

And I can't. I can't pull the trigger. I don't know why. I don't know anything anymore.

I just know I can't shoot him.

Noah puts his hand over the barrel of my gun—his Glock—and pushes it down.

He puts his forehead against mine.

"It's okay now," he says. "It's gonna be okay."

"Tell me it wasn't you," I whisper. "Tell me you aren't his son."

Noah removes the gun from my hand. He replaces it with the scroll of papers, pressing them firmly into my palm.

His mouth moves to my ear.

"Holden didn't have a son," he says. "He had a daughter."

Chapter 121

"HERE. IT SUCKS, but it's hot."

Officer Lauren Ricketts places the Styrofoam cup of coffee in front of me in the interview room at the substation. When I look up to thank her, I see black spots, and I feel the weight under my eyes.

"Rough night," she says, rubbing my back. "Tomorrow will be better."

Tomorrow is today. It's past five in the morning. And no amount of tomorrows will change it.

I look down again at the documents, still curved along the edges from having been rolled up in Noah's pocket for several hours. I read through them again, for at least the twentieth time. The first page, a piece of stationery bearing the name Lincoln Investigative Services. A letter to Holden Dahlquist VI.

You asked us to determine whether a woman named Gloria Willis, of Bridgehampton, mother of Aiden

Willis, gave birth to a second child approximately eight years ago.

Holden knew, or at least suspected, that he'd impregnated Aiden's mother.

The answer to your question is yes. Eight years ago, Ms. Willis did give birth to a second child at Southampton Hospital but left the hospital with her child only hours later, without filling out any paperwork. We believe that she abandoned this child later that evening at the Bridgehampton Police Substation (see attached news headline).

I flip the page. The news clipping I saw myself, at Aiden's house:

Newborn Abandoned at Police Station

The photo of Uncle Lang, holding the baby at the substation in Bridgehampton.

The next page, a photocopy of a handwritten note, the penmanship poor but legible:

Please find my daughter a good home. She is in danger. Don't ever let her know about me. Don't ever let her try to find me or the father. He will kill her.

My pulse banging like a gong, no matter how many times I read this note, a note from a terrified mother trying to protect her newborn daughter the only way she knew how—by abandoning her.

I flip to the next page, a court document:

> At a Term of the Family Court of the State of
> New York, held in and for the County of Suffolk,
> at Riverhead, New York
> **In the Matter of the Adoption of a Child Known as**
> **Baby Girl X**

I skip a bunch of the middle pages because they are legalese, just a bunch of lawyers' words. The punch line at the final page:

> IT IS HEREBY ORDERED that the petition of Gary and Lydia Murphy, for the adoption of Baby Girl X, a person born on a date unknown, at a location unknown, is allowed and approved; and it is further
>
> ORDERED that the name of the adoptive child shall be JENNA ROSE MURPHY, and that the adoptive child shall hereafter be known by that name.

I can picture her. Of course I can't in reality, but my brain isn't tracking reality now—I can picture my mother, visiting Uncle Lang like they did every summer, taking me from Lang, holding me in her arms and saying, *I'll love her. I'll love this child.*

A single tear, falling onto the page, a thick circular stain in the corner.

Still unable to believe it, though it makes all the sense in the world.

My physical differences from my parents and brother, especially the red hair. My nickname, *the red sheep of the family*.

Never quite feeling like I fit in.

Sometimes we tell our children little white lies, Chloe said to me.

She didn't tell me—none of them told me, not Mom, not Dad, not Lang, not Chloe. They kept me in the dark to protect me. Protect me from whom, they didn't know.

A little white lie.

And here I thought it was random—I thought I was a random victim at that house that day. When in reality, Holden was trying to kill me to end the Dahlquist bloodline. First he ran down Aiden's mother—my mother—with a car, then he had Justin scoop me up and bring me to the house to finish the job.

I would've died in that house if it weren't for Aiden, coming to avenge his mother's death.

Chief Isaac Marks pops his head in the door, measuring the look on my face before deeming it safe to enter.

"Murphy," he says. "We're done with Noah's interview. So you two are free to leave."

I nod and push myself out of the chair, my legs uncertain.

"Murphy, I—I'm sorry," he says. "I was a jerk. And I had you all wrong. I thought you were a loose cannon hassling poor Aiden for no reason. And then I—well, I admit for a time there, I—"

"You thought I was a serial killer."

He throws up a hand.

"That's okay," I say, "for a time there, I thought you were, too."

He laughs, which might, under the circumstances, be the best response of all.

"When Noah showed me those investigative records," he says, "and it turned out you were the daughter of—I mean, I thought you'd been playing me all along."

That's what Noah thought, too.

"Plus, your fingerprints on that knife—"

"I got it," I say. I may not like it, but I have so much emotion stirred up inside me right now, I don't have room for anger.

"Justin's spilling like a volcano," he says. "Now that we have him in custody, he won't shut up. He's proud of it. He says he's part of the legacy now, he'll go down in history, et cetera."

"I'm sure he feels that way."

"He told us about everything in 1994, too. Apparently, Holden saw you and your family walking to the beach one day, right past his house. He got one look at you and—I guess there's a strong resemblance to your biological mother. He followed you around the beach all day, then he hired an investigator, and—well, you know the rest. You got the investigator's file right there. Then he had Justin snatch you up and bring you to the house—"

"Isaac," I say, raising a hand. "I don't want to know the details. I don't remember and I don't *want* to remember."

"Sure. Yeah, sure, Murphy. Well, I'll see you next week, then. If you're ready."

I shake my head. "You need me to testify at the prelim?"

"That's not what I meant."

He places my badge and my gun on the table.

"You don't think I'm going to lose my best cop, do you?" he says. "I may be a horse's ass on occasion, but I'm not stupid."

Chapter 122

I WALK TO the cemetery on Main Street, the cemetery where Winston Dahlquist and his descendants are buried. The afternoon air is mild and smells of the rain this morning.

Just down from the Dahlquist plot, Aiden Willis is busy planting flowers in a vase by some tombstone. Back at work already. Always the same, the raggedy shirt, the baseball cap turned backward, the scarecrow hair. He surely takes after his father, not his mother.

Yesterday, the DA's office officially announced that it had no basis to proceed with murder charges against Aiden for the death of Holden VI. Aiden was too young at the time to have been charged as an adult, and the circumstances, they said, "strongly suggest that his use of force was justified."

That might be the understatement of the year.

Aiden stops what he's doing when he sees me approach, squints at me.

I don't really know what to say to him. I have no

sense of family with him. We couldn't be less alike. We've never known each other. We've never shared a single thing, other than a mother.

"Hey," I say.

His eyes scatter about, as always, never holding a gaze.

"You doin' okay?" he asks me.

"Me? Yeah, sure. Listen, Aiden, I'm sorry for the way I treated you. I thought—I thought you were a part of this. I had no idea it was Justin."

He nods, his eyes roaming around the ground at my feet.

"Did you?" I ask, uncertain if I should even ask. "All these murders? Did you know it was him?"

His eyes go blank a moment, as if he's lost in a thought—more accurate, probably, to say lost in a feeling. "Didn't know for sure," he says. "Couldn'ta ever proved nothin'. Who'd believe me, anyhow? I'm just a ditch-digger. He's got all that money and shit."

"And he had the knife you tossed out the window," I add.

For a moment, Aiden's eyes focus, though not on me, looking off in the distance, his mouth forming a small o. "He said he kept it somewheres for safekeepin'. Case I ever got any ideas, he said."

A not-so-subtle threat. *Don't mess with me,* Justin was saying to Aiden, *or the cops will suddenly find this bloody knife. Fuck with me and I'll send you to prison.*

He tortured Aiden. He made Aiden shoot up the school yard with him a year after Holden's death—one of the many things Justin has bragged about to the police—and who knows what else he said and did to him over the years.

"What about me?" I ask. "Did you know who I was?"

His eyes are still darting around, but a sheen of tears covers them. He shakes his head. "When you first came back to town, first time I saw you—you looked familiar, but I couldn't figure it. Then I finally 'membered where I'd seen you, from all that time ago when we was kids, that day at the Dahlquist house. I didn't know why you'd come back. Couldn't figure. But I didn't know that you were my—that we was—"

The flowers, halfway in the vase, start to tip over. Aiden reaches for them.

"You should probably get back to your work," I say.

Aiden fixes up the flowers, sets them down firmly, turns to me in his indirect, no-eye-contact way. "I's too young to know 'bout you at the time. I'da been only little when you was born. One time, when I's older, I saw a picture of her, with her belly."

I saw it, too. The photo from the scrapbook, with the baby bump.

"She said the baby didn't live. She got real sad."

Probably the same thing that she told Holden VI, that I didn't live, that I was stillborn.

A little white lie. To protect me, so Aiden wouldn't look for me. So Holden wouldn't look for me. So nobody would ever look for me.

His darting eyes, just for a single moment, make contact with mine before skittering away again. "You look like her," he says. "A good bit like her."

"I'm lucky. She was very pretty. And courageous. She

did a brave thing for me. So did you, Aiden. If there's anything I can—"

"You wanna see her grave?" he asks.

I start to speak, but a lump fills my throat. I nod and follow him.

It's a simple grave, farther to the south of the cemetery, an ordinary headstone kept up pristinely.

Gloria Jane Willis
March 5, 1964 – July 12, 1994
Our Beloved Mother

Our beloved mother. Even though, for all practical purposes, Aiden was an only child. Even though, as far as he knew, I didn't survive the birth. Still, he included me, the sibling he never really had, the sibling he never knew.

My—*our*—biological mother. The woman who gave me up to save me. A prostitute who surely wanted something better for herself, and for her son.

And for her daughter.

July 12, 1994—the day Gloria was killed in a hit-and-run. The day before the seven hours of hell, when I was plucked off the street and taken to 7 Ocean Drive, so Holden could take my life, too, and end any vestige of the tortured, maniacal Dahlquist bloodline.

I look over at Aiden, whose eyes have filled with tears.

"I still miss her," he says, his voice quaking. "You'da—you'da liked her."

"I know I would have." I take Aiden's hand in mine. "But you still have family. You still have me. You're my hero, Aiden. And you're my brother."

I lean over and kiss him on the cheek. He recoils slightly. I don't get the sense that a lot of women have kissed him in his life.

"Okay," he says awkwardly. His face brightens just a bit. "That'd be okay."

Chapter 123

I NESTLE MY feet into the sand and let out a long sigh. The beach is utter chaos in mid-August, kids running everywhere, boats and parasails and sand castles, but to me it feels like complete and total peace.

Four months, almost to the day, since it all happened.

Four months since Justin's murderous ways were exposed and he was taken into custody, a now-infamous killer who will go down in history with the legions of others. Someone told me they did a Google search on his name and got over ten thousand hits.

Hooray for him.

"Let's go watch," says Noah, sitting next to me.

"Not sure I want to."

"Oh, c'mon. Come *on*. You don't wanna watch?"

I relent, pushing myself out of the sand, fitting my toes into my sandals, my fingers intertwined with Noah's.

"Your hair's getting long again," I say. "Are you going back to Surfer Jesus?"

"Hey, be nice to me," he says, squeezing my hand. "I've been through a lot. I've been shot at by a cop two times."

"But she intended to miss each time," I add.

"So she says. So she says."

We climb onto the pavement of the parking lot and walk up Ocean Drive.

A thick crowd is gathered at the gate of 7 Ocean Drive. A couple of news crews as well. It's been like that ever since everything happened. They say there was a spike in tourism this summer due to all the people who wanted to come see this house.

So there will be a few people, some shop owners, who might be sorry to see what's about to happen. But I think most people will approve.

"Just in time," Noah says.

The wrecking ball slams into the roof first, crushing the slate inward, the spears and ornamental gargoyles disappearing in a satisfying rush, a collective gasp of awe from the crowd. They told me it will take hours to knock down the entire mansion. I told them I didn't care how long it took, I just wanted everything gone. The house. The tunnel and dungeon beneath. The carriage house.

It's my property, after all. That's what all the lawyers concluded after reviewing the trust documents. The property went into trust because nobody knew that Holden VI had left behind any offspring. So now it's mine.

It won't be for long. I wish I could open a museum or a shelter for battered women or something on this property, but this is prime real estate, and there are zoning laws designed to protect its value.

So I've put this massive lot up for sale, hopefully to a nice family who will build a nice new house with a very different future. The Realtors quoted me an estimate that's more money than I'd make in my lifetime, and far more money than I'll ever need. So I'll keep a fraction for myself and give the rest of the proceeds to Aiden Willis.

Another whack from the wrecking ball, this time taking out the wraparound balcony, the master bedroom where so many people lost, or took, their lives—centuries of horror gone with one crushing boom.

"I'm gonna miss that house," says Noah.

I laugh. It feels good to laugh. Odd, unusual, but good.

"But speaking of houses," he says, "those rooms aren't going to paint themselves."

Our new place, he means. Not far down the road from Uncle Lang's old house. A three-bedroom, two-bathroom in a nice, quiet spot. *Quiet* sounds good right about now. We cosigned the loan, on the salaries of a newly promoted detective, first grade, and the owner of a new handyman business.

Seeing this house, even in its deliciously beaten and battered form now, brings back everything from that final night.

I lean into Noah. "You were *that* sure I wouldn't shoot you?" I ask.

He cradles me with an arm. "Oh, yeah," he says. "It was clear that you were madly in love with me."

I smile to myself. I am, in fact, madly in love with this man.

I watch the wrecking ball do its work. I said I didn't want to watch, but now I'm fixated. Now I have to see it. I have to see every single piece of limestone battered and knocked to the ground. I need to see every inch of earth turned over—

Noah looks at me, sees the intensity in my face.

"Y'know what?" he says. "I changed my mind. This is boring. This house is old news. I wanna go to our new house."

This man understands me, sometimes better than I understand myself.

"Me too," I say.

We walk off, hand in hand, leaning against each other, the sun beating down on us.

Behind us, another boom, the sound of crushing rocks, another awed gasp from the crowd, but neither of us looks back.

[illegible] the case.

[illegible] Now [illegible]

[illegible] in my life.

[illegible] know what [illegible]

[illegible]

This man [illegible]

Milo [illegible]

[illegible]

[illegible] back.

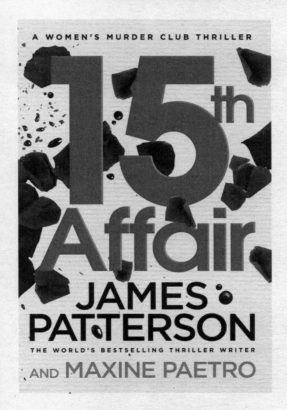

ALISON MULLER WASN'T classically beautiful, but she was striking, with swinging blonde hair and peekaboo bangs brushing the frames of her wraparound shades. Her black leather coat flared above the knees of her skinny jeans, and her purposeful stride was punctuated by the staccato clacking of her high-heeled boots.

That afternoon, as she cut through the golden-hued lobby of San Francisco's Four Seasons Hotel, Ali checked out every man, woman, and child crossing the floor, on the queue at reception, slouched in chairs in front of the fireplace. She noted and labeled the tourists and business-people, deflecting the stares of the men who couldn't look away, while on the phone with her husband and their younger daughter, Mitzi.

"I didn't actually forget, Mitz," Ali said to her five-year old. "More like I lost track."

"You *did* forget," her daughter insisted.

"Not completely. I thought your big day was tomorrow."

"Everyone wanted to know where you were," her daughter complained.

"I'll make it up to you, sweetheart," Ali said.

"When? With what?"

Ali's thoughts ran ahead to the man waiting for her in a room on the fourteenth floor.

"Let me speak to Daddy," Ali said.

She passed the stunning exhibition of modern art and reached the elevator bank at the northwest end of the lobby. She stood behind the couple in front of the doors. They were French, discussing their dinner plans, agreeing that they had enough time to shower and change.

Ali thumbed her phone, checked her e-mail and the *Investors Business Daily* headlines and the text from Michael asking if she'd gotten lost. Ali's husband came back on the line.

"I did my best," he said. "She's inconsolable."

"You can handle her, dear. I'm sure you can do it. I'll order her something online when I get home."

"Which will be when?" her husband asked.

God. The questions. The never-ending questions.

"After dinner," Ali said. "I'm sorry. I wouldn't blow you off if it wasn't important."

The elevator doors opened.

"Gotta go."

Her husband said, "Say good-bye to Mitzi."

Shit.

She said, "Hang on a minute. I'm losing reception."

Ali stepped into the elevator and stood with her back to the corner, her jacket parting to reveal the butt of a gun tucked into her waistband. The doors closed and the car rose swiftly and quietly upward.

When Ali got out at the fourteenth floor, she spoke to her daughter as she walked along the plush carpeted hallway.

"Miss Mitzi?"

She reached room 1420 and rapped on the door, and it opened.

Ali said into the phone, "Happy birthday. See you soon. Kiss, kiss. Bye-bye."

She clicked off, stepped inside the room, and kicked the door closed behind her as she went into Michael's arms.

"You're late," he said.

MICHAEL CHAN TOOK off Ali's glasses and sucked in his breath. He couldn't get over this woman—and he had tried. She smiled at him and he put his hands on both sides of her face and kissed the smile right off her.

One kiss ignited a string of them: deep, telling, momentous. Michael lifted Ali and she hooked her legs around his hips and he walked her into the luxurious blue-and-bronze suite backlit by the watercolor sunset over San Francisco.

Chan didn't notice the view. Ali smelled like orchids or some exotic musk, and she had her tongue at his ear.

"Too much," he muttered. "You're too damned much."

She was panting as he lowered her to the bed.

"Wait," she said.

"Of course. I'm a patient man," he said. His blood was surging, narrowing his focus. He put his hands on his hips and watched to see what she would do.

She looked up at him, her warm gaze flicking over his body and his strong features as if she were memorizing him. They met infrequently, but when they did, they pretended they were strangers. It was a game.

"At least tell me your name," she said.

"You first."

He pulled off her boots, tossed them aside. She sat up, shrugged off her coat, and shoved it over the edge of the bed. He plucked the gun from her waistband, looked through the sight, smelled the muzzle, and put it on the nightstand.

"Interesting," he said. "Hand-tooled."

He sat on the bed next to her and told her to lie down, and he lay next to her. He moved her bangs away from her eyes.

"Your name."

She reached down and ran her hand across the front of his pants. He grabbed her wrist.

She said, "Ummmm, I'm Renata."

"Giovanni," he said. "Prince of Gorgonzola."

She laughed. It was a terrific laugh. "Finally, I meet the Prince of Cheese."

Michael kept a straight face. "Correct. And you should never keep royalty waiting."

He stroked her cheek, then dipped his fingers beneath the neckline of her blouse.

"I think I may have met you once before," she said.

He freed the pearl buttons from their loops.

"I don't think so," he said. "I would have remembered."

He ran his hand over the tops of her breasts, then gathered up her hair, wrapped it around his left hand, and pulled her head back.

She moaned and said, "You paid me with three gold coins. I came to your room in the hotel overlooking"—she sighed—"the Trevi Fountain."

"I've never stayed in Rome," he said.

He turned her so that she faced away from him. He stroked the long side of her body down to her haunch and back. He enjoyed the soft sounds coming from her throat as she tried to twist away from him.

"Did you tell your husband?"

"Why would you ask me that?" she said.

"Because I want him to throw you out."

He undid the closure at the waist of her jeans, pulled down the zipper, got to his feet, and removed her jeans and all of his clothes.

He didn't hear the sound at the door.

This was unlike him. He had superior senses, but they were engaged. Ali was looking up at him with—what was that look in her eyes?

She said, "I heard a card in the lock."

A voice called out, "Housekeeping."

Chan said, "I didn't lock the door. You?"

Ali said, "Hell no."

Chan shouted, "Come back later," but the door was already opening and the cart was bumping over the threshold. He grabbed his pants from the floor and, holding them in front of him, he went toward the foyer.

He shouted, *"No! Wait!"*

The three shots were muffled by a suppressor. If Michael Chan had known his killer, it didn't matter now.

Lights out.

Game over.

Michael Chan was gone.

IT HAD BEEN a rough week, and it was only Monday.

My partner, Rich Conklin, and I had just testified against Edward "Ted" Swanson, a cop who had, over time, left eighteen people dead before the shootout with a predatory drug lord called Kingfisher took Swanson out of the game.

All of the SFPD had known Swanson as a great cop. We had liked him. Respected him. So when my partner and I exposed him as a psychopath with a badge, we were stunned and outraged.

During Swanson's lethal crime spree, he had stolen over five million in drugs and money from Kingfisher, and this drug boss with a murderous reputation up and down the West Coast hadn't taken this loss as the cost of doing business.

After the shootout, while Swanson lay comatose in the ICU, Kingfisher figured that his best chance of getting his property back was to turn his death threats on the lead investigator on the case.

That investigator was me.

His phone calls were irrational, untraceable, and absolutely *terrifying*.

Then, about the time Swanson was released from the hospital and indicted on multiple charges of drug trafficking and murder, Kingfisher's phone calls stopped. A week later, Mexican authorities turned up the King's body in a shallow grave in Baja. Was it really over?

Sometimes terrifying events leave aftershocks when you realize how bad things could have become. Kingfisher's threats had embedded themselves inside me on a visceral level, and now that I was free of them, something inside me unclenched.

On the other hand, events that seem innocuous at the time can flip you right over the edge into the dark side.

And that was the case with Swanson.

A dirty cop shakes up everything: friendships, public trust, and belief in your own ability to read people. I thought I had done a good job testifying against Swanson today. I hoped so. Richie had been terrific, for sure, and now the decision as to Swanson's guilt or innocence was up to his jury.

My partner said, "We're done with this, Lindsay. Time to move on."

I was checking out of the Hall of Justice at just after six when my husband texted me to say that he would be home late, and that there was a roasted chicken in the fridge.

Damn.

I was disappointed not to see Joe, but as I stepped outside the gray granite building into a luminous summer evening, I formulated a new plan. Rather than chicken for three, I would have a quiet dinner with my baby daughter, followed by Dreamland in about three hours, tops.

I fired up my old Explorer and had just cleared the rush-hour snarl on Bryant when the boss called me.

Against my better judgment, I picked up.

"Boxer," Brady said, "a bad scene just went down at the Four Seasons. I need you there."

The only scene I wanted to see was my little girl in clean onesies, and me with a glass of Chardonnay in my hand. But Homicide was understaffed, my partner and I had a fresh gap in our caseload, and Brady was a good lieutenant.

I said, "Were you able to catch Conklin?"

"He's on the way," said Brady.

I made a U-turn on Geary, and twenty minutes later, I met up with my partner in the sumptuous lobby of the Four Seasons Hotel. Conklin was as tired as I was, but it looked good on him.

"Overtime pay, Lindsay."

"Yahoo," I said with an appropriate lack of enthusiasm. "What did Brady tell you?"

"To be smart, thorough, and quick."

"Instead of what? Stupid, sloppy, and slow?"

Richie laughed. "He said the Four Seasons wants their hotel back."

We took the elevator to the fourteenth floor, and when the doors opened, we saw that the hallway was cordoned off and law enforcement personnel were standing at the exit doors, leaning against walls, waiting for us.

Conklin and I ducked under the tape and nodded to uniforms we knew, finally pulling up to the open door marked 1420.

The cop at the door signed us into the log, and I asked him, “Who called it in?”

“Hotel’s head of security. He responded to complaints of gunshots.”

“How bad is it?”

“Bad enough,” he said.

“Let’s see,” I said.

THE FIRST OFFICER stepped aside, revealing a naked male body lying faceup, about fifteen feet inside the deluxe hotel suite. He had been shot once in the forehead, once through the right eye, and had taken another bullet to his chest for good measure.

I said to Conklin, "What do you think? Midthirties? Asian?"

Conklin nodded and said, "That's an expensive watch. He's wearing a wedding ring. We're probably not looking at a robbery."

Someone called my name.

Charlie Clapper, director of San Francisco's forensic unit, came around a corner in the suite. "Boxer," Clapper said. "Conklin. Welcome to the

Four Seasons. How can we make your stay here more enjoyable?"

I said, "Tell me you've ID'd the victim and have the shooter in custody. And that by the way, the shooter confessed."

Clapper is a former homicide cop, a pro who knows what he's doing and never has to prove it. He laughed and said, "I guess miracles happen—but not here. Not today."

I peered behind Clapper. Lights had been set up and CSIs were processing the expensively furnished suite, which had soundproof windows and a high city view. There was a lot of blood around and under the victim, but the room behind him looked spotless.

I took in the silvery-blue carpeting and upholstery, the lightly rumpled bed, bedspread still in place. I saw no wine bottles or remains of a room service meal, and the TV was off.

It looked like room 1420 had only been used for a short time before what happened here went down.

Conklin asked Clapper to run what he knew so far.

Clapper said, "To start with, it looks like our

victim had company. We found fresh lipstick and a few long blonde hairs on a pillowcase. There's no wallet, no suitcase, no papers, no clothes, no shoes."

"Perfect score," said Conklin.

Clapper went on. "This gentleman checked in under the name Gregory Wang. He used a credit card with that name and the charge went through, but there is no Gregory Wang at the address on the card or anywhere.

"Also notable, the room has been thoroughly wiped down. No prints old or new. Entry was by a key card that was traced to a Maria Silva in housekeeping. Ms. Silva is now off duty, not answering her phone. A patrol car has gone to her address."

"What about *his* prints?" Conklin asked, indicating the victim.

"We ran the victim's prints and came up with nothing. He's not in the system, has never been in the military, or taught grade school, or been arrested. And wait. There's more," said Clapper. "There's a whole other crime scene right next door. Can't be a coincidence, but right now, I don't see the connection."

Also by James Patterson

ALEX CROSS NOVELS

Along Came a Spider • Kiss the Girls • Jack and Jill • Cat and Mouse • Pop Goes the Weasel • Roses are Red • Violets are Blue • Four Blind Mice • The Big Bad Wolf • London Bridges • Mary, Mary • Cross • Double Cross • Cross Country • Alex Cross's Trial (*with Richard DiLallo*) • I, Alex Cross • Cross Fire • Kill Alex Cross • Merry Christmas, Alex Cross • Alex Cross, Run • Cross My Heart • Hope to Die • Cross Justice

THE WOMEN'S MURDER CLUB SERIES

1st to Die • 2nd Chance (*with Andrew Gross*) • 3rd Degree (*with Andrew Gross*) • 4th of July (*with Maxine Paetro*) • The 5th Horseman (*with Maxine Paetro*) • The 6th Target (*with Maxine Paetro*) • 7th Heaven (*with Maxine Paetro*) • 8th Confession (*with Maxine Paetro*) • 9th Judgement (*with Maxine Paetro*) • 10th Anniversary (*with Maxine Paetro*) • 11th Hour (*with Maxine Paetro*) • 12th of Never (*with Maxine Paetro*) • Unlucky 13 (*with Maxine Paetro*) • 14th Deadly Sin (*with Maxine Paetro*) • 15th Affair (*with Maxine Paetro*)

DETECTIVE MICHAEL BENNETT SERIES

Step on a Crack (*with Michael Ledwidge*) • Run for Your Life (*with Michael Ledwidge*) • Worst Case (*with Michael Ledwidge*) • Tick Tock (*with Michael Ledwidge*) • I, Michael Bennett (*with Michael Ledwidge*) • Gone (*with Michael Ledwidge*) • Burn (*with Michael Ledwidge*) • Alert (*with Michael Ledwidge*) • Bullseye (*with Michael Ledwidge*)

PRIVATE NOVELS

Private (*with Maxine Paetro*) • Private London (*with Mark Pearson*) • Private Games (*with Mark Sullivan*) • Private: No. 1 Suspect (*with Maxine Paetro*) • Private Berlin (*with Mark Sullivan*) • Private Down Under (*with Michael White*) • Private L.A. (*with Mark Sullivan*) • Private India (*with Ashwin Sanghi*) • Private Vegas (*with Maxine Paetro*) • Private Sydney (*with Kathryn Fox*) • Private Paris (*with Mark Sullivan*) • The Games (*with Mark Sullivan*)

NYPD RED SERIES

NYPD Red (*with Marshall Karp*) •
NYPD Red 2 (*with Marshall Karp*) •
NYPD Red 3 (*with Marshall Karp*) •
NYPD Red 4 (*with Marshall Karp*)

NON-FICTION

Torn Apart (*with Hal and Cory Friedman*) •
The Murder of King Tut (*with Martin Dugard*)

ROMANCE

Sundays at Tiffany's (*with Gabrielle Charbonnet*) •
The Christmas Wedding (*with Richard DiLallo*) •
First Love (*with Emily Raymond*)

OTHER TITLES

Miracle at Augusta (*with Peter de Jonge*)

FAMILY OF PAGE-TURNERS

MIDDLE SCHOOL BOOKS

The Worst Years of My Life (*with Chris Tebbetts*) • Get Me Out of Here! (*with Chris Tebbetts*) • My Brother Is a Big, Fat Liar (*with Lisa Papademetriou*) • How I Survived Bullies, Broccoli, and Snake Hill (*with Chris Tebbetts*) • Ultimate Showdown (*with Julia Bergen*) • Save Rafe! (*with Chris Tebbetts*) • Just My Rotten Luck (*with Chris Tebbetts*)

I FUNNY SERIES

I Funny (*with Chris Grabenstein*) • I Even Funnier (*with Chris Grabenstein*) • I Totally Funniest (*with Chris Grabenstein*) • I Funny TV (*with Chris Grabenstein*)

TREASURE HUNTERS SERIES

Treasure Hunters (*with Chris Grabenstein*) • Danger Down the Nile (*with Chris Grabenstein*) • Secret of the Forbidden City (*with Chris Grabenstein*)

HOUSE OF ROBOTS SERIES

House of Robots (*with Chris Grabenstein*) • Robots Go Wild! (*with Chris Grabenstein*)

OTHER ILLUSTRATED NOVELS

Kenny Wright: Superhero (*with Chris Tebbetts*)
Homeroom Diaries (*with Lisa Papademetriou*)

MAXIMUM RIDE SERIES

The Angel Experiment • School's Out Forever • Saving the World and Other Extreme Sports • The Final Warning • Max • Fang • Angel • Nevermore • Forever

CONFESSIONS SERIES

Confessions of a Murder Suspect (*with Maxine Paetro*) • The Private School Murders (*with Maxine Paetro*) • The Paris Mysteries (*with Maxine Paetro*) • The Murder of an Angel (*with Maxine Paetro*)

WITCH & WIZARD SERIES

Witch & Wizard (*with Gabrielle Charbonnet*) • The Gift (*with Ned Rust*) • The Fire (*with Jill Dembowski*) • The Kiss (*with Jill Dembowski*) • The Lost (*with Emily Raymond*)

DANIEL X SERIES

The Dangerous Days of Daniel X (*with Michael Ledwidge*) • Watch the Skies (*with Ned Rust*) • Demons and Druids (*with Adam Sadler*) • Game Over (*with Ned Rust*) • Armageddon (*with Chris Grabenstein*) • Lights Out (with *Chris Grabenstein*)

GRAPHIC NOVELS

Daniel X: Alien Hunter (*with Leopoldo Gout*) • Maximum Ride: Manga Vols. 1–8 (*with NaRae Lee*)

For more information about James Patterson's novels, visit www.jamespatterson.co.uk

Or become a fan on Facebook